House of Rocamora

Other Books by Donald Michael Platt:

A Gathering of Vultures
Rocamora
Close to the Sun
Bodo the Apostate

House of Rocamora

Donald Michael Platt

www.penmorepress.com

House of Rocamora
By
Donald Michael Platt

Copyright © 2012 Donald Michael Platt

All rights reserved. No part of this book may be used or reproduced by any means without the written permission of the publisher except in the case of brief quotation embodied in critical articles and reviews.

ISBN-13: 978-1-942756-30-9(Paperback)
ISBN -13:978-1-942756-31-6 (e-book)

BISAC Subject Headings:
HIS045000 HISTORY / Europe / Spain &Portugal
FIC032000FICTION / War&Military
FIC031020FICTION / Thrillers / Historical

Front cover:
portrait of Vicente de Rocamora and
Back Cover: portrait of Abigail de Rocamora
by Pam Marin-Kingsley, website: www.pammarin-kingsley.com

Address all correspondence to:
Michael James
Penmore Press LLC
920 N Javelina Pl
Tucson AZ 85748
mjames@Penmorepress.com

For Ellen—
pithy says it all

The most extraordinary, if not the most profound, of
Menasseh's physician friends was Isaac, or Vicente, de Rocamora.

—Cecil Roth
A Life of Menasseh Ben Israel, Rabbi, Printer, Diplomat

Provinces and Cities where Rocamora Lived and Visited

All Dutch provinces freed from Spanish rule in the sixteenth and seventeenth centuries can trace their origin to a medieval county or a duchy. Their status changed when the Prince of Orange centralized them into the Republic of the Seven United Provinces: Holland, Zeeland, Gelderland, Utrecht, Friesland, Overijssel, and Groningen. The Republic's lands also included Drenthe, but without the autonomous status of the others.

Each of these "Netherlands" had a high degree of autonomy, co-operating with each other mainly on defense and on the international level in general, but keeping to their own affairs elsewhere.

The southern provinces, Brabant, Flanders, and Wallonia remained under the control of Spain until the Napoleonic era, after which they became Belgium in 1831.

Preface

Formerly the Spanish Netherlands, the Dutch Republic at the time of Vicente de Rocamora's arrival in 1643 had three other names: Holland (from *holzland*, wooded land) for its most prosperous and powerful province, the Netherlands (from *nederland*, low country), and the United Provinces. Spain controlled the Austrian Netherlands, the predominantly Catholic southern provinces and today's Belgium.

Because the Dutch Republic's local, provincial, and national systems of government were more complicated than the absolute and limited monarchies in the rest of Europe, here is a brief overview for the readers.

Each of the Republic's seven northern provinces had its own Estate, legislative council, which sent delegates to the national Estates General that met at The Hague. The local Estates and large municipalities such as Amsterdam had autonomy to tax and have their own universities, legal systems, and currencies. In each provincial Estate, wealthy burghers represented the towns and nobles the countryside. They shared power equally, with the exception of Holland where the body of nobles had one vote and the commoners eighteen.

In the national Estates General, each province had one vote and the right to veto. Its presidency rotated amongst the seven provinces weekly. All proposals regarding war and peace were sent to the provincial towns for discussion before their delegates voted in the Estates General.

Amsterdam (derived from Amstel Dam), where most of *House of Rocamora* is set, was governed and dominated by an oligarchic municipal corporation. It consisted of a thirty-six member legislative council, a tribunal of nine magistrates, an executive of four burgomasters, a treasurer, and a legal advisor with the title of Pensionary. Each town sent one delegate to Holland's provincial Estate.

Looming over the loosely connected Dutch Republic, the non-republican *Stadhouder*, literally guardian/steward of the State, commanded the army and navy, granted pardons, nominated magistrates, but had no judicial or fiscal authority. The provinces of Groningen and Friesland also had *Stadhouders*. The national and provincial *Stadhouders* came from the House of Orange-Nassau, descended from the family of Willem the Silent, who led the initial revolt against Spain. The *Stadhouders'* powers waxed and waned during periods of war and peace. Their political supporters were called Orangists.

To secure their power, the commoner controlled Estates passed laws that forbade the granting of new titles. By the time Vicente de Rocamora arrived in Amsterdam, the Republic had no more than thirty landed noble families.

Chartered by the Estates General, the VOC, *Vereenigde Oost Indische Compagnie*, United East-Indian Company or Dutch East India Company, operated as a government unto itself with powers to wage war, negotiate treaties, coin money, and establish colonies.

The religion of the United Provinces was Protestant in the majority, the strict Calvinist Dutch Reformed Church being the most dominant sect but not absolute. There were also Remonstrantors, Collegiants, Quakers, and Mennonites. Jews were tolerated as guests in seventeenth century Amsterdam, and Catholics had the most severe restrictions placed on them.

Delineated social classes existed. Unemployed rabble filled the bottom. Above them in ascending order were peasants, artisans and others who worked with their hands. Steps higher as equals came Calvinist ministers, lawyers, teachers, clerks for the great companies, apothecaries, surgeons, and physicians. Next came the landed nobility, and ensconced at the apex merchant oligarchs controlled the government of Amsterdam, each of the Seven Provinces, and the Dutch East India Company.

Author's Notes, the author's translation of David de Barrios' twenty-two stanza *Aplauso Harmonico* praising Rocamora's life, abbreviated genealogy of the royal houses of Orange-Nassau and Stuart, value of money and cost of living appear at the end of *House of Rocamora*.

Fictional Characters
In Order of Appearance

Jacobus Velde (and family), a surgeon.
Cornelia Pauw, Rocamora's landlady.
Dirck van Noordwijk, aristocratic soldier and diplomat.
Mina Dekker, owner of a bakery.
Samuel de Santcroos (and family), wealthy merchant, shareholder of the Dutch East India Company.
Abraham da Mexia a member of the *Ma'amad*.
Elijah da Nuñes, a member of the *Ma'amad*.
Joseph da Costa, a member of the *Ma'amad*.
Gaspar Enríquez aka Hendrijks, sea captain and pirate.
Paulus Vanderpoel, a banker.
Matthias Poons, a professor at the University of Leyden Medical School.
Cornelius Palen, a Calvinist minister.
Gisebert Hagedorn, Professor at the University of Franeker Medical School.
Gustav Krogh, Gaspar Enríquez-Hendrijks' First Mate.
Roosjie Poons, wife of the professor.
Nikolaes Lertsma, Pedel at the University of Leyden.
Jan and Julia van der Waag, Rocamora's patients.
Nieto brothers, owners of a bordello.
Miriam, servant of the de Rocamora household.
Pablo de Royaya, Rocamora's friend from Valencia.
Benjamin de Ferrar, friend of Mexia, member of the Congregation.
Madame Yèyīng, woman of mystery.
Lyzor, Miriam's love.
Delia Schiffer (and family), Moses de Rocamora's love.
Geitl, servant who replaces Miriam.
Abel Muelen, ship captain.
Jacob de Rocamora, Moses' son.
Rebecca da Silva, Jacob's wet nurse.
Joan Woodhill, Lady Fairfield, Jacob's lover.

Holland is a country where the demon gold
is seated on a throne and crowned with tobacco.
—Salmasius

Part I
Adjustment
1644

Jews may be granted citizenship solely for the sake of trade ...
but not a license to become shopkeepers.
—Amsterdam Ordinance of 1632

1.
First Winter in Amsterdam

"¡Madre de dios!"

Don Vicente de Rocamora, born into the *caballero* caste, erstwhile Dominican friar and royal confessor for Infanta María, and who might have become Inquisitor General of Spain, lost his footing on the slick pavement and landed on his Spanish dignity. He stood and brushed snow from his cloak grateful he had no broken bones.

Have I traded the inferno of a Madrid summer for the icy hell of an Amsterdam winter?

Bells chimed the hour of eight in the morning. The clock enslaved others to Time but symbolized for Rocamora his new freedom with no required prayers at lauds, matins, and other canonical hours, and no Infanta, Count-Duke, and Inquisitor General demanding his services.

With a scented handkerchief, something he carried from his first days on the stinking streets of Madrid, Rocamora wiped moisture from his curled mustachio and spade goatee, less flamboyant than those of the Count-Duke de Olivares, his barber had trimmed them in a popular style after portraits by the recently deceased Flemish artist Sir Anthony van Dyck.

A strong North Sea wind knifed through Rocamora's clothes and burned his face and ears. He had purchased garments more for current fashion than climate. This day, he wore a black doublet, vest, and pair of breeches of fine wool beneath a cloak too thin for the frigid weather. His white blouse, flat collar and cuffs were of linen, and a black felt hat decorated with ostrich plumes atop a low crown and wide brim pinned to one side. Instead of shoes, he had on a pair of turned-top boots and inside them stockings too thin for his chilled feet.

By way of contrast, many Amsterdammers had no shape because under heavy cloaks or padded dressing gowns, the men had donned multiple waistcoats and breeches, and Rocamora speculated how many layers of clothing the women had beneath their long coats. Bundled roundly, the children reminded him of balls the Dutch rolled in a game they called *kegelen* played with nine pins.

Rocamora proceeded with caution on the icy bricks and cobblestones to avoid slipping again. Three-sided tents faced the frozen canals in which vendors offered choices of tea, single and double strength beer, more powerful spirits, and assortments of meats and cakes. Rocamora had enough of the cold and entered the nearest tent. He pushed through the crowd to a fire burning in a drum where he lit his pipe and warmed himself.

In relative comfort, Rocamora watched Amsterdammers of all ages, castes, and both genders playing and speeding along the ice on iron blades twice the length of their feet, the front edges curved upward like ships' prows on wood frames attached to their boots. He marveled at the swiftness and balance of peasants carrying baskets of eggs and produce, tradesmen their wares, and others who pushed small children and the elderly in armchairs affixed to smooth slats of wood. The most skilled skaters leaped, turned and spun in one place. All made room for plumed horses pulling painted sleighs, their jingling bells adding to shouts and laughter.

This is a world unlike any I have seen. Can I become part of it?

Before Rocamora ordered hot tea, portly surgeon Jacobus Velde, an acquaintance made the previous November, approached with two quart-size pewter *flapkans* of beer. A pair of skates hung from his neck.

"Mynheer Isaacus. A most delightful surprise to see you."

"Good morning, Mynheer Jacobus."

The Dutch custom of Latinizing names amused Rocamora. In his mind, he forever would be Don Vicente de Rocamora y Cornel even though he took the name Isaac that day of his rash act the previous October.

Velde handed Rocamora one of the tankards. "Drink and warm your innards."

Rocamora preferred not to imbibe so early in the day, but the Dutch considered it rude to refuse a drink of their national brew in the company of friends. He also had yet to become used to seeing women, youths, and small children toping no less than the men.

"Perhaps you will allow me to loan you my skates and give you your first lesson. You will soon discover it is easier to skate than walking on ice."

"Another day, Jacobus."

"Consider tomorrow. Our canals and lakes do not remain frozen for very long. There will be competitions later today and every day until they melt. If the ice is in good condition, one can skate from Amsterdam to Leyden in less than an hour and a half."

"Impressive."

Velde purchased sausages and cakes from a vendor, and Rocamora took small polite bites not to offend Velde. He hoped to avoid falling into the Dutch practice of *overvloed*, the gluttony for which they were notorious throughout Europe.

"Isaacus, do you see those men and boys on the ice striking a small wooden ball with those sticks curved at the end? One side tries to hit that post and the other defends it. We call the game *Groote Kolven*, another of our popular sports. We play it on ice in winter and on grass in summer."

Rocamora watched two opponents collide. "And which makes new patients for you surgeons."

"Yes, smashed noses and broken limbs are not uncommon. Isaacus, even though we have been acquainted for a few months, I respect your wisdom. I need your advice on a matter of great importance."

Velde's request did not surprise Rocamora. Despite his Spanish reserve, strangers often initiated conversations with him regarding the most personal subjects. The same as when he confessed and counseled penitents in Spain, Rocamora listened, nodded sympathetically, said little, and most of the time they made their own decisions. He waited for Velde to continue.

"But this is not a convenient time or the right place. I have business, some sawing of bones this morning, Is the hour past noon agreeable to you?"

"It is."

"Then let us meet at *The Three Crows* on Haarlemmerstraat, near the docks."

Rocamora did not tell Velde about his planned liaison later in the afternoon with Mina Dekker, a young and voluptuous strawberry blonde widow who inherited a bakery near the Town Hall. He had tested his newly trimmed lance with Mina this past December and several times each week since.

Rocamora put aside his *flapkan*. "I also have people to see this morning, Jacobus."

"But you have not finished your beer."

"It has been enough for me, and I thank you."

After Rocamora parted from Velde, he reflected on their budding friendship that began at a public anatomy demonstration. The surgeon had recognized him by name, which many did in Amsterdam because of his fame as Empress María's confessor when she was Infanta of Spain. Whenever they met for a midday meal at a tavern, Rocamora found Velde to be a well-meaning, congenial, and informative companion who offered much valuable information about medicine, life in the municipality, and nuances of the Dutch language. He preferred to master everyday talk and the local idioms and jargon before achieving academic perfection in their difficult tongue.

Rocamora's ruminations about Velde ended when he sensed someone following but saw no suspicious individuals along the canals. The vindictive Holy Office never hesitated to send assassins to eliminate its enemies or at the very least spies to report on their movements and activities. Rocamora believed he could deal with anyone the Inquisition might hire. He carried a dagger, and his walking stick held a sharp sword.

2.
Vlooienburg

Rocamora arrived without further mishap at Saint Anthony's Lock and bridge over the frozen Oude Schans Canal. On the other side lay Jodenbreestraat, Jews Broadstreet, and the Iberian Jewish district called Vlooienburg, derived from *vloedborg*, embankment against flooding. Situated near the Amstel River, Vlooienburg was not a confining ghetto, and the Jews of Amsterdam wore no identifying badges, caps, or caftans. Although they could live anywhere in Amsterdam, most chose to cluster close to their synagogue, Talmud Torah, which made it easier to associate with their coreligionists and fellow exiles. Unlike anywhere else in Europe, here Christians resided amidst Jews, most of them painters and dealers in fine art.

Rocamora crossed the bridge and stepped onto teeming Jodenbreestraat. Vendors hawked tempting savory foods. Men strolled to and from the synagogue. Others gathered in groups talking and gesturing. Women with small children carried their purchases from marketing.

Whenever Rocamora appeared on the streets of Vlooienburg, many of its inhabitants regarded him with awe and curiosity because of his former position at the Spanish Court. Others stared with expressions of suspicion or hostility. They resented, even hated him for having been a member of the Dominican Order that persecuted them and their families. Some feared he might be a spy for the Inquisition.

Rocamora passed men wearing boots and spurs bearing themselves with all the pride and dignity of *hidalgo*s and *caballeros*. As in Spain, the poorest wore great cloaks to cover worn, often threadbare garments. Wealthy merchants preened like grandees in silk and the finest wool doublets beneath their fur cloaks. Gold threads, pearls, and precious gems decorated the clothing of their women. The choice of colors, regardless of material, rivaled the austere requirements of the Spanish Court, mostly dull grays, blacks, and violet with glossy accessories of brownish yellow, orange-brown, and dark blue. A rare few rode in carriages or coaches with coats of arms painted on the doors.

Rocamora heard Spanish, Portuguese, Catalan, Valencian, French, and Italian spoken by the residents of Vlooienburg, which identified the lands of their origins. Most were polylingual of necessity. Rabbi Menasseh told him in Vlooienburg one needed Hebrew for prayer, Latin and Greek for a classical education, Portuguese for daily conversation, Spanish for literature and fine arts, and Dutch for dealing with municipal officials and doing business with Christians.

Rocamora learned Hebrew, Greek, and Latin from his mentor Don Lope and at the College of Confessors of Santo Domingo in Orihuela. Valencian Spanish was his native tongue, and he spoke Castilian for the twenty-two years he lived at the Alcazar. Similar to Spanish, Portuguese had been easy for him to master. From Rocamora's days on the docks of el Grau through his years at Court, to Amsterdam, he had become fluent in French and proficient in English, German, and now Dutch.

Rocamora came to Vlooienburg to visit a man reputed to be one of the most honest in Amsterdam who dealt in precious gems. His supply of escudos was diminishing faster than anticipated. He turned the corner and knocked on the door of a narrow, three-story home with a typical brick façade. An elderly woman, Judah Touro's widowed sister, opened it.

"Doña Ribcá, is Don Judah at home?"

The woman squinted at him. "I recognize you now. You were at the *berit milah* of my nephew's son."

And my own.

"Yes, I was. I am Don Vi—Don Isaac de Rocamora."

"Please come in. My brother is at the synagogue and will return shortly I am preparing our midday meal and must leave you."

"Thank you."

Her glare reminded Rocamora to touch the silver mezuzah etched with the six-pointed Star of David on the doorframe with the first two fingers of his right hand and kiss them to show love and respect for God and His commandments written on the tiny rolled scroll placed inside. On one side of the tiny parchment was the *Shemah*, Hear oh Israel, the Lord our God, the Lord is One, and on the verso another of God's names, *Shaddai*, the acronym for *Shomer Daltot Yisrael*, Guardian of Israel's Doors. That Jews fearlessly identified their houses with mezuzahs further confirmed for Rocamora the religious tolerance of the Dutch.

In the vestibule, he heard scraping and coughing coming from the basement. Curious, he descended the stairs and saw a young woman seated by a brazier rubbing two diamonds together. She wore a heavy drab grey wool robe over her clothes and a floppy white cap with starched points that touched her shoulders.

"Doña Abigail?"

Her welcoming smile warmed Rocamora more than any brazier or fireplace could on this winter day.

"*Capitán*, how delightful to see you after these many months. I thought you might have returned to Spain."

"That, I can never do."

"Of course. You have come to see my uncle?"

"Don Judah, yes."

"He is at the synagogue."

"So your aunt told me. Perhaps, I should wait upstairs. You are not chaperoned."

"Vlooienburg is not Spain or Portugal."

Sometimes I wonder.

"Please come closer and warm yourself by my brazier. And tell me, why do you wish to speak with my uncle?"

Rocamora opened a small pouch and placed two gems on her table. "I can appreciate their superficial beauty, but I do not know what price to ask if I sell them."

"I must confess, *Capitán*, I do not know why you have chosen my uncle. There are greater merchants in Amsterdam."

"People have assured me that I can trust Don Judah to tell me their true value."

While Abigail studied the gems, Rocamora reflected on why she addressed him by the rank he held in Cardinal-Infante Fernándo's army. Nine years passed since that day he introduced himself as *Capitán* Vicente de Rocamora to Abigail and her father at their home in Antwerp. He remembered his reaction when the impressionable girl told him they would wed. A child's fantasy, he had thought that day.

"You hold them so close to your eyes. Perhaps you need to wear *quevedos*."

"What are *quevedos*?"

"A famous satirist of that name wore spectacles and made them popular in Madrid."

"Was he a friend of yours?"

"An acquaintance."

Abigail returned the gems to Rocamora. "Be assured, my uncle will give you an honest appraisal."

"May I ask what is it you were doing?"

"Bruting, polishing diamonds. After a stone has been cut or split to achieve a natural eight-sided shape, I rub one crystal face against the other, and the box below catches the grit. Next, I use the grit to grind the tip to a crude facet. The dust removes any scratches on the surface and refines the cut."

"An impressive skill." He did not like the sound of Abigail's cough and the chill in the basement. "For how many years have you been polishing?"

"Since I was a child helping my father, may he rest in peace."

"It is not good for your well-being to work in so dank and damp a room, and I believe you could rid yourself of that cough by placing a linen gauze over your nose and mouth so you do not inhale the diamond dust."

"I have been given no other place to work and sleep, but I shall heed your advice about the gauze."

"And to soothe your nose, throat, and lungs, I recommend peppermint."

Rocamora experienced an attraction to Abigail unlike any before, not with the *morilla* Moraíma, not even with María. More than her features and intelligence pleased him. She had self-assurance and an innate serenity beyond that of the Empress. Each movement of her body and hand had a natural grace suggesting dance rather than mere gesture. When Abigail spoke, her voice enveloped him in velvet, and there was her wonderful smile.

What is happening to me? What am I thinking? Abigail is five years younger than my daughter Brianda would have been had she lived.

"Don Isaac?" Judah Touro stepped into the basement.

"Good morning, Don Judah."

Abigail stood. "May I serve you tea, *Capitán*?"

"No, thank you."

Judah searched Abigail's face. "Don Isaac, I am honored to welcome you to my home."

"I have come here to ask for your advice regarding gems." Rocamora saw disappointment etched on Judah's face. "I have heard of your unblemished reputation for honesty and discretion and that what I ask and reveal here will go no farther."

"Abigail, perhaps it is best you leave this room."

"No, let her stay. I trust your niece. Doña Abigail was instructing me on the fine art of diamond polishing."

"My niece is the best in Amsterdam, and that mill … she has two … and many other valuable possessions are part of her *dotar*, her dowry."

Abigail blushed. "But I have yet to accept any suitor."

Rocamora now understood that Judah hoped he had come to inquire about his suitability as a potential husband for Abigail.

"Don Judah, I need information about diamonds and other gems. I told Doña Abigail that I appreciate their beauty but lack the practiced eye and experience to differentiate the fine points of quality."

Judah held one of Rocamora's diamonds to the candlelight. "Value is dependent upon the stone's weight and quality of transparency or brilliance, its lack of blemish, spots, and other flaws. The price is further dictated by the supply and demand of the market. These are undoubtedly of the finest quality. Where did you obtain them?"

"When Empress María was Infanta of Spain, I confessed her. She often rewarded me with gifts."

"Our congregation, the entire city, all know of your past. A collector would value them higher if you could prove their provenance."

"My word is my provenance."

"Don Isaac, do not take what I say to be an insult, but in the diamond market a man's word may not be good enough." He studied the gems further. "Even so, small as they are, these stones are worth many guilders."

"How many?"

"A general guess? Let me see." Judah weighed and inspected each gem. "Somewhere between fifty to a hundred guilders each. Perhaps more, but not less."

"*Capitán*, you should price other stones of similar quality sold by jewelers."

"Abigail is right. Study the current market so you can negotiate the price you want from a position of strength."

"Perhaps I shall ask for your or Doña Abigail's assistance, for I have seen that haggling in the marketplace is a natural skill if not an art, and I have had no experience in the game."

"I can give you the names of several honorable merchants."

"Don Judah, your assistance and honesty are greatly appreciated, and please, say nothing of my gems to anyone."

"You have both our words."

"*Capitán*, will you stay and share our meal?"

"Yes, please do."

Rocamora took the paper on which Judah had written names of trusted merchants. "I thank you, Don Judah, Doña Abigail, but I cannot accept your kind invitation this day."

"*Capitán*, you are always most welcome here."

3.
A Summons

Rocamora left the Touros shaken by his reaction to Abigail. He could well imagine making his place in Amsterdam with so intelligent, accomplished, and attractive a woman. If he had read Abigail and Judah correctly, they would be agreeable to his wooing. Never one to believe in witchcraft and the prophecies of *sabias,* wise women, Rocamora never forgot Moraíma's prophecy he would have three loves and children. Moraíma, the beautiful *morilla* mistress of Philip IV and unattainable María had been the first two.

Walking along Jodenbreestraat toward St. Anthony's Lock, Rocamora questioned if he wanted to become part of this small, restrictive community and wear new masks of conformity. He enjoyed his new freedom too much to consider a life of routine and obligation for now. Despite his dream of becoming a physician, the Siren's song of a *pícaro's* life also beckoned him no less than when he parted from Moraíma so many years ago. Why should he not spend the remainder of his allotted years living the life of a free spirit?

"Don Isaac … Don Isaac de Rocamora."

Rocamora turned and greeted thirty-nine year old Rabbi Menasseh ben Israel, an energetic man of short stature, and, in his estimation, the greatest individual he had encountered in the Sephardic community. Born Manoel Dias Soeiro in Portugal, Menasseh had been so precocious in Talmudic studies he was ordained a rabbi in Amsterdam at age seventeen.

Menasseh's writing and publishing history impressed Rocamora. The rabbi had established one of the first Jewish printing presses in Amsterdam. His energy, broad range of interests, and talents reminded Rocamora of Olivares, the giant who had dominated Spain for more than twenty years.

"We are well met, Don Isaac."

"As always, Rabbi."

"I need to speak with you, but the Breestraat is too crowded." Menasseh guided Rocamora around a corner to a quieter street. "Please do not take offense at what I have to say. Some here in Vlooienburg are questioning why you have not joined our community, and in truth I am disappointed you have not."

"You told me I must wait three years before I can join your congregation."

"You can become part of our community at any time."

"I have been studying Dutch and immersing myself in their language and customs. I would have poor manners not to learn all I can about our tolerant hosts."

"Not their gluttony and drinking, I trust. In any case, I was going to send my pupil, young Bento d'Espinoza, to give you my message. I have assumed the task of informing you that you have been summoned to appear at Talmud Torah."

Rocamora stiffened. "Summoned? By whose authority and for what?"

"The authority of the *Ma'amad*, our Supreme Council."

So, here in Vlooienburg, these Jews also have their own la Suprema, *Supreme Council of the Holy Office.*

"From whom or what do they derive their authority?"

"They are the leadership of our community elected from those who have full rights of membership in the congregation."

"You mean the *poderosos*, your oligarchs."

"It often turns out that way. Unfortunately, wealth often earns more respect than learning or innate virtues, but you should know this. In the synagogue or in the law court of the *Ma'amad*, no one may oppose its orders and commands or circulate writings containing adverse criticisms of the council's decisions and actions. The *Haham*, our sages of the congregation, enjoy the same authority."

"Your sages?"

"Yes, the leading rabbis"

"I am not yet a member of your community, so what questions can they possibly put to me?"

"You may be the most exceptional refugee ever to have come to our community. No one else lived at the Spanish Court for so long a time. No one else was an intimate of the Count-Duke de Olivares. No one else confessed Queen Isabel and Empress María when she was Infanta of Spain. No one else might have been Inquisitor General. That is why some in our community fear you may be a spy or even an assassin for the Inquisition. Will you honor the summons?"

"Tell me, Rabbi, does your *Ma'amad* question every man who has left Spain and Portugal?"

"No, but to repeat, you are unique, a former royal confessor and member of the monastic order that persecutes us as no other. And, you participated in *autos de fé* and burnings at the *quemaderos*."

"I cannot, I will not deny my past. If I choose to appear, will you be there?"

"I am the presiding rabbi this week."

"I shall honor your summons. At what hour?"

"At ten tomorrow morning. By the way, a stranger to our community has inquired about you. He is Dutch, a large man with the bearing of a soldier, but he would not give his name or his reasons for seeking you."

"I shall be alert to him."

"I saw you leaving Don Judah's home. His niece is a virtuous young woman, one of many we have here in Vlooienburg. Have you considered marrying?"

Rocamora feigned confusion. "What?"

"Remember, you will not be a true man in our community until you marry and have children. I know not what wealth or lack of it you brought with you from Spain, but you will have a choice of wealthy widows and daughters of successful merchants with great dowries. Our eligible women and girls far outnumber the men available for marriage."

Rabbi, author, book publisher. Did Menasseh also wear the hat of matchmaker?

Menasseh took an envelope from his doublet. "One last thing before we part. This letter arrived for you."

Rocamora could not imagine who might have written him. The plain wax seal had no identifying mark from ring or stamp. "Who sent it?"

"It was enclosed in another missive sent by my esteemed friend, Dr. Immanuel Bocarro."

"The renowned physician and mathematician? Why would he write me?"

"He did not say." Menasseh squinted at Rocamora. "Of course you are aware that Bocarro is physician to Emperor Ferdinand III and his family."

And María is Ferdinand's wife.

Menasseh interrupted Rocamora's speculations about the letter's contents. The rabbi took his arm and stopped in front of a house larger than most near the bridge. "Don Isaac, if you can spare the time, there is someone I would like you to meet. I believe you will find the experience most interesting."

4.
Jewish Eyes

"Don Isaac, that mansion next door on the corner belongs to the merchant, Daniel de Pinto, and this is the home of Rembrandt van Rijn, our greatest artist. As you can see it is also larger than most, for it covers two lots."

Rocamora hesitated on the steps. "We may be disturbing him."

"He enjoys meeting new people." Menasseh rapped on the front door. A voluptuous woman with hair the color of copper opened it. A small boy with blond curls clung to her skirt.

"Rabbi Menasseh, please enter, you are always most welcome here."

They stepped into a spacious vestibule the Dutch called a *voorhuis*. "Mevrouw, I have brought with me the esteemed Don Isaac de Rocamora, former confessor to Empress María. Don Isaac this is Vrouw Geertje."

"I am caretaker of Rembrandt's home and dry nurse for his son Titus."

Rocamora offered a slight bow. "Mevrouw."

"Rabbi, the master will be pleased to see you and meet your friend. You know your way. There is never any need for you to stand on ceremony and be announced, and I must feed Titus."

"If you do not mind, I shall take Don Isaac on a tour of the rooms on the way to his studio."

"Of course. Mynheer Isaacus, you may purchase whatever you like if you meet the master's price."

Never before had Rocamora thought about purchasing paintings and drawings he admired. In Spain, those of modest means and his own *caballero* caste hung crucifixes or icons of Jesus, Mary, and saints on their walls. The collection of fine art was left to the royal family and the wealthy. Tempting it might be, he would not spend guilders on a painting or drawing while his future was uncertain and he had no income and home.

Geertje left with Titus, and Menasseh led Rocamora from the vestibule, into a *sydelcamer*, side room, where several dozen canvases painted by Rembrandt and other artists hung on the walls.

"It is a veritable museum, Rabbi."

"Not exactly. Geertje is right. Everything is for sale, and believe me, Don Isaac, there is much more to see. Have you ever observed the process of engraving?"

"I have not."

Menasseh took Rocamora into a large room. "Rembrandt must have sent his apprentice on an errand. No problem, the process of engraving is simple to explain and complicated to execute. Rembrandt etches his scenes and portraits on these copper plates, after which he inks and makes prints from this press on those moist sheets of paper. They are less costly than his paintings, and he may be making engravings for a book I am writing."

Rocamora studied several etchings drying like wash on clotheslines. "Brilliant, absolutely brilliant what he can do with a few lines."

"Come with me, Don Isaac. I want to show you where Rembrandt keeps assorted objects and rarities he uses for his paintings."

They went into a great hall. They went into a great hall filled with a grand collection of oddities. It included seashells, corals, stuffed animal skins, and weapons from all over the world. Cabinets and drawers bursting with drawings and etchings by Rembrandt and other artists could not be closed.

"One could linger here for several days and still not see all, Rabbi."

"That is true. Rembrandt is no stranger to auctions."

Rocamora followed Menasseh through an anteroom filled with fine furniture and cabinetry where more paintings covered the walls and onto the top floor studio, a room of good size filled with light streaming in through large windows.

Rocamora hesitated at the stairs. Rembrandt munched on a chunk of bread and drank from a goblet of wine while staring at a drawing on an easel. He had seen Rembrandt for the first time the previous October at Daniel Touro's home sketching the family and guests during the *berit milah* of his host's son.

Rocamora compared Rembrandt's appearance with that of another great artist, Velázquez, always well groomed and conscious of his handsome mien. Rembrandt, by way of contrast, was a disheveled unkempt man of gross peasant features and wild hair. Rocamora amused himself imagining how this rumpled genius would have fit into the Spanish Court.

Rembrandt saw Menasseh and embraced him. "Always delighted to have your company, Rabbi, and who is this you have brought to my studio?"

"I have the honor of introducing you to the esteemed Don Isaac de Rocamora who ...."

"... was Empress María's former confessor. Mynheer Isaacus, I have looked forward to meeting you, and I welcome you." Rembrandt went to a side table. "Will you join me in a glass of wine?"

"Yes, thank you."

"Rabbi?"

"I respectfully decline."

Rembrandt poured white wine into two goblets and handed one to Rocamora. "News of your defection from the Spanish church and monarchy has excited all in Amsterdam."

"And our Sephardic community. I wanted you and Don Isaac to meet. I took the liberty of taking him on a tour of your home to show him your paintings and etchings."

"Wonderful. Then please tell me, Mynheer Isaacus, what are your impressions?"

"Like no one before, you have managed to penetrate and reveal the essences of your subjects' beings. You show more truth in their eyes than any artist I have seen, any book I have read."

"You must have met Velázquez and seen his paintings every day when you lived at the Alcazar."

"Peter Paul Rubens too at the time he visited in the capacity of a diplomat, and I saw works by many other painters of great repute in the royal collection. That is why I can say without flattery you are the greater master."

A hearty laugh shook Rembrandt's stomach. "If you have seen all that, your praise has true currency. When you purchase something of mine, I shall deduct that amount from the price. And so, Mynheer Isaacus, which of my paintings, drawings, and etchings have you selected?"

"More than I am able to count, but as you know, I am recently arrived in Amsterdam and have no permanent home. After I establish myself, I most certainly will purchase something of yours."

"I shall hold you to it. And now, Rabbi, have you completed your book you wish me to illustrate?"

"Not yet."

Rembrandt offered more wine, which Rocamora refused. "I regret I must leave now. Mynheer Rembrandt, I thank you for your hospitality and the opportunity to see your great work. Rabbi …."

"One moment, Don Isaac. Mynheer Rembrandt, you often use our people to pose for your scriptural paintings, drawings, and etchings. Don Isaac has a most interesting face, do you not agree? I believe he would be an excellent subject for you."

Rembrandt moved closer to Rocamora "Most exceptional. I have never before seen eyes like yours." He went to his palette, mixed several colors, and applied the result to paper. "Yes, that is it, the patina copper acquires if it is not polished. After I perfect this verdigris tint, I will use it for a pair of eyes in a painting I have in mind, but I cannot use him for one of my Jewish subjects, not even for a drawing or etching."

"But why?"

"Rabbi Menasseh, my friend, cannot you of all people see? Look closely at his eyes. No disrespect to Mynheer Isaacus, who like all of us, must have experienced the travails and disappointments of life and the loss of loved ones. Yes, look at those eyes. Unusual of color they may be, but he does not have the exceptional eyes of your people who have suffered so many torments and persecutions throughout the centuries. He does not have Jewish eyes."

5.
Van Noordwijk

After he left Menasseh and Rembrandt, Rocamora went to Dam Square to read daily bulletins posted on the walls of the Town Hall next to the Wisselbank and pamphlets announcing the latest government decrees, results of battles and diplomacy, and reports about Spain. Groups of men gathered at the city's center all hours of the day to discuss business, government, and war. Adjacent and perpendicular to the Town Hall was the imposing *Nieuwe Kerk*, New Church, and next to it the *Waag*, where officials weighed and measured goods for taxation. The square also served as a marketplace for dry goods, fowl, meats. produce and flowers in season.

Rocamora saw a trio of soldiers on the steps of the Town Hall staring at him. One of the cavaliers nodded at a burly blond who matched Menasseh's description. Wary of strangers, he gripped his walking stick when the soldier left his companions and approached. Despite the two inches of extra height added by the heels and soles of his boots, Rocamora faced a man more than a head taller.

The soldier spoke in heavily accented Spanish. "You are the renowned Dominican friar, Don Vicente de Rocamora."

It was not a question, and Rocamora responded in Dutch. "Before I reply, will you do me the courtesy of identifying yourself?"

"Yes, of course. I am Dirck van Noordwijk, Captain of the *Stadhouder's* Guard."

"You are correct. I was Don Vicente de Rocamora, but no longer a Dominican and hardly renowned. I am now Don Isaac de Rocamora and a Jew. How did you know who I am?"

"My companions over there identified you."

"I am not acquainted with them."

"Despite your modesty, your reputation precedes you. They have seen you reading the bulletins every day, and it seems everyone I have spoken with in Amsterdam has heard of you. I have been seeking you on behalf of our *Stadhouder* who wishes to meet you. It is not every day our Republic becomes a sanctuary for a member of the Spanish Court who was more than Empress María's confessor when she was Infanta of Spain and Queen of Hungary. We could not have captured a greater prize in battle. You also served the

Count-Duke de Olivares, the *de facto* ruler of Spain until recently, as his spy and master of codes. You were an intimate friend of their greatest soldier, Cardinal-Infante Fernándo, and you came within a hair's width of attaining the position of Inquisitor General."

What else have they learned about me?

"I have been given the honor of escorting you to The Hague, Don Isaacus."

Rocamora recovered from his surprise. He should have expected the *Stadhouder* or his minions to question him about his intimate knowledge of the Spanish court, government, military, and personalities. Rocamora loosened his grip on the stick. He instinctively trusted van Noordwijk, who had an innate charm and genuine affability.

"I cannot refuse the Prince of Orange. When do we leave?"

"I have other duties to perform in Amsterdam. Would you please meet me here the day after tomorrow at ten in the morning. I will provide a mount for you."

"*In twee dagen tot wij opnieuw samenkomen.*"

"Yes, until we meet again in two days. I must say that I am impressed with your command of our language, Don Isaacus."

"It would be disrespectful and ill-mannered not to learn the tongue of my host country and sanctuary."

"Well said, and so until then, *Ga met God.*"

6.
One Who Must Remain Nameless

Rocamora entered the room he rented at the home of Vrouw Cornelia Pauw, plump widow of a wool dyer, in the respectable Jordaan District of guild masters, clerks, professionals, and ministers. Jordaan came from the French word *jardin* for garden, and its streets were named for flowers like Rosengracht where he lodged.

He lit a candle at his table by the fireplace and hesitated before opening the letter. One of Cornelia's Chartreaux kittens had adopted him, and it leaped into his lap for warmth and affection. She bred Chartreaux because their lush silver blue coats made them desired by furriers and by the affluent for pets.

Rocamora named the kitten Hombrecillo, little man, after the midget court *bufón*, Sancho de Fonseca. The royal fool had been his most loyal friend inside the Alcazar until he ingested poison after his wife Inéz died of fever.

Rocamora sliced the wax seal with his dagger and opened the envelope. He smiled when he read the familiar numeric code he had taught María. Rocamora placed a blank sheet of paper beside the letter, and when he decrypted the first words, he experienced disappointment.

> To the most esteemed and illustrious Don Vicente de Rocamora,
>
> I am the physician Immanuel Bocarro, and I write this letter to you on behalf of One who must remain nameless.

Yes, the Empress would not condescend to write me directly.

> That Person demands to know if it is true you are now residing in Amsterdam amongst heretics, and worse, that you have joined the community of abominable cursed Jews.

Good, no mention of my circumcision.

The Person for whom I am writing cannot imagine a former Royal Confessor could ever contemplate so loathsome a choice and condemn his soul to everlasting damnation. That Person prefers to believe he has sought temporary sanctuary from his many enemies.

Sanctuary, yes. Living as a Jew, not yet.

That Person demands the courtesy of a response so those calumnies and lies can be disputed and proven false.

Rocamora lit his long stemmed clay pipe, stroked the kitten, and considered how best to respond. Soon memories intruded, and he saw María in the context of sunny days.

He relived that first moment when the human Hombrecillo, whom he had rescued with the midget's wife from brigands, brought him to the Infanta's apartments. She had been more golden within the gloom of the palace than a sky filled with noon suns.

He remembered her confessions, many of them intimate, and the satisfying penances he had given her.

He recalled their conspiring together against Charles, Prince of Wales, whom she refused to marry unless he converted to Catholicism.

He retained clear memory of that day in the gardens of the Casa de Campo when María seemed about to reveal her true feelings for him before Prince Charles dropped from the wall and interrupted the one confession he most desired to hear.

He closed his eyes and wished he had the skills of Velázquez so he too could have captured that telltale smile María bestowed upon him the day the artist completed her portrait. It had been the fatal revealing smile seen by Olivares and the Austrian Ambassador, which convinced them that the Queen of Hungary's confessor must never accompany her when she left Spain for the Empire.

Rocamora imagined what might have happened had he kissed María's lips during their meeting in the antechamber and how the end might have played out had he carried her away. Would she have played Lucretia to his Tarquin or Juliet to his Romeo?

He could not find the words to begin his reply. Should he write the truth? His mentor Don Lope would have advised him to tell the empress of his Jewish blood and end his dream of attaining the unattainable. He heard more voices speaking from the grave: his worldly older kinsman and greatest friend Ramón, Señor de Ballebrera and Knight of Alcántara, suggesting a reply more ambiguous to learn what María's next move might be, and Hombrecillo urging him to burn the letter and forget María for all time.

Not yet ready to write a response, Rocamora opened his great trunk with its many confounding locks and secret compartments that contained his reserve of gold coins, precious gems, and poems he had written for and about María. He held the cross his mother had given him, which contained the three mysterious clues to their origins: Sep, Natronai, and Bodo. He uncovered the silver crucifix of the Dominican Order he wore for twenty-five years.

Rocamora prevented the kitten from leaping inside, collected his poems, and read each verse. He saved for the last, his favorite of all.

María

I send this letter to you, my love,
On the wings of a milk-white dove,
Sweetened with cinnamon water,
And scented with spring flowers
From our lost Garden of Eden.

I remember the golden sun of your hair,
The soft May-blue sky of your eyes,
The blooming pink rose of your lips,
The perfectly matched pearls of your teeth,
And the dulcet nightingale-song of your voice.

Do you hear me call your name in the wind,
Taste my tears of remorse in the rain,
Hear my heartbeat in the distant thunder,
Echoing your dainty footsteps
In the corridors of memory?

Regardless of any rumors the Empress might have heard, Rocamora believed that without absolute proof of his apostasy she would remember him as her Dominican confessor. For the moment, however, he was not prepared to craft a clever response.

Hombrecillo clung to Rocamora's shoulder when he went into the kitchen. His landlady, Vrouw Cornelia, sat by the fire reading her bible. The kitten leaped from Rocamora's shoulder to the floor where its brothers and sisters pushed for space at a large bowl of cream.

"Mynheer Isaacus, your bath was satisfactory?"

"As always."

"Bathing several times each week. I cannot understand why."

"It is something that was denied me in Spain. I cannot bathe often enough."

"Do you know how many pots of water I must boil for your bath in winter?"

"I have counted them, and I thank you. It saves me the time and expense of going to the bath houses."

"Those vile places of corruption. Never visit them." She closed her bible. "You are going out again?"

"I am meeting a friend at a tavern."

"Taverns and inns, all of them, places of sin. You have been my best boarder. I do not want to lose you. Hurry home before night falls. The streets of Amsterdam are dangerous after dark, especially for the unwary."

Now comes her daily lecture.

"Beware of the women, for in the taverns when they sit next to you or on your lap to tempt, they are skilled at removing your purse. Also be wary of the tavern owners. An unsavory lot, all of them. They commonly cheat drunken customers by double billing and diluting the wine, which is nothing more than watered syrup. And at each table is a sawdust bin where the whores can empty their glasses to speed a fool's drinking and themselves to avoid *dronkenschaap*."

No different from the garitos *in El Grau and Madrid.*

"You should find yourself a virtuous woman and marry her."

It seems everyone in Amsterdam wants me to wed.

7.
Language of Flapkans and Mussels

How shall I ever find Velde in this man made fog?

Rocamora's eyes watered the instant he entered the raucous tavern. He coughed and pushed deeper into the crowded maw of *The Three Crows* where each customer smoked a pipe. Rocamora detected aromas of trance inducing ingredients and many customers sitting in varying degrees of stupor. Velde had told him tobacconists often added the hallucinogenic substances black henbane seed, belladonna, thorn apples, or cannabis sativa.

At each table men ate and drank, smoked, wenched, and gambled every variation of knucklebones, cards, and the usual obsessive wagering on the absurd: who could swill from a tankard the fastest, on which plate a fly would land, or which toper would leave with which woman.

By now, the height and heft of the general population led Rocamora to believe the Dutch had to be the tallest people in Europe. He remembered the Spanish clergy reviling the Protestant Netherlanders for their wallowing in gluttony and drunkenness. Velde often said with pride *overvloed* was part of the Dutch national character.

Their silent language of gestures he had become familiar with amused Rocamora. If a patron showed interest in a whore for a liaison, he thrust a forefinger in the bowl of his pipe. When a wench sought a customer, she touched her breast and crotch; or she might open the top of a *flapkan* and expose the tankard's maw.

Rocamora found Velde at a table drinking beer, fondling a plump partridge seated on his lap, and wagering with a man at an adjacent table how many pieces of mutton were in his neighbor's steaming *hutspot,* the typical Dutch stew of carrots and potatoes mixed with chunks of pork, beef, mutton, or goat in a seasoned meat sauce. The surgeon's face was red, and his beatific smile suggested he was already in a state of what the Dutch called in their difficult to pronounce language *beschonkenheid,* tipsiness.

Velde greeted Rocamora, pushed the girl to her feet, and ordered a *hutspot* and bowls of mussels for them both. "Another tankard for me, Lise, and a fresh one for my friend. Ah, Isaacus, I can see that you have not yet adapted to the smoke of Amsterdam."

Rocamora sat and dabbed his eyes with a handkerchief. "Does one ever?"

"We have a saying. A Hollander without a pipe is a national impossibility, akin to a town without houses, a stage without actors, and a spring without flowers."

Rocamora agreed that was no understatement. Because tobacco was plentiful and inexpensive, the populace smoked everywhere, even in their churches, and smoke infused their clothing, hair, and furnishings.

Several wenches, whose capacious bosoms overflowed from their sweat-stained bodices, clustered around Rocamora and competed for a place on his lap. Polite yet authoritative, he sent them away.

"No girl here to please you? Surely you are not still keeping your vow of chastity."

Rocamora did not reply, and Lise served their *hutspot*. Another wench, whose breasts seemed about to burst from her low cut bodice, brought mussels and beer. She opened Rocamora's tankard and smiled a gap-toothed invitation. "These mussels may be closed, but mine is always open."

Velde slapped her behind. "My dear Clara, not even a canal boat can fill your *kweido*."

"And your *pezel* is so small it makes an ant look like a great ship." She leered at Rocamora. "But, you, Mynheer, I am sure you could sail a great route with your *jacht*."

Rocamora understood her metaphor of a hunting boat. "I shall be docking this night at a different harbor."

"If another ship arrives there first, remember to anchor at mine."

Velde sent Lise and Clara away and raised his tankard to Rocamora. "Life does not get better than this. I am honored, as always, to share a table with you."

Rocamora acknowledged the toast and sipped his beer while Velde guzzled. "You seem to know every whore in *The Three Crows*."

"And they amuse me. Let me assure you, though, that I love my wife and children too much to do more than jibe and jest with them. Even when I repair broken limbs and sew knife wounds at the *plugge-kits* ...."

"Your brothels."

"I am no *muylpeeren* ...."

"A fool who pays for women."

"Wonderful, my friend, you have acquired the language of the streets."

"Only the words, never the diseases."

"And I too am fortunate to have avoided them."

Rocamora speared a carrot from the *hutspot*. "I have never before tasted sweeter carrots or seen any with so intense an orange color than those here in Amsterdam."

"Our growers cultivate only the best to honor the memory of William the Silent, Prince of Orange, who founded the House of Orange-Nassau and the Netherlands as a state."

"Now, Jacobus what is it you wished to discuss with me, and can we go to a table where it is quieter? I am barely able to hear you."

"Impossible." Velde spread his arms.. "Look about you. More customers than tables. All of them eating, drinking, gambling, and wenching." He moved his chair closer to Rocamora and lowered his voice. "One can make an even better business with an establishment like this if separate rooms were added for gambling and others for discreet liaisons. That is the owners' plan. They will offer me the opportunity to purchase shares should they expand, and I am thinking of investing enough guilders to become a partner."

Rocamora withheld comment and waited for Velde to continue.

The surgeon pointed at a corpulent man whose eyes disappeared between low brow and full cheeks. "That fellow over there, Hugo Graacht, is the proprietor of *The Three Crows*. Two magistrates are his principal partners. Ah, your face. I read volumes of skepticism in your expression. Yes, I can guess what you are thinking. They would be putting my money and those of other investors at risk, not theirs, and controlling the figures they put in the account ledger. I can see it clearly now. A good business for them, bad for me. Thank you, my dear friend for your wisdom. Better to keep my money in the Wisselbank and make small investments at the Bourse."

Rocamora reflected upon the countless times his silence and laconic questions motivated individuals to arrive at decisions they wanted to make in the first place.

Whom we seek for advice is predetermined by the answers we want to hear.

"I must go now, Jacobus."

"But why?"

"I have promised to meet another."

"I hope it is with some fair doxy, but I am not one to pry." Velde raised his hand when Rocamora reached into his coin purse. "Put that away, my friend. I invited you, and you gave me valuable advice."

"As I appreciate yours." Rocamora stood, raised his walking stick in a salute, and left.

8.
Alluring Scent of Marzipan

Although dusk came early during an Amsterdam winter, the Amsteldammers continued to skate on the frozen canals aided by torches they carried and light from tent fires. More revelers filled streets and alleys going in and out of taverns and brothels along Rocamora's route. He used his walking stick to discourage aggressive *nagtlopers* and *pluggen*, women of the streets and their flesh mongers.

Ay, those harsh sounding difficult to pronounce but amusing Dutch words.

In Spain, prostitutes were euphemistically called *mujeres perdidas*, lost women, when *puta* was not used.

Rocamora rapped on the bakery door. Someone unbolted and opened it, and a pleasing scent of marzipan wafted toward him. A plump strawberry blonde in a shift held a candelabrum to his face.

"You are late."

"Mina, my beauty, I regret the inconvenience, but circumstances arose that prevented me from being on time. No, do not narrow your lovely eyes. It was not a member of your fair gender but a friend who needed advice. May I be allowed to make amends?"

"I should slam this door in your face for that and for ignoring me."

"These two days away from you have been torture. I have yearned to breathe more deeply of your delicious marzipan scent."

"You are too charming a rogue, but I am weak. Your unusual green eyes, your rich voice that sings even when the words are ordinary …."

"The goddess of love favors me, for I have found myself a poetess, whose lush couplets caught my attention from the start."

"My wicked cavalier." Mina thrust her bosom against Rocamora's chest and kissed him. "Come inside, and I will allow you to make your apologies."

They passed her ovens, which Rocamora thought to be an apt metaphor for his carnal destination, and he breathed aromas of dough and spices Mina used in her pastries pleased his olfactory senses, marzipan his favorite ingredient of all. Her sugary confections were the most popular in Amsterdam, but this night, other offerings satisfied his carnal desires.

A sigh escaped Mina's lips when the final grains of sand dropped yet another time to the bottom of her hourglass on a nearby stand. "You have more than made up for your lateness although …."

"What is it?"

"Sometimes, it seems you are not really here in mind and spirit."

Rocamora did not speak. Protesting would do no good, and he preferred to let Mina reveal her thoughts.

"Even now, it seems you are detached. Are you thinking of your former life in Spain, some woman you left behind?"

"No, Mina, my one thought is how to convince you to let me stay in bed with you."

"I want that too, but now you must go. My apprentices will be arriving soon. We have to bake fresh breads and prepare confections for my customers. Will you promise to be on time tomorrow?"

"You have my word."

Rocamora was not yet ready to tell Mina their liaisons would be ending soon. After the worst of winter passed, he intended to travel throughout the United Provinces and visit the medical schools at Leyden, Utrecht, and Franeker before deciding where to matriculate.

Hombrecillo leaped into Rocamora's arms when he returned to his room. He stoked the fire, lit a candle, and sat at his table. He waited for the purring kitten to settle in his lap and wrote a reply to Bocarro's letter in the same code, He dared not address this letter personally to María.

> To the most esteemed and illustrious Doctor Bocarro ….
>
> Please inform the Person who inquired about me that I pray She is well and happy and that I am honored to be the subject of Her thoughts, as She is forever in mine.

That is true.

> The Person asked if I have become a Jew. Assure Her of this. I have not joined their community. I do not worship at their synagogue. I do not live amongst them.

No lies, simply a withholding of the entire truth.

> Please inform that most esteemed Personage I have come to Amsterdam to seek sanctuary from those who wish me harm and to study Medicine.

Now that is the absolute truth.

> After I have my license to practice medicine, I shall so inform you, which information, I trust, you will relate to the Person on whose behalf you have written me. In the meantime, please continue to write me about Her health, may it improve.

Rocamora read his letter several times before signing it. Yes, any spy could verify all he had written. He would not be living with Jews or joining their community and congregation in the near future while he studied medicine.

"Ay, Hombrecillo, if María were to summon me, should I go to her?"

9.
Supreme Council

The following morning, Rocamora appeared before the *Ma'amad*, which reminded him of that terrifying day in 1621 when he was interrogated by the Supreme Council of the Inquisition. The inquisitors questioned Rocamora about the Propositions to trap him into confessing heretical beliefs, expressing blasphemy, and to determine if he was worthy to be appointed a royal confessor. Before and now he concealed his true thoughts. No black hoods, however, the men of the council dressed the same as any Dutch burgher except for those peculiar twisted white threads hanging beneath their doublets, which identified them as Jews.

Rocamora saw too close a parallel between the *Ma'amad* and the Inquisition. Both exerted despotic religious control. Thanks to Menasseh, Rocamora had a clear idea of what to expect when he appeared before them. The rabbi had given him a copy of his *Thesouro dos Dinim*, a handbook explaining Jewish rites and rituals for New-Christian refugees, and his *Conciliador*, which explained scripture for those who were not yet sure about accepting the Law of Moses.

The rabbi had written that the immortality of the soul depended upon the three essential principles of Judaism: existence of God, divine origin of the Torah, and reward or punishment after death. They were less extensive than the Propositions required by the Holy Office Rocamora followed in Spain.

Rocamora did not fear these men. Unlike the Inquisitors of *la Suprema*, the *Ma'amad* could offer no harm. At worst, they might ban him from joining a community he was not sure he wanted to join.

Rocamora remembered his lineage, what he had been in Spain, and affected a haughty manner after Menasseh invited him to sit with the interrogators at the oval table in an attempt to make the atmosphere more collegial. He threw his cloak over the left shoulder in imitation of the current fashion and assumed the regal manner of royals he had seen sitting on throne-chairs.

"Don Isaac, consider this to be merely an informal meeting of our council. We appreciate your answering our summons and willingness to respond to our questions and concerns."

Rocamora did not speak, and Menasseh next introduced him to the four wardens called *parnassim* and the treasurer-secretary. Except for the rabbi, they were of the wealthiest families in the Sephardic community. Although in Amsterdam a short time, Rocamora had learned much about them by name.

He marked Joseph da Costa, a portly trader in corals and spices, as neutral and likely swayed by the strongest personality.

Abraham da Mexia, a shriveled sciatic gnome, regarded him with overt hostility. So did his cousin Elijah da Nuñes, a sour man of skin and bones whose face, as the saying went in Spain, seemed to carry Lent in it. They were partners in the tobacco business.

Samuel de Santcroos, a significant shareholder of the Dutch East India Company and possibly the wealthiest member of the congregation, had a welcoming expression and the most intriguing face. Rocamora speculated about the merchant's broken nose and scar across his forehead. His name appeared often in documents he had seen in Spain.

Santcroos was typical of rich and powerful Sephardim living in Holland. They imported tobacco, tea, sugar, fruits, spices, coral and precious gems from the New World, Africa, and Asia. The most prosperous had significant Iberian connections, usually Judaizing relations or other contacts in high places, which gave them access to worldwide markets controlled by Spain and Portugal.

A fashionable hat obscured the face of the treasurer, Solomon Curiel, a younger man bent over sheets of paper ready to take notes.

Menasseh spoke first. "Don Isaac, I welcome you on behalf of the Council. I want to say everyone was impressed with your bold initiative to circumcise yourself, but some members of our congregation are disappointed that you have not yet joined our community. Will you please explain why?"

"I needed time to recover."

"That should have taken no more than a few weeks," Mexia said. "I spoke with my cousin, the esteemed physician Ephraim da Bueno, who assured me that this Rocamora has had more than enough time for that. It has been months since your theatrics. Why have you delayed taking instruction in Torah and Talmud?"

"I have been immersing myself in the language and customs of my Dutch hosts and preparing myself to study medicine."

Nuñes scoffed. "You could do that and still be part of our community."

Menasseh commanded silence. "Perhaps we should first explain to Don Isaac what it means to be part of our community."

Rocamora listened disappointed when the rabbi explained the laws and the degree to which the *Ma'amad* held authority over each member of the synagogue. No one could marry, divorce, or bring a lawsuit against a fellow member without its consent. No book and no treatise of a religious or political nature in any language could be printed without its permission. The council even regulated education, trade, gambling and fighting, all based on Jewish law and traditions.

Rocamora had not yet recovered from his astonishment how these Iberian Jews brought to Amsterdam their own version of the Supreme Council of the Holy Office, the Inquisition, with equivalent Familiars, spies, threat of excommunication, and Index of Forbidden Works.

"So the Dutch have allowed you to have a separate government here in Vlooienburg."

"To a degree, Don Isaac," Santcroos said. "You must always remember that we are guests of the Dutch. Jews cannot engage in most trades run by guilds. Furthermore, marriages, even casual carnal liaisons with Christians, all are forbidden. We may not employ Christian servants, we cannot hold public office, and our children may not attend their schools."

"Still," Menasseh said, "we must never forget that here in Amsterdam we have more freedoms, peace, and security than anywhere else in the world. We enjoy protection of their law, the right to reside anywhere in the city, and, yes, Don Isaac, we have religious, social, and economic autonomy. But understand this. When the magistrates decided we could reside in Amsterdam as guests of their municipality, they told us in no uncertain terms we must never tolerate heterodoxy within our community."

Nuñes looked at his notes. "Do you, Don Isaac, accept that there is an omnipotent God, the Creator, that Moses and the prophets revealed truth under Divine inspiration, and that there is another life after death, in which good people are rewarded and the wicked are punished?"

Rocamora took time to consider a response. He would never voice here his long-held views regarding religious and ritual dogma even though he wanted to tell them that he accepted no absolutes and believed in no theology. This was neither the time nor place, unless he wished to break now with these Jews. Better he should apply a variation of the same mask he had worn in Spain.

Mexia forced a derisive laugh before Rocamora could speak. "It matters not what he answers. We Portuguese are suspicious of you Spaniards. More so than in Spain, our forebears in Portugal were responsible for the survival of our religion in spite of restrictions, persecutions, torture and death. We are the true *hombres da nação*, men of the nation chosen by God to maintain Judaism and observe the Law. That is why we survived your Inquisition and mourn our kin you Dominicans martyred."

From hombres de negócio, *men of business in Spain, to* hombres da nação, *men of the Israelite nation. How pretentious.*

Questions and comments came rapidly from Mexia and Nuñes while da Costa nodded approval at each. Rocamora sustained an impassive mask of insouciance. They engendered no fear unlike the Supreme Council of the Inquisition when they interrogated him more than two decades ago.

"Why have you shown no remorse for your former Christian life?"

"Why did you not leave Spain sooner?"

"He wanted to become Inquisitor-General."

"That accursed order. While a Dominican, did you persecute Jews?"

"Of course he did."

Rocamora let them rant so he could further gauge their personalities. Mexia's antipathy was palpable. Nuñes followed his lead. Da Costa looked to them for guidance.

Santcroos did not hide his annoyance at their questioning. "Please, let Don Isaac answer the first question before you pose another."

Mexia would not be silenced. "Who is this Rocamora anyway? Can we believe anything he says? I suspect he has not a single drop of Jewish blood. His eyes, that unusual green color, not even the Ashkenazim, those strange Jews from central and eastern Europe, have such eyes. He has eyes of the *goyim*. I still believe him to be a spy or informer sent by the Inquisition to ferret out the real names of Jews who have sought sanctuary here, and to identify our kin who use false identities in Portugal and Spain. We all know what happens next. Our brothers and sisters will be denounced, arrested, tortured, and humiliated at the Inquisition's abominable *autos de fé*, followed by burnings at the *quemadero*, which also has been done to so many of us in effigy."

Santcroos touched Mexia's arm to silence him. "Why would Don Isaac perform his own *berit milah*?"

"Everyone knows those Christian fanatics are trained to tolerate pain," Mexia said. "Do they not flagellate and scourge themselves daily? Even if he is not a spy, he has been in Amsterdam more than four months. He is not studying Torah, and he lives in the midst of gentiles near their churches."

Santcroos glared at Mexia. "So do I Don Abraham. Don Isaac, let me assure you of this. No one in this community is required to become a scholar of Torah, Talmud, and Mishna. That we leave to our sages."

Mexia persisted. "We have no place here for one who has preached a false religion, and worse. I can name eyewitnesses who now live amongst us and were present when Rocamora persecuted our people."

Menasseh demanded silence. "Don Isaac, you have heard our concerns. We are aware our religion is foreign to you. That is why we require education of refugees in our customs and practices. Are you now prepared to join our community?"

"I first must become a physician."

Mexia scoffed "At your age?"

"Was not your great Rabbi Hillel also a student at my age?"

"Presumptuous." Nuñes again read from his notes. "You have been observed consuming cakes and cheeses of gentile manufacture and mixing dairy and meat products including the flesh of unclean swine."

"You have set spies upon me?"

"For the safety of our community."

Menasseh turned to Rocamora. "I can assure you it was not ordered by the *Ma'amad*."

Santcroos spoke before Mexia and Nuñes could utter another word. "My apologies, Don Isaac. Unfortunately, there are many in our community who have a propensity for spying and informing and time for little else. Rabbi, Señores, I believe in time Don Isaac will observe all our regulations and traditional customs."

Mexia snorted. "I strongly disagree. He lives here in Amsterdam as a Christian, not as a Jew. Never forget that this Rocamora was a Dominican. One can find in monasteries, convents and abbeys in Portugal, Spain, France, and Italy friars and nuns of *converso* origins, all of them idolaters. Perhaps he has already succumbed to the lure of humanism, and thus of secularism."

"We all know your views Don Abraham," Santcroos said. "But let us now reduce this session to a simple question and save valuable time. Don Isaac, are you now prepared to join our community?"

"After I return I shall give my answer."

Menasseh gasped surprised "Return? Where are you going?"

Mexia forced a scornful laugh. "He is returning to Spain, and spy that he is, he will report our names to the Inquisition."

"You waste both breath and venom. I have no intention of ever returning to Spain."

"Of course not," Menasseh said. "Perhaps since you have been immersed in the teachings of the false church and know its doctrines and dogma so well, you will write polemical tracts attacking its falseness, which I shall be delighted to publish."

"I have no desire to attack the sincere beliefs of others. I say it again. I first want to devote all my time to becoming a physician." Rocamora stood, his fists clenched on the table. His forceful voice resonated throughout the room and cowed his antagonists. "Now you, Mexia, and you, Nuñes, you have been speaking with the certitude of absolute ignorance. You know nothing of my plans or intentions. I must postpone my joining your community because *Stadhouder* Frederick Hendrick has summoned me to The Hague."

Rocamora enjoyed the expressions of surprise on their faces and their open mouths from which no sound came.

10.
Transactions

Menasseh accompanied Rocamora outside to the steps of the synagogue. "I want to reassure you that the council is generally more restrained and level headed, and I cannot understand why Mexia and Nuñes were so hostile."

"There are men everywhere who are suspicious by nature."

"Be assured of this. We want you to learn our customs and rituals so you do not flaunt them in ignorance. We do not demand daily attendance at Talmud Torah for prayers. Outward conformity is all that is required by the congregation, for who but the Lord, Blessed be He, can know what is in a man's heart."

"That is true, Rabbi." Rocamora glanced in the direction of Don Judah's home. Were he to marry a woman of this community, he would have to wear the mask of an observant Jew for the rest of his life. Rocamora thought it best to change the subject. "How best can I send a letter to the Imperial palace with my response to Doctor Bocarro?"

"I know of no one I can trust who is going to the Empire in the immediate future."

Santcroos joined them. "Don Isaac, I rebuked Mexia and Nuñes for their rudeness to you. Pay no further attention to them."

"I had not intended to do so, Don Samuel."

"I overheard your wish to send a letter to Bocarro. One of my agents is leaving for the Imperial palace next week. You can be assured he will deliver your message."

Rocamora handed Santcroos the envelope. "I thank you, and please emphasize it must be handed personally to Bocarro."

"You have my word."

Menasseh went inside the synagogue, and Santcroos invited Rocamora to ride in his carriage, one of the few he had seen in Amsterdam, pulled by two chestnut horses, with coachman, and servant in dark green livery. "Don Isaac, I will take you anywhere you wish."

Rocamora told Santcroos where he resided and settled in the burgundy velvet seat opposite him. He measured the merchant and concluded that beneath his genial façade lay a tough-minded man, a hard man.

Santcroos rapped the ceiling with his stick for his coachman to move the horses. "Don Isaac, will you come to my home this evening at seven? I have something of great importance to discuss with you."

"Has it anything to do with la *Cofradia de los Judios de Holanda*?"

A hearty laugh shook Santcroos' belly. "Of course you would be well informed about the Jewish Brotherhood of Holland."

Rocamora's residual loyalty to the Count-Duke prevented him from describing Olivares' rages upon hearing the news another Spanish ship laden with gold or silver had been captured by pirates or sunk. "I also read reports about your depredations in the dossiers of the Holy Office."

"But you were never an inquisitor."

"True, but I had access to their files because Olivares made sure his financiers were protected, and for a significant bribe, he allowed some to flee."

"Are you the one who alerted my brother-in-law, Miguel de Tejera, may he rest in peace, that he had been denounced for Judaizing?"

"That was in 1637. Yes, I arranged his escape."

"For that alone, I am eternally grateful to you."

"I am sorry to hear he is deceased."

"Yes, in Venice two years ago."

Rocamora decided he could trust Santcroos with more than delivering his letter to Bocarro. He needed to settle his financial affairs before going to The Hague. Rocamora had no idea what *Stadhouder* Frederick Hendrick might ask. A possibility existed that he might be away from Amsterdam for a long while.

"Don Samuel, will you come with me to my room? I have some items of value to show you, and I need your advice how best to convert them to guilders."

Santcroos' carriage caused a stir on the street where Rocamora rented his room. People gaped open-mouthed, and Vrouw Cornelia greeted the merchant as if he were royalty.

"Please, sit here, Mynheer and let me offer you refreshments. I have cakes, cheeses, and beer."

"We can visit with you for a few minutes. Don Samuel is a busy man, and we have business to discuss."

"A small glass of beer will be enough, Mevrouw."

"Yes, of course, of course, I will be but a minute." Cornelia left and returned with a tray of tankards filled with beer for the three of them and a plate of assorted cheeses." "I cannot tell you how honored I am to welcome so famous a merchant in my humble home."

"It is a lovely home, Mevrouw, but who is this?"

Hombrecillo had climbed to Rocamora's lap. "My companion who adopted me. I will be distressed to leave him behind."

Cornelia choked on her beer. "You are going away?"

"Tomorrow, I regret to say."

"For how long?"

"It may be for a week or much longer."

"You are the best lodger I have had. I will save your room for you, if you pay for it."

Santcroos winked at Rocamora and charmed Cornelia with a smile. "You should reduce the fee for my friend because he will not be eating and drinking here."

She thought for a moment. "I will halve it until he returns."

Rocamora stood. "And now we must leave you."

Santcroos also rose. "I thank you for you hospitality, Mevrouw Cornelia."

"You are welcome any time."

Santcroos grimaced when he entered Rocamora's room. "Why, this is no larger than a monk's cell and inadequate for a man of your blood, experience, and abilities."

"A bed, table for writing, and a fireplace for warmth are all I need until I become a physician." Rocamora showed Santcroos the gems he taken to Judah Touro. "And here are the names of merchants he said I could trust to give me a fair price."

Santcroos did not hide his appreciation. "Superb specimens. Apparently flawless. And yes, they will deal with you honestly."

"Even if I require payment today? Would they not offer an amount below their value if they see I am in haste?"

"Yes, they would. I assume their provenance comes from someone in the Spanish royal family. It has been reported that the Infanta gave you many gifts."

"I have more to show you." Rocamora held Hombrecillo and opened his trunk. He removed a small object wrapped in rags and another covered in purple velvet with the Habsburg coat of arms stitched in brilliant colors and gold threads. He did not touch the compartment that contained the ruby ring and lock of hair María gave him in the secret vestibule outside her bedroom the last time he saw her in Spain. He not yet ready to part with them, if ever.

Santcroos gasped when Rocamora untied the rags and handed him a golden cross of diamonds, rubies, sapphires, and emeralds. "Infanta María gifted it to me the day I became her confessor and spiritual director."

"A religious abomination, Don Isaac, yet an object of great beauty." He studied the gems. "Again flawless, each one flawless."

Rocamora removed the velvet cloth and handed Santcroos a flat box of polished mahogany an arms width horizontally and half that length vertically. "Infanta María gave me this for exposing a heretic cult."

"Begoña, the *alumbrado*. I attended his *auto de fé* and still can hear your brilliant sermon even though it was fifteen years ago."

Rocamora well remembered the *alumbrados*, the enlightened, also known as *illuminati*, heretics all who sought personal mystical union with the Holy Spirit through copulation. Another world. Another time.

Santcroos opened the flat box that became a miniature Flemish triptych of the seven sacraments painted in vivid tempura. He took it to the window and studied every square inch of the painting. "A masterpiece. And this velvet covering assures its provenance. Don Isaac, you have brought a fortune in gems and art with you to Amsterdam."

"I want to sell my silver Dominican's cross and chain as well."

"Yes, it can be melted and reformed by a silversmith, perhaps as *kiddush* cups for the blessing of wine, a most fitting transformation."

"But can I get a fair price for them?"

"Yes, and this day you shall have it. I will purchase them myself. Don Isaac, I wish to prove I can become your good friend, and, therefore, I shall pay you a collector's price, a fair price."

Rocamora masked his reaction to the enormous sum Santcroos offered. "That creates another problem. How can I hide so many guilders from theft?"

"Have you not used the services of our Wisselbank?"

"Only to exchange escudos for florins."

"I see I must explain our banking system to you. I leave my wealth there, so you should have no fears regarding yours. Come with me, and I will introduce you to our great exchange bank."

"Leaving one's money in the hands of strangers is a new experience for my friend."

"I understand, Mynheer Samuel." Banker Paulus Vanderpoel opened a thick ledger. "The Wisselbank is now in its thirty-fourth year. It regulates the supply of money and rates of exchange in Amsterdam and prevents the use of foreign coins in domestic trade because many are likely to be debased, clipped, and counterfeited. We neither lend money, nor do we offer credit. Our charter forbids such practices in order to guarantee monetary stability, which is backed by the City of Amsterdam."

Vanderpoel held the note for the amount Santcroos purchased the gems, crosses, and triptych. "Like this note, the guilder is used mostly for paper transaction, the silver florin and lesser coins, *stuiver* and *penningen*, for daily transactions. The current rate is sixteen florins to your Spanish *escudo* or guilder coins, and the Carolus guilder engraved with a profile of Emperor Charles V is currently worth one and a half times their value."

Vanderpoel prepared to write in his ledger. "Here I will debit Mynheer Samuel's account for the amount of his note to you and credit your new account minus our fees."

"I suspected you are not a charity and charge fees to pay wages and cover expenses."

"Of necessity, Mynheer Isaacus. We credit deposits of gold and silver for five-percent less than their mint price, and we add a maintenance fee. One-quarter percent for silver, and half a percent for gold, which the depositor must pay every six months to extend the period of deposit. Also, we charge a fee of ten guilders for the first account, three guilders and three *stuivers* for each additional account, and two *stuivers* for each transaction over three hundred guilders."

Santcroos said to Rocamora, "For significant purchases, you can earn three to five percent above the guilder's value in the market place because the bank's paper is more reliable than the potential of false, impure, or clipped coins, and less cumbersome to carry."

"Paper transactions?"

"Precisely."

Rocamora considered what the banker and Santcroos had said. He had much to learn about the ways of buying and selling. "I have heard men may become wealthy in a short time at something called the Bourse. What can you tell me about it?"

Vanderpoel closed the ledger and wrinkled his face as if smelling the foulest odors. "In my opinion it is a place of sin, no different than a gambling den. At the Bourse, one speculates to make a profit. There you may purchase stock in an overseas venture, gambling, for want of a better word, that the cargo will arrive safely and an enormous profit will be gained."

Rocamora remembered Catalina's disastrous experience with paper futures. "Or lose all as many did when your great tulip bubble burst."

"Exactly. It is less risky to hide your money on your person or under your mattress than to risk it in such speculation at the Bourse, with all due respect to you, Mynheer Samuel, of course. Is there anything else I can do for you, Mynheer Isaacus?"

Rocamora emptied his purse of gold escudos on the desk. "I wish to exchange these for florins."

Outside the Wisselbank, Santcroos lingered with Rocamora before they parted. "I heard you counting in Spanish. I have lived her most of my life, and although I am fluent in Dutch, I too continue to count in my native tongue. So do all I deal with in Vlooienburg. An interesting phenomenon, do you not agree?"

"If the count is accurate, it should not matter."

"True, so very true. I will introduce you to the Bourse another day so you will see for yourself if it is heaven or hell for the speculators."

"I suspect it is both."

11.
Mina's Secrets

Mina tried to prevent Rocamora from leaving their bed. "You are abandoning me so soon, my handsome Isaacus?"

"I have another obligation this evening."

"But I will see you tomorrow."

Rocamora sat beside Mina on the edge of her bed. "I wish it were so, but on the morrow, I leave for The Hague."

"The Hague? Well, it is but a short journey. When do you return? No, I can see it in your eyes. I shall not see you again. You have tired of me."

"No, lovely Mina, it is not that. Do you not remember I told you of my plans to visit the university towns and decide which medical school to attend?"

"I did not think you would be leaving so soon. Must you become a physician?"

"It is my true calling."

"Do not stay away too long. I have many who would be my suitors, but I prefer you above all others."

Is she proposing marriage? It is well I am leaving.

"I cannot say when I will return."

Mina slapped his shoulder. "Villain. Then I must make other plans for my future. I have not told you before, but two men would wed me in an instant were I to say yes."

Clever woman, hoarding lovers the same as having guilders in reserve at the Wisselbank.

"I am sure you have more than two."

"Yes, but Peter and Carl are the best of the lot, after you of course. You are a wise man, Isaacus. The guild masters envy and resent that I, a woman, have the most successful bakery in Amsterdam. They have pressured me to wed one of them or sell. I need a man to protect me.

Rocamora did not speak while he dressed and Mina described each of the men she preferred. Peter, the handsome young and strong apprentice she inherited from her father, wanted her to go with him to New Amsterdam and open a bakery there. Johannes, a prosperous older widower magistrate from Delft, had four children.

"What do you think, Isaacus? Whom should I choose?"

"The lives they offer you cannot be more different, one of adventure in the New World with a young man, and the other of predictable comfort and children for you to raise."

"Yes, yes, you have given me the best advice. I shall sell this bakery to one of the guild masters, and go with Peter to New Amsterdam. There we shall make a life together, and I will give birth to my own children."

Rocamora breathed deeply of his favorite scent in the bakery and took a marzipan infused pastry from a bowl at Mina's bedside.

"Beast. You always preferred my confections to me."

He bent and kissed Mina for the last time. "They and you are one and the same and shall always be so in my memory of you, my sweet Mina."

12.
A Tempting Offer

Rocamora had yet to become used to the fronts of Dutch homes, especially those of the wealthy, so unlike the *palacios* in Spain. In Amsterdam, houses were set a mere few steps away from the streets with plain exteriors, except for columns at the top of steps, carved lentils over the front doors, and many windows. Santcroos' mansion on Herengracht between Utrechtsestraat and the Amstel, a fashionable district, was the grandest of all.

In contrast with the exterior, its interior was more sumptuous than the Astórquia *Palacio* in Madrid where Rocamora's kinsman Ramón once resided and served as companion for an elderly duchess. The merchant had filled the great hall with richly upholstered furniture, vivid tiles, paintings by great masters, and exotic objects from all continents. Many servants stood in attendance.

Santcroos and his family awaited Rocamora in the great hall. The merchant's wife, a slender woman who looked older than her husband, wore a silk dress the color of wine from the Rhône, its billowing sleeves decorated with gold thread and precious gems, a linen collar and cuffs, and a cap of the finest lace.

"I am delighted to present the esteemed Don Isaac de Rocamora, who was confessor to the Empress when she was Infanta of Spain, and who honors our home with his presence. Don Isaac, my wife, Doña Rebecca."

"Señora."

"Don Isaac."

"My son David, to be bar mitzvahed later this year, and my daughters Lea, Sara, and Rachael."

Rocamora exchanged greetings with the boy, who wore doublet, breeches and hose of the finest silk, and with Santcroos' girls, whose silk and velvet dresses detailed in gold and covered with pearls would have created envy at the Spanish court.

"You have a lovely wife, a handsome son, and beautiful daughters, Don Samuel, and I thank you for inviting me to your home."

"My wife and children will be supping separately, for we have serious business to discuss." Santcroos brought Rocamora into a banquet hall worthy of a royal palace and introduced him to a short lean man of weathered complexion and hard, suspicious eyes. "Don Isaac, this is Don Gaspar Enríquez, my partner in certain ventures, and known by the Dutch when in Amsterdam as Gaspar Hendrijks."

Gaspar wore a blue turban. His flaring mustachio resembled a Turkish Janissary, and silver filigree earrings reminded Rocamora of his dead *pícaro* friend, the Arab Yusef.

"Don Gaspar, this is the esteemed Don Isaac de Rocamora, formerly Vicente, and confessor for Empress María when she was Infanta of Spain."

"Your reputation precedes you, Don Isaac."

"As does yours, Don Gaspar"

"Mine? How so?"

"Both Crown and Holy Office are aware of your notoriety."

"Well aware I should imagine."

Santcroos invited them to sit at one end of a shiny ebony table large enough to accommodate several dozen guests on chairs upholstered in floral aqua and orange shantung silk under an elaborate crystal and gold chandelier. Dozens more candles on candelabra and sconces illuminated the room to near daylight.

"Currently, Don Gaspar captains *The Avenger*, one of the ships we finance to capture Spanish gold and silver from the New World. I sailed with him when I was younger. We took many a prize at sea and from our raids ashore upon the colonies of Spain and Portugal."

A servant poured wine into jeweled gilded goblets, and Santcroos raised his. "Don Isaac, again I welcome you to my home."

"The honor is mine."

"Because you will be meeting with the *Stadhouder*, I have written a letter to Prince Frederick Hendrick. Will you deliver it on my behalf?"

"Am I to be told of its content?"

"Better than that, you may read each word before I seal it."

"I wish your colleagues in the *Ma'amad* trusted me the same."

Hendrijks hit the table with his fist. "Whiners all. Too many wear the cloak of martyrdom and victimization instead of the armor of vengeance."

Rocamora liked the pirate's attitude. He might have been a typical Valencian for whom vendetta was a way of life. "I could not agree more."

"I like to think you do. I must admit I was not pleased when Don Samuel said you would be joining us. You were after all a Dominican, a member of that accursed Order that allowed my family to perish in the dungeons of Seville. Still, I trust the judgment of no man more than my friend and partner here." Gaspar raised his goblet to Rocamora. "You look fit enough to sail with me."

Rocamora remembered his boyhood dreams of sailing for the Crown and soldiering against Protestants and Muslims. "Were I a youth, I would join your crew, but after I participated in battle at Nördlingen in 1634 and rode through the ravaged Germanys in winter, I had seen my fill of war. I have come to the United Provinces to be a physician. Even if I were to accept your offer, I would not return in time to matriculate at a medical school by the end of August."

"What is a year or so in the life of a man if he can return with great wealth? I am offering you the additional pleasure of taking retribution against the persecutors of our people and your own enemies in the Holy Office. Think about it. I do not sail for another week."

"I may not have returned from The Hague by then."

"Even so, Don Samuel has told me much about your most interesting life in Spain. I believe you can be of great help to take from our oppressors their gold and silver and to weaken their kingdoms financially."

"You seem to be doing well enough without me."

"You know the ways of the Inquisition. Perhaps after you obtain your license to practice, you could sail with us as a physician, and, if necessary, infiltrate one of their prisons and help to release our people."

During a repast of assorted fruits and cheeses with light wine from Maas River vineyards, Rocamora listened to Gaspar's tales of pirating. Santcroos added his own experiences and adventures when he was younger. "I would be sailing still with Don Gaspar if I did not have family and community obligations. Those may have been the happiest years of my life."

"Don Isaac, I can see by the light in your eyes that I have tempted you to join my crew."

"Meaning no offence, Don Gaspar, but please understand this. For the first time in my life, I have complete freedom to do and be whatever I wish. I prefer not to place myself under the command of any sea captain who has absolute authority over life and death aboard his ship."

"And I prefer Don Isaac to remain on land for my own purposes."

"And what are they, Don Samuel?"

"In time, Don Isaac, in due time."

13.
To the Hague

"I regret I must leave you, my little *hidalgo*."

Rocamora rubbed Hombrecillo's belly and locked his poetry and the de Rocamora genealogy chart in his trunk. He considered taking the kitten with him but decided against it. Best to think only about himself during a journey filled with uncertainties.

Rocamora carried on his person a dagger and coin purse filled with florins. He placed in one pocket of his doublet a small box with the ruby ring and a lock of hair the Infanta had given him and several Carolus guilders in the other. His satchel held one change of clothes, a brace of wheel locks, a supply of herbs, spices, and ointments for medicinal purposes, and teas supplied gratis by Santcroos. He did not forget his walking stick.

Rocamora found Vrouw Cornelia in the kitchen preparing a typical midday meal of meat and vegetable stew and another course of fish cooked with prunes. "Mevrouw, I do not know how long I shall be away."

"I will store your trunk in my attic. I shall miss our conversations."

"We will have many more after I return."

Rocamora arrived early at the Town Hall and filled the time reading the latest bulletins posted on the walls. Both sides continued to suspend campaigning during winter in the war between King Charles and the English Parliament. An end to the general European wars remained elusive although peace talks had begun.

Van Noordwijk came out of the Town Hall, greeted Rocamora, and took him to a pair of powerful black Frisian horses tethered nearby.

Rocamora stroked his mount before climbing onto the saddle. "A fine steed you have brought for me."

"The best from my stables."

They rode at a trot through the congested streets of the city, and Van Noordwijk leaned toward Rocamora. "You sit the saddle as one with your mount, like a centaur, and now I remember. I was told you were of the *caballero* caste, Señor de Benetorrente, and kin to the Marqués de Rafal and the Conde de la Granja de Rocamora."

"Yes, the *caballero* I was born to be."

"I have been admiring your silver spurs."

"They were my father's."

They cantered in silent companionability along linden and elm lined roads beside the canals careful to avoid frozen ruts and holes that might injure their horses. Rocamora noted the towns in Holland were relatively close to Amsterdam when compared with distances between Madrid and the other great cities of Spain. Haarlem, which they bypassed, lay a mere six miles from Amsterdam across Lake Brassemer, Leyden about fifteen, and The Hague less than thirty.

Along their route, countless windmills and dykes controlled water levels on drained land the Dutch called polders. More people skated on frozen canals than were on the roads. Rocamora recalled Velde's assertion that one could skate from Amsterdam to Leyden in an hour and a half.

Van Noordwijk and Rocamora stopped at a roadside tavern north of Leyden. "We will rest our horses here and share a midday meal."

They dismounted and tethered their mounts by a frozen trough. Rocamora broke the ice with his walking stick so the horses could drink. Inside the tavern, van Noordwijk told a groom to bring their beasts feed. He ordered a pot of stew, bread, cheese, and *flapkans* of beer. They were the only patrons and went to the fireplace to warm themselves.

"Tell me, Mynheer Isaacus, what do you think of your Dutch hosts?"

"That I appreciate your tolerance goes without saying." Rocamora preferred van Noordwijk do the talking. "I have so much more to learn about your countrymen."

"First, you should know that the Dutch, especially the Amsterdammers, are a people driven to make money. That is our strength. Men of ability can rise to the top regardless of origins. Despite all that, the hereditary nobility is still influential in government administration and the military."

Their food and drink arrived, and they sat at a table closest to the fire. Rocamora wanted to know more about van Noordwijk. "Given your rank and position, may I assume you are of the nobility?"

"Yes, I became an officer of the *Stadhouder's* guard because I am related by blood on my father's side to the House of Orange-Nassau. My mother is English, kin to the Howard family. Our hereditary lands are near Gouda. My father participated in the marriage negotiations that led to the union between our Prince Willem and Princess Royal Mary Stuart, daughter of King Charles."

"Will you become an ambassador like your father?"

"I am merely a captain of the guard and an emissary in training, but, God willing, one day I shall be posted to England. I trust I am not being disrespectful, Mynheer Isaacus. I must say that I have difficulty imagining you as a Dominican in a hooded robe. How and why did you choose that path?"

"That is a long story. Suffice it to say, I was forced into the Order. When I was a boy, I wanted to soldier for the Crown."

"Which you did at Nördlingen. I would not be surprised to learn you are a master of all arms. Which style of swordsmanship do you fancy, the Italian or the French school?"

"I apply each when necessary and prefer the English school most of all."

"The English school? I am not familiar with it. Ah, I see a wry smile. You are jesting?"

"Not at all. Think about this. More common than fighting a formal duel is the likelihood of encountering trouble in taverns, inns, lonely roads, and the dangerous streets of cities and towns. A man should also know how to use a chair, overturn a table, or throw a bowl, a *flapkan*, and on the streets a loose brick. That can be the difference between survival and death."

"I see there has been a gap in my education at arms, but why call it the English style?"

"The English are reputed to be more practical, whereas Spaniards, Italians, and French of their aristocratic and knightly castes prefer to fight according to their codes of honor instead of using common sense. They leave the dishonorable methods of killing to their *matones*, paid assassins."

"Then forgive me if my eyes wander, for now I must study the furniture and objects in this tavern should a brawl occur."

"As I did the moment we entered."

They shared a good laugh, and Rocamora felt a bond of friendship developing with van Noordwijk despite the twenty-year difference in their ages. The young man reminded him both of Juan de Rocamora, because of his affable manner, and Stauffacher, the giant fierce Swiss who wielded his ancient double-blade battle-ax with deadly effect at Nördlingen.

Late afternoon, they entered The Hague. By now, they had dispensed with formalities.

"Dirck, it seems to be more a place of residence than commerce and much quieter than Amsterdam."

"That is why the water of our canals is so clear. After the ice melts, you will see no barges laden with goods."

They rode past the edge of a natural park van Noordwijk identified as The Wood. "Over there, you can see caged wild animals and beyond is a lake stocked with fish."

Rocamora thought it paled in size and construction when compared to Buen Retiro, the magnificent palace and vast grounds Olivares built for Philip IV in the Prado.

Van Noordwijk led him to an adjacent community of imposing homes. "These mansions are residences of ambassadors, and the *Stadhouder's* palaces are over there by that church spire. The brick manse we are approaching is our home when we are in The Hague. I will send a servant to the palace to inform the Prince of Orange we have arrived. Most likely, you will be presented at court sometime tomorrow. In the meantime, we have the house to ourselves. My father is in England, and my mother and sisters are at our estate near Gouda. We shall spend the night here."

They dismounted in the courtyard, and grooms took their horses to the stables. The sparse though neat interior of van Noordwijk's home surprised Rocamora. The worn furnishings suggested near penury. After Rocamora washed dust from hands and face in the kitchen, he joined van Noordwijk by a fire where they lit their pipes.

"Would it be possible for me to bathe before I retire for the night?"

Van Noordwijk stared at him surprised. "A bath? Why would you want one?"

"It is my habit to do so several times a week."

"More a vice than a habit, I should think. We have no tub, but I can have my servants prepare a pot of hot water so you may wash."

Rocamora masked his disappointment. "I would appreciate that. Dirck, because the *Stadhouder* is Prince of Orange, shall I address him as *Uwe Hoogheid*, Your Highness?"

"I have neglected to mention that French is the preferred language at our Court due to the influence of the *Stadhouder's* wife. Princess Amalia is the daughter of Admiral Coligny from the great Huguenot family. Do you speak French?"

"*Mais oui*, fluently."

"Excellent. Our court has adopted French manners and titles. You must address Prince Frederick Hendrick as Monseigneur, each member of the Estates General as Most Mighty Seigneur, those of the Admiralty as Noble and Austere Seigneurs and their wives as Madames, burgomasters as Monseigneurs, and any surgeon, lawyer, and guild president you encounter as Maître. Were you to practice medicine at Court, you would be Monsieur le Docteur. For now, you will be addressed as Monsieur."

Better that than friar.

14.
House of Orange

They entered Noordeinde, the *Stadhouder's* palace, the following afternoon. Rocamora wore the change of clothes he had brought: his black doublet, vest, and breeches of the finest wool, cape with purple velvet lining, boots and spurs, and cavalier's hat with ostrich plumes. Van Noordwijk dressed in the French style with sash and badge showing his rank of captain of the guard. Hammering and shouts of workers assaulted their ears.

"As you can see and hear, Isaacus, the palace is being expanded. Frederick Hendrick is lengthening the main section and adding wings on either side."

In a crowded antechamber decorated in the French style, Rocamora saw pages wearing Spanish breeches and heard officers speaking French and German. While they waited, he reviewed what he had learned in Spain from spies and reports about Frederick Hendrick.

The fifty-nine year old Prince of Orange and Count of Nassau became *Stadhouder* of the United Provinces of Holland, Zeeland, Utrecht, OverIJssel, and Guelders in 1625. Rocamora admired his diplomatic skills. In 1635, Frederick Hendrick allied with France and Sweden against the Habsburgs, and a subsidy from Cardinal Richelieu guaranteed he could continue waging war against Spain. In 1641, he also allied with England when his son Willem wed Mary Henrietta Stuart, daughter of Charles I and Henriette Maria, younger sister of Queen Isabel of Spain.

"Monseigneur will receive you now."

The Court Chamberlain led them to a small reception salon considerably more informal than the Spanish Court. No dais, in a semi-circle Frederick Hendrick and his wife Amalia of Solms-Braunfels sat on plain mahogany armchairs with seat cushions upholstered in velvet, their son Willem next to the *Stadhouder* and their daughter-in-law, Princess Royal Mary Henrietta Stuart, daughter of Charles I beside Amalia.

Mary's lady-in-waiting stood behind her. Rocamora saw the young woman smile at van Noordwijk. Her delicate beauty and pale skin bordering on yellow suggested unhealthiness.

Upon first evaluation, Rocamora found Frederick Hendrick to be courteous and affable, diffident on the surface, but something about his intelligent eyes revealed a determined man. Princess Amelia impressed Rocamora as *muy varonil*, a forceful masculine woman who would not tolerate opposition to her wishes. Handsome and haughty seventeen-year old Willem wore armor and reminded him of Cardinal-Infante Fernándo. Unlike his father, whose mustachio and spade beard were graying, Willem's face lacked hair except for a downy mustache over his lower lip. Willem's petite twelve year old wife, Princess Royal Mary, had both the pleasing features of her father and a resemblance to her aunt Isabel, the late Queen of Spain.

Frederick Hendrick beckoned Rocamora and van Noordwijk to approach closer and sit opposite. Servants brought them tea and small pastries. "We welcome you, Monsieur. We are delighted that so accomplished and well-placed a person familiar with the Spanish Court and its inhabitants has come to live in our beautiful land. That is why I have summoned you, for I can think of no one else in our Republic who is better informed to tell us about King Philip and his court."

"Thank you, Monseigneur, Madame." Rocamora had prepared in advance how best to phrase what he intended to divulge. "When I left Spain, His Majesty trusted no one more than his Queen. She is the one person most responsible for the downfall of Olivares."

"Which may soon contribute to the peace we desire."

"But not before we have taken the southern provinces," Willem interrupted.

Frederick Hendrick raised a hand to silence his rash son. "Why did King Philip remove the man who had been the true ruler of Spain for so many years?"

"The Count-Duke attempted to do too much and made enemies when he tried to reform and centralize the government. Defeats in war, losses of Roussillon to France, and Portugal to independence sealed his fate."

Frederick Hendrick gave his son a meaningful look. "Yes, Olivares' greatest fault was to overreach. Now, tell me about the quality of the men who replaced Olivares."

"They are men of considerably less ability. All of them together do not equal the Count-Duke. Philip listens only to his queen."

Rocamora's evaluation pleased the *Stadhouder*. "So we have heard."

"If I may add, Monseigneur, their new Inquisitor General, Diego Arce y Reynoso, will benefit the United Provinces in the long run. He is an inflexible bigot who rigorously enforces the *limpieza*, Spain's blood purity statutes."

"And if you had become Inquisitor General? Yes, we know you were the favorite of a significant faction."

"Working with Olivares, I would have encouraged the Crown to repeal the statutes or at the least ignore them. That is another reason why the reactionaries were our enemies."

"We have seen reports that you were more than a confessor and servant of Olivares. Were you not a captain who participated in battle?"

"Only one. At Nördlingen."

"A great victory for the Cardinal Infante, but one that shall soon be reversed," Willem said.

Frederick Hendrick again gestured to silence his son. "To the best of your knowledge, Monsieur, does Spain wish to continue the war?"

"In principle, yes, but the kingdom is exhausted financially and war weary in spirit."

"Weary of war against our United Provinces, but perhaps we can use Spain for a lever against their greatest enemy, France. I am sure you know that King Philip's sister Anne, Queen of France, was given the Austrian Netherlands by their father Philip III as part of her dowry when she married Louis XIII. Unfortunately, the French have designs far beyond Brabant and Wallonia. The expansionist policies of their de facto ruler, Cardinal Mazarin, have caused many of us to be more concerned about the French than our most hated enemy Spain. Did you learn anything about their plans while you served Olivares?"

"Based on reports I read, the Alps, Rhine, and Pyrenees are the natural borders France desires, which means Mazarin would take Rotterdam if he could."

"And the Empire, Spain's Austrian cousins? Do you believe the Emperor desires an end to war, or is he being duplicitous?"

Rocamora described his journey from Antwerp to Madrid through the devastated German principalities eight years earlier. "I cannot imagine the situation there improving until they have peace."

Frederick Hendrick waited until his wife finished whispering to him. "We know you were the confessor and spiritual director for Empress María when she was Infanta of Spain and Queen of Hungary. Is it true no man in Spain is closer to his female penitent than even her husband and father?"

"So it is said, Monseigneur."

And so it was with María and me.

"We have reliable information that Empress María influences the Emperor's policies."

"Her Imperial Majesty has always been a woman of strong personality." Rocamora saw Amalia smile when he described how María was the one royal not to panic during a fire at Aranjuez, King Philip's summer palace, and Olivares' reference to her as "That block of ice."

The *Stadhouder* intervened before Amalia could ask another question. "We want your opinion, Monsieur. Will the Empress advise her husband to continue the war to the end, or will she encourage him to seek peace?"

Are they thinking of sending me as an emissary to María?

Rocamora sipped his tea to delay his response to the *Stadhouder*. The María he remembered would have converted the English by force to Catholicism had she wed Charles Stuart. He also recalled the Austrian Habsburg preference for expanding their holdings through marriage rather than war.

"Monseigneur, of all the Spanish and perhaps Austrian Habsburgs, Empress María is by far the most intelligent. She is not one to demand her husband fight to the last Catholic standing. I believe she and the emperor would prefer peace for another reason. The Ottomans are encroaching on the Empire's Hungarian lands. Catholic France allied with the Muslim Turks against the Habsburgs in the previous century. Why should the French not ally with them again for reasons of state?"

"You have confirmed what has been reported to me and have been most helpful."

Rocamora took an envelope from his doublet. "Monseigneur, Samuel de Santcroos asked me to deliver this to you."

Frederick Hendrick broke the seal, read the document, and passed it to his son. "Santcroos has offered us excellent terms to provision our army and navy."

Princess Mary spoke for the first time. "Monsieur, were you present at the Alcazar when His Majesty King Charles, my father, visited Spain?"

"I was."

"Come to my suite after this audience. I want to hear everything you remember about my father."

"He can do it here and now," Amalia snapped.

Rocamora saw repressed anger cloud Mary's face. While still serving Olivares, he had read reports that although a child of ten when she wed Willem in 1641, the Princess Royal had considered The House of Orange inferior to the Stuarts. He would do well to cheer her.

Rocamora switched to English and described how all at *la Corte* remarked on her father's handsome looks and fine taste in art. Omitting his own role, he related every detail of Charles' gallant but failed courtship of the Infanta. He spoke as if delivering one of his eloquent sermons, whispering forcefully here, raising his deep voice there, and pausing before the delivery of a telling line, which enthralled all, even Amalia. He added flattering anecdotes about Mary's aunt Isabel, Queen of Spain, and emphasized how she triumphed over the powerful Count-Duke de Olivares to become, as King Philip IV expressed it, "my chief minister."

Mary had tears in her eyes when Rocamora finished. "Would the Infanta have married my father if he converted?"

"Yes, Your Royal Highness."

Rocamora spoke the truth. Although María did not love Charles, she would have wed whomsoever her brother chose for her.

The *Stadhouder* broke the extended silence in the salon with a return to the French language. "I now understand better how you acquired a reputation for eloquence, Monsieur. What is it you plan to do here in the United Provinces?"

"I intend to become a physician."

"A physician? We thought you might serve us."

"I have come to the United Provinces because of its deserved reputation for tolerance. In gratitude, should you request them, I do offer my services howsoever you may request them."

"Well said. Tomorrow, I want you to meet with my officers and advisers. They will have specific questions for you."

Frederick Hendrick dismissed Rocamora and van Noordwijk. Outside the palace in the torch lighted quadrangle, they waited for grooms to bring their horses.

"Isaacus, did you notice the auburn-haired young woman with the vivid blue eyes standing to the side of Princess Mary?"

"I did. She never took her eyes from you."

And God help you, Dirck, for she is fragile, not built well for childbearing, and may not have a long life.

"Her name is Arabella Douglas. She is the one I adore. If we can obtain our parents' consent, we shall wed. It will be difficult. Fair Arabella is of the impecunious aristocracy. My father prefers I wed a merchant's daughter and bring some necessary wealth into our family."

"Have you unmarried sisters?"

"Two."

"Let them marry the burghers' sons, and you marry for love."

Van Noordwijk's laughter drew the attention from all in the courtyard. "That is the best suggestion I have heard."

"I wish you good fortune with your Arabella."

"Thank you, Isaacus. After you meet with the *Stadhouder's* men, will you return to Amsterdam?"

"Not immediately. I want to visit your university towns, Leyden, Utrecht, and Franeker, and decide which has the best medical school for me to attend."

"That will be time consuming. Although Leyden and Utrecht are relatively close to The Hague, Franeker is a several hundred mile journey from here because of the winding and poor condition of our roads, especially in the north."

"I have lived in Amsterdam during my brief time in your country and would like to learn if other communities are more congenial to my temperament."

"What are your impressions of The Hague?"

"A lovely town, from the little I have seen, but too small. I am a son of the great city of Valencia and lived in Madrid for twenty-two years."

"But if you were asked to serve our *Stadhouder*?"

"Then my residing here would be one of obligation to the Prince of Orange, not one of choice."

15.
Leyden

The freeze passed, the ice melted, and waterways again opened to traffic. After several days answering questions posed by the *Stadhouder* and his generals, Rocamora stood with van Noordwijk on a tree lined canal embankment before boarding one of the vividly painted passenger boats.

"It is not too late to accept one of my horses for your journey."

"Thank you, Dirck, but I prefer to experience your public transportation and mingle with the populace. I can learn much from them about the different provinces. I also thank you again for your hospitality and friendship."

"And I for your friendship and wisdom."

"I wish you well with your courtship."

"I foresee no barriers, and I thank you for giving me your itinerary should the *Stadhouder* further request your services."

"I still may be a difficult man to find."

Rocamora waved a final farewell to van Noordwijk and boarded the passenger boat while the boatman attached harness and ropes to the powerful draft horse that pulled it along the embankments. Geography and means of transportation determined his route. Canals, rivers, and roads linked The Hague to Leyden and Haarlem in the north, to Delft and Rotterdam in the south, Rotterdam to Utrecht and Arnhem in the east. From Arnhem, he would let the River IJssel carry him north to the Zuider Sea and take land transport beyond to Franeker in Friesland, unless he decided to travel southeast along the Rhine to the Empire and María. He could postpone that decision until the last moment.

Rocamora chose to backtrack and visit Leyden first because it had what many considered to be the greatest university and medical school in Europe and it was situated on the coast. If possible, he preferred to live in a community where he could look out to sea even if the geography disoriented him. Raised on the eastern shore of Valencia, Rocamora had not yet become used to facing a broad expanse of water and seeing the sun set instead of rising above the horizon, which affected his sense of direction.

Rocamora had no schedule to meet, no one to whom he must answer. He continued to revel in his new freedom to do and be whatever he wanted and to live wherever and however he chose. Although Amsterdam was a great city with many potential patients for a physician, Vlooienburg was confining and small when compared with the wider world. Could he live there or anywhere without donning a mask of religious conformity?

Aware several women stared at him with interest, Rocamora thought about the possibility of marrying after he established his practice. Twenty-seven years ago, Moraíma foretold he would have three great loves. Whomsoever the third might be, he would leave that to Kismet.

Behind its deep moats, brick façade and bastions, Leyden was a noisy city. The staccato sound of *klumpen,* wooden shoes, on the tightly packed brick pavements, reminded Rocamora of gypsy castanets.

Leyden's medical school was the first in Europe to require clinical teaching instead of awarding degrees solely on disputes. Rocamora attended several lectures at the medical school, all given in Latin and Greek, languages with which he was familiar and which eliminated barriers for the many foreign students attending the school. He had learned more about medicine and healing from Don Lope than most of the physicians, surgeons, and apothecaries he met. True, the Leyden professors were aware of the newest practices and medicines, and Rocamora appreciated most their freedom to dissect corpses and advance the science of anatomy. Still and despite their knowledge of the Englishman Harvey's proof of how blood circulated in the human body, most bled their patients to cure many aliments.

Rocamora visited the teaching hospital, St. Cecilia, where professors lectured at patients' bedsides on Wednesdays and Saturdays, and he spent many hours in the university's botanical gardens. He wanted to learn about unfamiliar healing plants and herbs indigenous to the Netherlands, England, and others brought recently from the European colonies and through trade from all over the world.

One of the professors, a genial man of advanced age, approached him in the gardens. "Mynheer, I have seen you at my lectures. You are not a student here. Perhaps a visiting physician or surgeon?"

"Neither."

"I am Professor Matthias Poons."

"And I am Don Isaac de Rocamora."

"Rocamora? The Dominican who was Empress María's confessor and joined the Jewish community in Amsterdam?"

Rocamora suppressed a smile at that common reaction to his name. "I am that man."

"An honor to make your acquaintance. May I ask why you are visiting our university?"

"I may matriculate here or at one of the other medical schools. I want to visit all before I come to a decision."

Poons squinted at Rocamora's features through his spectacles. "At this stage of your life?"

Rocamora worried they might not let him matriculate because of his age. "How old do you think I am?"

"Early to mid-thirties, in appearance, but impossible if you were the Empress' confessor. Well, that is not my concern. Your fellow students may be as young as sixteen, but the typical age is twenty-one give or take a few years. Your age should not be a problem, nor your religion. I can assure you the university is free of ecclesiastic control."

"So I have heard."

"I can count on the fingers of one hand the number of your faith enrolled here and have three or four digits to spare. Be assured that you would be treated no differently than others. No religious oaths are required because we want our students and professors to worship however they choose, or not at all as the case may be."

"That is good to know."

"I am certain you will return to Leyden, for our medical school is the best in all Europe. Should you visit Franeker, I suggest you introduce yourself to my great friend, the eminent Professor Gisebert Hagedorn, and give him my regards."

"I shall."

"I must say, Mynheer Isaacus, that your Dutch is excellent."

"That is good to hear. Perhaps we shall meet again."

16.
Leisurely Journey

From Leyden, Rocamora traveled less than ten miles by canal to Haarlem also called *Bloemenstad*, City of Flowers. Set along coastal dunes and expansive fields of tulip beds, the city was renowned for its water used to brew the best beer in the Netherlands and for bleaching. Rocamora marked Haarlem as a place where he might live and practice medicine because of its reputation for religious tolerance and proximity to the sea.

At Haarlem, Rocamora reversed direction and took the canals south to Delft, famous for its vivid blue and white pottery with designs of Chinese influence. Beyond Delft, he traveled to the great seaport of Rotterdam eighteen miles from where the Maas and Rhine Rivers ended at the North Sea. From Rotterdam, he went eastward to Gouda, where he sampled its wonderful cheeses, and beyond toward Utrecht fifteen miles away on the River Vecht.

By now, Rocamora had become used to the disadvantages of canal travel: waiting at bridges and dikes along the way because of transshipments and the demands for tolls and taxes. Aside from learning much about the geography, flora and fauna, and regional customs of each province, he found his journey to be medically instructive.

Physicians and apothecaries he encountered agreed that continual mists and humidity caused headaches, rheumatism, and insomnia. The common folk trusted cures Rocamora thought absurd. The desperate accepted any random mixture of animal, plant, and insect prescribed by apothecaries and quacks. For curing ringworm, some believed in an ointment based on boiling a green lizard in wine and oil or a mash of fifty earth snails. Potions to enhance appearance were no less strange. Oil of earthworms for hair growth was one. To replace loss of hair, some washed the bald spot with a mix of honey, candy wine, boy's urine, and milk. For depilatories, one had a choice of many applications: ant's eggs, juice of henbane, hemlock, seeds of fleawort, blood from both bat and tortoise, and juices from ivy and radishes.

Vanity made all classes susceptible to cures of suspect efficacy. For unsightly fatty lumps and bumps, some used an ointment of goose grease and turpentine. Women who worried about oversized or sagging breasts bound them in bandages and washed them in white wine and rosewater. Those of wealth who wished to lose weight might bathe in a mix of claret, wormwood, calamint, chamomile, sage, and assorted flowers believed to have curative properties.

Quackery thrived everywhere regardless of country and religion. So did a certain vice to tempt the gullible.

On the deck of the canal boat taking him to Utrecht, Rocamora watched a sleek, well-dressed man with rings on most fingers teach three young men a card game. Their long, pointed yellow wooden clogs and coarse woolen garments identified them as farmers.

In Spain, Rocamora learned the game as Thirty-One. In the United Provinces, the Dutch called it Bone-Ace for the ace of hearts. The cards had face value, the aces one, and the royal cards ten. They were dealt from the bottom of the deck, two cards face down and the last face up. If a player received the ace of hearts as a face card, he won the round. Otherwise, the wager went to the gambler who reached thirty-one or came closest to it without going over.

The young men said they understood the game. No surprise to Rocamora, the scoundrel drew low card and dealt one of the farmers the bone-ace face up, giving him the first pot. His friends won the next several rounds and accepted the stranger's suggestion for an increase in stakes. They lost each of the subsequent two rounds.

A minister stood beside Rocamora. "An abomination. They will pay for this in hell. So will the boat master for allowing it. Gambling ruins families and sets bad examples for the children."

"You are absolutely right, Reverend, for they are losing all their winnings and the rest of their money to the dealer."

"You disapprove of gambling?"

"Whenever I see cheating."

The minister squinted at the cards. "Cheating? How so?"

"I will show you, but first ….." Rocamora prodded the dealer hard with his walking stick causing him to drop the deck of cards "You, return all their money."

The dealer stood with hand on the hilt of his dagger. "Why have you interrupted our game? Who are you?"

"You have clever hands. Need I explain? I said return all they wagered. Your winnings too."

The look in Rocamora's eyes and authority of his voice cowed the cheat, who complied. Two of the young men seized the scoundrel before he could scurry away. The third scratched his head. "Mynheer, how was he cheating us?"

Rocamora decided to play the role of a virtuous man. "If I show you, will you swear before the Lord, this honorable minister, and all these witnesses that you will repent your sin of gambling, a curse that leaves families destitute and will guarantee you eternal damnation in Hell?"

The farmers so promised and their fellow passengers added amens. Rocamora held the ace of hearts for all to see, placed it at top of the deck face out, and dealt card after card without disturbing the bone-ace. He placed the ace of hearts at the bottom of the deck and repeated the exercise except to give himself the bone-ace when he called it out.

"That is how this son of Satan cheated. If you cannot see what I am doing, how can any of you ever win at cards and other games?"

The minister raised his bible. "Wait. Do not release him. What shall be done with this vile creature?" Passengers offered punishments from hanging, through tarring and feathering, to lashes or a thorough beating.

Rocamora quieted them. "If this miserable sinner repents and swears to mend his wicked ways, I would say spare his life although he must suffer some form of punishment."

"I repent and promise never again to cheat at cards."

Rocamora detected insincerity in the man's eyes and tone of voice. "This scoundrel would have picked these farmers clean, so why not let the punishment fit his crime? Strip him of his clothes and rings and let the waters of the canal cleanse him."

Laughter and agreement greeted Rocamora's suggestion. The farmers stripped and pummeled the cheat, took his rings, and heaved him overboard into the cold water of the canal.

The minister watched the rogue flail in the water trying to stay afloat. "Do you think he will drown?"

Rocamora looked at the sky. "That is up to the Lord."

"Amen. You have given those wayward farmers a superb lesson that I shall include in my sermon, but what shall be done with his clothing and rings?"

"They are of fine quality. Why not auction them to these passengers and donate the money to your church?"

"I should have thought of that. Are you perhaps a reformed gambler, for who else could have known he was cheating?"

"I do not gamble, but whenever I can, I do the Lord's work by turning the tools of the Devil against his evil minions in my humble way."

Tears filled the minister's eyes. "Well spoken. Mynheer, you must come to my church in Utrecht on Sunday. I am the Reverend Cornelius Palen."

"And I am Isaac de Rocamora."

"A Spaniard? But your Amstel Dutch is flawless."

"I now reside in Amsterdam because of its tolerance."

"De Rocamora. You are a Jew?"

"Yes, I am."

"Then perhaps my sermon will inspire you to convert."

Rocamora had visited Sunday services along his route and heard sermons different from those he had given in Spain. The dour Calvinists believed everyone was damned with no free will contrary to teachings of the Catholic Church, except for those of an Elect predetermined by God to be saved as evidenced by their piety and commercial success in this world. The Calvinists' conviction that everyone was a sinner except those born to be of the Elect went far beyond the beliefs of his intolerant kinsman, Tomás de Rocamora, the Dominican Provincial of Aragón.

On his first Sunday in Utrecht, Rocamora attended Reverend Palen's bare-bone church to hear his sermon against gambling. Typical of other previously Catholic churches, it had been stripped of statues, paintings, and crucifixes. Rocamora listened astounded when the minister also railed against the building of paved roads claiming such luxuries led to greater sins.

17.
May Day

Rocamora decided not to matriculate at the relatively new medical school at Utrecht established in 1636 because it had fewer professors and facilities than Leyden. Heavy spring rains turned the rutted roads to mud causing cart and carriage wheels to sink into the slime, which was why he preferred to continue by boat to Arnhem. The weather provided another contrast with sunny Spain. Most days were cold with misty sunshine and frequent drizzles. With the rains, flowers bloomed, and Rocamora admired tulips, grape hyacinths, and daffodils in parks, gardens, and fields creating palettes of color any artist would have envied.

"Boatman, why have we stopped here?"

Late morning on the thirtieth day of April, the canal boat docked near a waterfront inn and tavern in Gelderland a good ten miles to the west of Arnhem.

"Mynheer, tomorrow is the First of May, one of our national holidays, and everyone will be celebrating. It is best we reserve our rooms here. The Crimson Tulip is one of the finest and cleanest country inns in the United Provinces. They know me and always treat my passengers well."

Rocamora paid for a small but immaculate room. Other establishments he stayed at along the route had dormitories with straw on the floor for bedding and no tubs for bathing. The Crimson Tulip was renowned for its cuisine, and Rocamora ordered a full meal of breads, cheeses, prune soup flavored with ginger, minced ox-tongue with green apples, and a dessert cream of milk, sugar, cinnamon, and eggs beaten with chopped parsley and apples. The local beer was tolerable.

After a siesta in his room, Rocamora watched a group of youths erect and decorate a maypole in a field with paper streamers and gilded branches. Girls flirted and teased the boys, who responded with bawdy songs.

At misty dawn the following day, festivities began in earnest with drinking and exchanges of presents. Children flew kites, walked on stilts, and somersaulted on the great lawns. Dressed all in green, boys and young men sang and danced around the maypole with nubile girls wearing garlands in their hair, which reminded Rocamora of paintings portraying nymphs chased by satyrs in wooded glades and meadows.

In the afternoon, older folk bowled ninepins on the green, younger men wagered to see who could roll a heavy disk the farthest, and later boys played a rough game of Groote Kolven pthis time on grass instead of ice.After a collision and piling of bodies, one of the boys lay on the ground screaming and holding his useless left arm. The other players called for someone to find the town surgeon, but he had passed out from guzzling too much beer.

Rocamora pushed through the crowd, kneeled beside the boy, and saw he had a fracture at the elbow. "Bring me two slats of wood and something to tie it."

"Are you a surgeon?" one of the villagers asked.

"I have been taught by the best. Hurry. We want his bones to knit." Rocamora pointed at two of the sturdiest boys. "You, carry him to the inn. I have medicine for his pain."

At the inn, patrons cleared a table for the boy to lie on, and Rocamora returned from his room with an opiate. He told the innkeeper to brew it for a tea. A townsman arrived with two slats, which Rocamora bound to the boy's arm. After a few minutes more, the tea calmed his patient.

"Take the boy home, and when your surgeon is sober, he can attend him."

All applauded Rocamora and offered him unlimited beer. The sun began to set, and torches and lamps illuminated the town. Imbibing increased, judgment decreased, and with it decorum and modesty. Beer flowed faster than the Rhine, and that night at the inn the patrons caroused, gambled, and wenched.

An inebriated woman thrust her bosom against Rocamora's face "I have soft pillows for you this night.

Rocamora gently pushed her away. "I prefer my own bedding."

The following morning Rocamora boarded the canal boat to Arnhem, also known as the Green City on the Rhine because it lay between thick verdant forests. He lingered in Arnhem longer than intended strolling through its many parks and dithering. Should he continue along the great river into the Rhenish Palatinate and beyond to Austria and María or follow his original route to Franeker?

In the game of life no different from chess, each move had intended and unintended consequences. Rocamora believed his journey through the Rhenish Palatinate to Austria would be easier than his travels during the winter famine of 1634-35 on his way back to Spain when he saw victims of atrocities and feral starving men and women reduced to cannibalism. Surely,

Bocarro would arrange a meeting with María. That he might learn much about medicine from the renowned physician was another incentive.

On the grass under the shade of great oaks, Rocamora next imagined all possibilities should he appear before María. Would she be pleased or set the guards upon him? Perhaps her response would be a disappointing formal audience and curt dismissal, which would not be worth the time and effort of the journey. Even if María greeted him warmly what then? Impossible for him to be the Empress' confessor, and he was not qualified to be her physician.

During his ruminations, Rocamora experienced a puzzling phenomenon. Ten years had passed since he had last seen María, and he could no longer remember her features clearly. Unaware he had fallen asleep, Rocamora did not understand why Moraíma's face had replaced that of María. He was sixteen again with the *morilla* on a bed of orange blossoms.

"I see you with three loves. Yes. Three loves, one of them not yet born. And you will have many children."

"If I love you, Moraíma, why would there be others? Who are the others?"

"I see a golden fire, flaming brilliantly, but burning under thick ice. I also see a ruby and a pearl."

"Tell me, Moraíma, what does it all mean?"

Moraíma vanished, and Abigail appeared.

Rocamora awakened startled by the noise of children playing nearby. Twice now, he had dreamed of Moraíma's prophecy and Abigail. His first love had accurately foreseen his second love, Infanta María, and that he would wear many masks while playing a significant role on a great stage. Ruby and pearl, was that her image of his third love? Was she Abigail?

18.
To Franeker

Rocamora decided against going to Vienna. He left Arnhem the first week in July and traveled by passenger boat northward along the River IJssel, a tributary of the Rhine, to Kampen near the Zuider Zee. He visited more towns and villages along the way, none of which compared to Amsterdam and Haarlem.

In Kampen, Rocamora had no choice but to go by land to Franeker because canals were rare in the north. He stared both curious and dismayed at the coach, a long cart drawn by four horses and covered by a waxed cloth stretched over iron hoops. He approached the coachman.

"Good morning, Mynheer, this will be my first experience in one of your coaches. May I ask what you are doing with that leather cloth?"

"It is a sail we use according to the wind to achieve greater speed. To which town are you traveling?"

"Franeker in Friesland."

"We should be there in thirty hours including time to change horses and stop to refresh ourselves at inns and taverns along the way."

"How can you be so precise?"

"We have a fixed timetable along our regular routes. If we do not break any axels or wheels, or overturn in a ditch, we can do fifty to sixty miles a day."

"Are highwaymen common?"

"That scourge ended several decades ago. The authorities used to hang those criminals on the spot along the routes to discourage others."

Rocamora paid extra for an outside seat. All roads he had traveled were the same in Spain, the Germanys, France, and now the United Provinces, with ruts and grooves that guaranteed a swaying bumpy ride. After another look at the narrow high wheels of the cart, he entered the post inn, gave a serving girl some marjoram, and asked her to brew a strong potion of the herbal tea to lessen the effects of motion sickness.

The coach carried a full load of twelve passengers, most of them Frieslanders. Rocamora's keen ear for languages identified a mix of Danish and Low German in their regional dialect. A lively young peasant couple from Sneek sat in his row, and the wife beside him held a basket on her lap filled with cheese, bread, carrots, cucumbers, and apples.

Regional clothing continued to fascinate Rocamora throughout the journey. The Friesland men dressed no differently from sailors in short doublets, billowing trousers, and felt caps. The women wore long summer dresses of coarse material, blue aprons, red or yellow stockings, and an exposed bodice with an undergarment that flattened their chests.

They left Kampen precisely at six in the morning. Rocamora took in the countryside so different from the other more populated provinces. Along the coast of the Zuider Zee and still in Gelderland, they passed the Gooi, an expanse of wooded dunes. Farther inland, he saw great forests and heaths with flocks of sheep.

The peasant woman with her husband's permission offered cheese and bread to Rocamora and a soldier seated behind him who had lost a leg. The cheese had bits of clove in it, which created a pleasant sensation on his palate, and the bread was infused with enough sugar to taste more like a cake.

The soldier pointed at the woods. "Plenty of wild boar there. Used to hunt them with my father when I was a lad. Perhaps they will serve boar meat and good mutton at the next rest stop, and strong drink, which I sorely need."

Rocamora felt compassion for the soldier, a handsome young man whose limb had been severed mid-thigh and probably too recently for a wooden leg to be attached. At the first rest stop, he helped the veteran from the coach and into the tavern.

"I suggest a strong brandy to encourage sleep on the coach."

"An excellent suggestion, Mynheer. The double beer I had at the last tavern did not help much."

"Feel free to address me as Isaac."

"And I am Karl."

"Are you in much pain?"

"I feel a throbbing …."

"And the sensation that you still have your leg?"

"Yes, how did you know?"

"It is a typical reaction for those who have had limbs amputated."

"Are you a surgeon?"

"A great friend of mine was. I used to help him restrain his patients."

"It took four men to hold me down while that butcher sawed. I could bear all now if the coach did not bounce and shake." A serving girl approached. "A bottle of aquavit. And two cups."

Rocamora was not sure he heard correctly. "Aquavit?"

"Our regional eu de vie."

After she brought the bottle, Karl poured and touched cups with Rocamora. "To your health."

"And yours." Rocamora experienced another surprising taste sensation, the aroma and taste of caraway seed. "A strong brew."

"I truly pray it is."

After the brief stop, the coach crossed the River IJssel and veered northwest into Drenthe, a sere infertile province, and onward to the east and Friesland. Rocamora saw inviting lakes for bathing but few canals. He also noted the early sunrise around five in the morning and sunset nearer to nine in the evening.

No mishaps, and after thirty hours, the coach arrived on schedule in Harlingen at noon. Rocamora had several hours to wait before he boarded a canal boat for the final seven miles to Franeker. He spent the time sitting on a grassy dike staring at the North Sea and several of the Frisian Islands on the horizon while remembering his boyhood on the palm lined beaches of Valencia. He had a sudden intense craving for melons and purchased pears, the fruit closest to them in sweetness and texture.

In Franeker, Rocamora chose to stay in one of the homes where university students rented rooms. They had gone to their towns and cities for the summer, and the landlord was delighted to have a paying guest. Rocamora's room had clean bedding, offered privacy, and most important of all, the landlord provided a tub for bathing.

19.
Tests

Gisebert Hagedorn, a bald cherubic man in his fifties with rolled shirtsleeves and wearing a bloodstained leather apron, welcomed Rocamora in his laboratory at the university where he was probing the heart of a dissected cadaver. "Isaac de Rocamora, the Dominican confessor of Empress María who fled to Amsterdam?"

"The same, and I am surprised my reputation has preceded me this far north."

Hagedorn put away his instruments and wiped his hands on a leather apron. "I received a letter from my good friend Professor Poons at Leyden. He said you would be coming to Franeker."

"I have toured the Leyden and Utrecht medical schools, and now I wish to see yours before I decide which to attend."

"To become a physician."

"Yes."

Hagedorn removed his apron and squinted at Rocamora. "You are not a young man."

"Is there an age barrier?"

"No, no of course not, nor do we care about a man's religion." City bells chimed the hour, and Hagedorn donned his doublet and hat. "Come, let us adjourn for a midday meal. Dissecting always gives me a hearty appetite for meat, and the best tavern in Franeker is across the street from the university."

The tavern offered many choices. Rocamora chose wine from the Rhine and salmon seasoned with garlic and dill. Hagedorn selected ale, a leg of mutton with mint sauce, oysters, and mussels. Rocamora let the professor select their vegetables, bread, and cheese.

"Now please tell me, Mynheer Isaacus, why you wish to become a physician at your stage of life."

"It is a calling I would have heeded when a young man, but I was forced into the clergy."

"As happens so often in Catholic lands, I have been told. Have you any knowledge of medicine?"

Rocamora described for Hagedorn the many skills of his boyhood mentor. "Don Lope introduced me to the medicine of the Arab Ibn al-Nafis,

Vesalius, and Lusitanus. I also observed the better physicians at *la Corte* most prominent amongst them the Royal Physician Fernando Cardozo."

"An excellent schooling it seems in both medicine and surgery. What did you think of the medical schools at Leyden and Utrecht?"

"I have rejected Utrecht and most likely will matriculate at Leyden, unless Franeker can persuade me otherwise."

"We are not yet Leyden's equal, but we are superior to most other European schools of medicine. We have our own botanical garden and hothouse with exotic plants, which I shall show you after our meal. Our university also has respected departments of Theology, Law, Physics, and Philosophy. Because of our excellent reputation, we draw students from Scandinavia, Poland, the Germanys, England, and Scotland."

Their drinks arrived, and after they touched *flapkans*, Hagedorn abruptly switched to Latin. "What did Hippocrates say when the brain is severely wounded?"

Rocamora replied without hesitation, "*Quibus perscissom fuerit hic nicesse est februm et bilis vomitum superveniere.* When the brain is severely wounded, fever and vomiting of bile necessarily intervene."

"Your Latin is excellent."

Rocamora responded accurately to further questions about Hippocrates' diagnoses and cures:

"In cases of protracted severe fever accompanied by dry tickling coughs and minimal expectoration, there is usually not much thirst.

"When the urine is transparent and white, it is bad. It appears principally in cases of phrenitis.

"During quartan fevers, if blood flows from the nostrils it is a bad symptom.

"In a chronic disease an excessive flux from the bowels is bad.

"Diseases that medicines and the knife do not cure, fire cures; and those which fire cannot cure are incurable."

Hagedorn raised his flapkan in a salute. "I am impressed."

"I have been studying curricula and refreshing my competence in Latin and Greek."

Food arrived, and Hagedorn continued his interrogation between bites. "Mynheer, what does Galen say about the humors?"

"Galen held that the body is governed by a system of fluids he called humors: blood, phlegm, yellow bile, black bile. Each body has a complexion specific to the individual and reflects a tendency to one of the four humors. The humoral complexion of men is hot and dry, women cold and wet, a defective version of a more perfect male body. Because a man's body is hotter, his reproductive organs stay more comfortably outside his body. Colder, female reproductive organs are instead tucked inside the body to maintain warmth."

"Continue, please."

"Galen believed four humors combine to form the chyle, a mix of lymphatic fluids. They are divided along two physical axes, wet-dry and warm-cold. Blood is warm and wet. Phlegm is cold and wet. Choler, also called yellow bile, is warm and dry. And melancholy, black bile, is cold and dry. The humors are balanced against the four elements. Earth, air, fire and water, and the four seasons. A healthy body exhibits a mix of all four humors. When one humor predominates, physical or mental illness results."

"And how are those illnesses treated?"

"According to Galen?"

"Of course."

"Galen recommended applying polar opposite treatments. When a fever is warm and dry with an excess of choler, the physician should prescribe a cold bath or cool towel. A cold and its resulting phlegm should be treated with warmth and dryness."

"How does the complexion of the patient aid the physician in his diagnosis? And can you give me specific examples?"

"Those who are sanguine tend to be cheerful and energetic. The phlegmatic appear to be lethargic and cheerless. Yellow bile reveals a choleric temperament. Such individuals are quick to lose their temper. And depressed melancholics suffered from an imbalance of black bile, which leads to melancholy."

"You know more than my students, and I suspect, as much as most professors."

"Yet there are new discoveries each day in the treatment of patients and healing herbs that I need to learn."

"And so you shall wherever you decided to matriculate. We treasure our freedom to seek knowledge and to experiment."

After their meal, Hagedorn took Rocamora to the university's botanical gardens. "Are you familiar with Harvey's treatise on the circulation of blood?"

"I agree with him that blood flows the same in every human body regardless if one is of high or low birth. *Sangre azul*, the blue blood claimed by the royals and aristocrats of Spain does not exist."

"So dissections have proven. Did you know that Rene Descartes matriculated here in 1629?"

"No, I did not."

"Have you read Descartes?"

"Yes"

"And your thoughts?"

"I care little for his eschatology but agree with his metaphor that the body works like a machine, that it has the material properties of extension and motion, and that it follows the laws of physics. His conclusions are definitely contrary to Spanish beliefs that one is born physically superior according to caste, that noble blood is linked to nobility of spirit and social status, and the opposite characteristics are proof of a man's base blood."

Hagedorn led Rocamora into the hothouse filled with tropical plants and fruits. "Yes, science has proven that the lowest peasant and worst criminals have the same intricate structure of muscles and tendons, bones, and circulation of blood as you and I and the *Stadhouder* himself. However, we cannot ignore Descartes' conclusions regarding the human soul."

Rocamora preferred to substitute another word for soul. "Do you agree with his argument that the mind interacts with the body at the pineal gland?"

"Pineal gland or not, it is obvious to me that the mind controls the body and at times the body controls our behavior."

"And yet Descartes cannot explain why you became an esteemed professor and physician, and others are criminals or drunkards."

"Our bodies may be alike, but it must be something inexplicable connected to the brain that causes one to take a higher road than another. In any case, you should refrain from expressing these opinions in front of certain professors who still prefer Galen and letting of blood."

Rocamora gasped when he saw melons, round familiar orbs, that contained the succulent fruit he had been craving. "Is it possible to purchase them?"

"No, but I shall arrange for you to have one tomorrow."

Over the next languid summer days, Hagedorn introduced Rocamora to the pleasures of sailing and line fishing at nearby lakes and along canals and estuaries. On the beaches, they gathered shellfish, dined, and drank well. The professor also managed to bring melons for Rocamora. Early in August, Hagedorn invited him to his office for a smoke and conversation.

"Have you come to a decision? Our school year begins in a few weeks."

"Your friendship and generosity and the reputation of your medical school tempt me, but I believe I cannot endure your long, dark and cold winters."

"Then you will return to Amsterdam and go on to Leyden?"

"Yes."

"You may arrive too late to matriculate there."

Rocamora did not want to tell Hagedorn of his plans to travel to England. "If so, that will give me another year to be better prepared."

"You are already well prepared as it is. When you have a thesis, I can assure you of this. If you present it to our faculty without having attended any of our classes, even if it is in the middle of our school year and if you defend it well, we will give you your license to practice."

"I thank you and will keep that in mind."

Jews must not vilify Christianity; Christians must not
be converted to Judaism; Jews may not have relations with
Christian women.
—Netherlands Decree of 1616

Part II
Becoming Don Isaac?
1644-1647

20.
Montezinos

Rocamora returned to Amsterdam in September of 1644 too late to matriculate at Leyden. Vrouw Cornelia complained he was too thin. She pulled him into her kitchen and served bread, cheese, fish soup, and beer. Hombrecillo had grown. When Rocamora reached to pet the Chartreaux, it hissed and scratched his hand.

"Have you forgotten me so soon, my little friend, or did you resent my leaving you?"

Watched by Hombrecillo, Rocamora later wallowed in a long bath, something he had been able to do infrequently during the past several months. He decided Amsterdam would be the best place for him to live unless England had some pleasant surprises. Because he must wait another year to matriculate at Leyden Medical School, Rocamora hoped to meet the great Harvey and other physicians reputed to be in the forefront of scientific knowledge.

Santcroos could help him select the best passage across the North Sea to England and perhaps write letters of introduction to men of influence there. Although war continued between King and Parliament, from what he had been told, only small parts of the country were affected by the strife.

After Rocamora settled in bed, Hombrecillo leaped onto his stomach, turned its behind to his face, and purred. "I take your insult for a sign of truce, *amigo*."

The following morning, Rocamora learned from workers at Santcroos' dockside warehouse that the merchant and his son had gone to Talmud Torah. When he arrived at the synagogue, he joined an excitable crowd of both Jews and Christians climbing the three steps between ornate wrought iron benches and passing two-by-two through the entrance, indistinguishable from each other by their clothes but not by language. The Sephardim spoke Spanish and Portuguese and the Protestants Dutch or English. All discussed the likelihood that someone named António de Montezinos, also known as Aaron Levi, had found descendants of the Lost Tribes of Israel in New Grenada. The most repeated words Rocamora heard from Jew and Christian alike were Messiah and Anointed One.

They pressed into a bare vestibule where observant Sephardim washed their hands from a tap with soap, but on this day, many ignored the ritual and ascended the stairs on either side. Inside the stifling synagogue, wooden floor planks squeaked at each step despite its usual covering with sand to silence the clumping sound of boots. Above, men filled the grilled galleries reserved for women that ran the length of the building. Silver chandeliers hanging from ceiling beams and the gallery to the right held hundreds of candles to illuminate the synagogue. More candles flamed in glass lamps along the walls. Congregants and guests sat at every chair and on each table used for studying. More occupied the five rows of benches beneath the gallery to his left.

Unlike the Christian churches and cathedrals where priests and ministers faced their congregations, rabbis preached from a platform in the center called the *tiváh*, three feet high surrounded by railings and facing benches perpendicular to it. At the far end of the synagogue, a shut cupboard contained scrolls of the Torah.

Fortunate to find a place to stand at the back, Rocamora saw Santcroos in the front row where oligarchs of the congregation had permanent seats. Several city magistrates and other civic dignitaries sat near the *poderoso*.

Montezinos stood with Menasseh on the *tiváh* flanked by rabbis and wardens of the *Ma'amad* in their high-back chairs. Rocamora studied the lean sun-bronzed Spaniard who had yet to speak. Not much taller than Menasseh, Montezinos had Mediterranean features and might have passed for Italian as well as Spanish. He wore plain black doublet and hose, boots, spurs, and a feathered hat at a jaunty angle. The explorer swaggered and exuded confidence while he waited for the murmuring to subside. And why not? Even if Montezinos were a poor speaker, his words would carry the value of gold for a receptive audience eager to believe whatever he said.

The last of the murmuring subsided, and Menasseh effusively introduced Montezinos. Renewed muttering from congregants and guests indicated their impatience for the rabbi to finish. Their restlessness and impatience reminded Rocamora of similar emotions Spaniards exhibited before *autos de fé*, *quemaderos*, and bullfights.

Allowed to speak, Montezinos thanked the rabbis and leaders of the community for giving him this opportunity to share his unique experience and began his tale. Rocamora appreciated his powerful manly voice and the way he commanded the stage. Montezinos strutted, gestured, and seemed to look every man in the eye. Each word from passionate whisper to dramatic bellow commanded their full attention no less than any dynamic *alumbrado* hypnotizing his cult.

Rocamora believed the first part of his tale. Montezinos had been prospecting in the Quito Province of New Granada with several companions and their Indian guides. When they climbed through the Cordilleras, a high range of mountains, a strong blizzard forced them to seek shelter in a cave.

Montezinos paused satisfied he had everyone waiting for his next word. He raised his voice so those farthest from him could hear. "That was when our Indian guides told us the storm was God's punishment upon the Spaniards, but not for our conquest of their kingdoms. … it was for … and I repeat this verbatim … for their mistreatment of … of a Holy People."

Many stood. Jews shook their fists and cursed Spain and Portugal for the martyrdom of family members and their forced exile. Dutch Protestants did the same in remembrance of atrocities committed by the Duke of Alba and his soldiers during their war for independence.

Montezinos waited until their anger subsided. "I did not find any Holy People and returned to Quito. Before I could make plans for a second journey, Familiars of the Inquisition arrested me for Judaizing."

While those beside him excoriated the Inquisition, Rocamora believed Montezinos must have voiced his assumption that the Holy People could be one of the Lost Ten Tribes of Israel. That would have been enough cause for his companions to denounce him.

Montezinos waited for silence. "The Holy Office soon released me for lack of evidence. By that time, I had become an obsessed man, but no longer did I hunger for gold. I wanted to find the Holy People. I convinced my Indian guides that I was one of them, and they agreed to lead me to my brethren."

Montezinos described his second trek with the Indian guides and led his audience along the same trails describing each rock, flower, and blade of grass until their impatience to meet the Holy People became near unbearable. By now, Rocamora had marked the explorer to be more than a skilled rhetorician. No liar either, Montezinos had the eyes of a zealot and spoke with true fervor. The man believed everything he said, which gave him credibility.

"After more than two weeks traversing the northern side of the Cordilleras, we came to a small clearing at the edge of a forest. My guides whistled in imitation of birds, and four Indians emerged from the brush. After a long conversation in their language, which I did not understand, my guides convinced them I was one of the Holy People."

Rocamora appreciated another of Montezino's dramatic pauses, during which all implored him to continue.

"The Indians embraced me and then each other. You can imagine my surprise when they recited in Hebrew … yes Hebrew … our *Shemah* … yes, the *Shemah*. Hear, oh Israel, the Lord our God, the Lord is One."

Montezinos stopped speaking, this time not by choice. No one could have been heard over the din in the synagogue. Calmer men shushed their neighbors, and he resumed his tale, his voice now raspy. "Although the natives' skin had been baked brown by the sun, I could see from their noble features and bearing that they were Hebrews."

More shouting, many wept.

Montezinos again quieted his audience. "The Indians brought me to a village where I was given the warmest of welcomes, and my guides interpreted the tribal elders' story. Most were descendants of the Lost Tribe of Reuben. Please … let me continue. Others were Levites, the same as I, for as many of you know, my real name is Aaron Levi."

Montezinos repeated how they and their forebears had lived in the jungle for centuries having been driven from their lands by Tartars. Their dream had always been to reestablish contact with the main body of the Jewish people because they had forgotten Hebrew, much of Scripture, and most rituals.

"I was reluctant to leave them, and before I departed, they made me promise to send missionaries so they could be instructed in the Law of Moses. Therefore, without question, I have found a Lost Tribe of Israel in the Americas. Only England remains to complete our people's dispersal to the four corners of the world, as prophesied in Scripture, and then our Messiah will come and redeem us to Zion."

Menasseh rose and waved a document. "This is an oath the *Ma'amad* has requested our honored guest to sign affirming all he has said."

After Montezinos complied, Jews and Christians rushed to the platform screaming their questions. Practical and clear-thinking in daily affairs these Sephardim and Protestants might be, today Rocamora thought they were naive for believing Montezinos had found a lost tribe of Israel. No one asked for proof beyond his words. No one suggested a more logical reason for the Indians' recital of the *Shemah*, that Judaizing *conquistadores* who came to Peru with Pizarro a century earlier could have taught the prayer to indigenous savages.

Moved by Montezinos' revelations, several Protestants standing beside Rocamora quoted prophecies from Scripture, all with the same theme: after the Children of Israel had been dispersed to the four corners of the earth, the moment would come for them to be returned to Zion thus heralding the appearance of the Anointed One.

Rocamora thought it best to leave before anyone asked his opinion of Montezinos, but Menasseh stopped him on the steps. The excitement in the rabbi's eyes betrayed his belief in explorer's tale before speech confirmed it.

"Wonderful, is it not, Don Isaac? Jews have been found in China, India, and now in the New World. One place is left to be populated by our people, which will most certainly herald the Anointed One and restore us to Israel from the four corners of the world according to the prophecies of Isaiah,

Daniel, and others in Scripture."

The man Rocamora most admired and whom he considered his greatest partisan in the Sephardic community now disappointed him. Besotted with messianism, Menasseh believed Montezinos without empirical evidence.

Santcroos apologized for interrupting and took Rocamora aside. "I did not know you had returned."

"I arrived late yesterday."

"We must speak. Will you come to my warehouse this afternoon?"

"Yes, and I have much to discuss with you."

Rocamora left the synagogue steps before Menasseh drew him deeper into a discussion about the Messiah, but when he turned the corner at Jodenbreestraat, Bento d'Espinoza caught him.

"Don Isaac."

"Good day, Bento."

"You heard Montezinos?"

"I did."

"And I. Do you believe he found a lost tribe of Israel?"

Rocamora would not reveal his thoughts to the precocious twelve year old. "What did you think, Bento?"

"I thought it is irrelevant because there cannot be any Messiah."

He patted the boy's shoulder and increased his pace to create distance between them. "My advice is to keep such thoughts to yourself."

21.
An Interval of Sanity

"Mynheer Isaacus, it is a great honor to meet you. My husband has spoken often and well of you. I hope you will tell me what the Empress is like."

The surgeon's typically narrow three-story home was a few blocks from his residence in the Jordaan District. Rocamora thought Velde and Johanna were well suited to each other, both being cheerful, plump, and with features so similar they might pass for twins. Like their parents, nine year old Peter, seven year old Kaethe, and three-year old Claudia's cheeks were apple red. Rocamora could not resist making coins appear and disappear from their faces and clothes as he had done often in Spain at orphanages and in the homes of families he confessed.

Velde calmed his children when they demanded more. "Be careful, Isaacus, they may bankrupt you when they become wiser and demand florins."

Because of his playful nature, Rocamora assumed a stern expression and recited a homily in the same deep, passionate, and compelling voice he had used in Spain during his sermons. "Remember this, children, greed is one of the Seven Deadly Sins. Money comes and goes with the wind, but virtue is eternal. Peter, Julia, and Claudia obey your parents, or the treasure of coins in your noses and behind your ears will disappear forever."

"Mynheer, my children adore you. You would be an excellent father. My husband and I know a young widow …."

"Johanna is right. Vrouw Paula will fall in love with you at first sight, and perhaps you with her, for she is wealthy."

"Marriage is not part of my immediate plans."

"You may think differently after you meet her."

"Perhaps, Jacobus, but I did not leave servitude to Crown and Church to be enslaved so soon by matrimony."

Velde kissed his wife. "Being a slave to love is not so terrible."

"Are marriage and love the same?"

"It can be."

"I am not yet ready to gamble my life on that thin hope."

Velde invited Rocamora to share their midday meal in the kitchen where copper pots and pans shone at a brightness that rivaled the sun. The surgeon provided an ample amount of beer, and Johanna served a hearty meal of mutton with carrots and spinach followed by fresh fish with currants, plums, and berries, and a honey cake ringed by cinnamon bark and marzipan.

The marzipan reminded Rocamora of Mina. When he stopped at her bakery on the way to Velde, the new owner told him she married her apprentice and sailed for New Amsterdam.

After the meal, Velde invited Rocamora to sit with him in his basement surgery for conversation, more beer, and a smoke. Jars containing preserved organs, fetuses, hands and feet filled shelves lining the walls. Surgical tools and a table for operating could not be cleaner.

Velde offered Rocamora tobacco. "It is good to see you after these many months, my friend. I worried you had made a rash decision and returned to Spain."

"As you know, I was invited to The Hague, and I am sorry, Jacobus, that I cannot tell you more."

"I understand although I am disappointed you have not matriculated at one of our medical schools. Have you decided not to become a physician after all?"

"That is still my goal, but I wanted to see the medical schools at Leyden, Utrecht, and Franeker before making my choice."

"And which one have you decided to attend?"

"Leyden."

"Excellent, the best and closest to Amsterdam. Now tell me about your adventures, for surely you must have had many having been gone these many months since February."

"First, I want you to know that being with you and your family has been an antidote to the madness I experienced this morning." Rocamora went on to describe Montezinos' tale and the reaction of the congregation and their Protestant guests. "I am disappointed that so many men of brilliant mind can be credulous and succumb to the myth of messianism. Faith often triumphs over empiricism and common sense."

"How true it is. I am sure that the most extreme Protestant believers, the English dissidents living here in Amsterdam, went to see Montezinos."

"They did."

"No people, not even our Calvinists, are more obsessed with what the English call Old Testament Scripture. Day and night, they quote passages relating to Jesus' Second Coming, which they believe to be imminent. But let us now speak of the real world. What shall you do until next August? There will be pressures from the Iberians to join their community. You cannot postpone your decision forever."

"I know."

"Now, tell me the truth. Did you reject our offer of an introduction to the widow Vrouw Paula because some Spanish or Portuguese beauty caught your eye, or better yet, the daughter of a wealthy merchant or a rich widow?"

Velde's question prompted self-doubting. Could he have a happy family like Velde's and a home filled with love and laughter? Had Abigail married? If he wed her or anyone else, how many children would they have? What kind of father would he be? If his sons lacked physical courage or the ability to succeed at studies, could he still love them? If they misbehaved, could he beat them? And what if his daughters were ill favored of appearance and temperament unlike his lost Brianda? Could he show them love?

"Isaacus, your silence, did I offend you with my question?"

"No, of course not."

"I said it before, and I say it again. We can introduce you to any of several amiable women of means who would welcome you to their beds and warm your thin Spanish blood during our long and cold winter nights."

Rocamora touched *flapkans* with Velde. "That is something I shall keep in mind. And now, tell me. Did you decide to invest in the expansion of *The Three Crows*?"

"No, and I am grateful to you for your advice, which convinced me not to take the risk, for those who invested lost all. Last month, the owner disappeared with close to twenty-five thousand guilders. His magistrate partners and the investors have yet to find him. I suspect he is probably on some boat headed for a faraway colony if he planned well. It would have been wonderful to be someone important when I entered my tavern and bath house."

"You are somebody important, one of the best surgeons in Amsterdam and a monarch in your home."

"Perhaps you are right, but even though I love my wife and have a happy home, there are times when I dream of living another life."

"So do we all."

22.
Like Minded

Rocamora entered the great maw of Santcroos' warehouse. Redolent with the pleasant scent of spices, herbs, and sandalwood unlike the noisy docks outside reeking of rotting fish and refuse, the vast interior burst with goods from all over the world. Santcroos stood beside his son David between open crates and burlap bags. A downy lip image of his father, the boy counted the merchandise inside and recorded it in a ledger.

"Most impressive, Don Samuel."

A broad smile creased Santcroos' face. "We are the center of world trade. If you cannot find what you want in Amsterdam, it does not exist." He affectionately squeezed David's shoulder. "You remember meeting Don Isaac de Rocamora."

"Yes, Father. Welcome to our warehouse, Señor."

"David has been blessed with the gift of numbers. I have absolute confidence he will continue taking accurate inventory while we speak, Don Isaac."

Santcroos took Rocamora to his office and told a servant to bring them tea, cheeses, and tobacco for their pipes. A large map of the world covered one wall. Ledgers filled shelves and cabinets. Rocamora sat opposite Santcroos at a carved desk covered with neat stacks of manifests. After he described his impressions of the *Stadhouder* and Prince Willem, Santcroos handed him a draft from the Wisselbank with four figures written on it payable to the bearer.

"What is this, Don Samuel?"

"A modest amount for your delivery of my letter. Frederick Hendrick has accepted my offer to be provisioner of his army and navy."

Rocamora stiffened. Although he accepted many gifts from Infanta María, which he could not refuse, he did not like being the recipient of another man's largesse. Generosities always came with strings attached. "I gave your letter to the Stadhouder out of friendship, Don Samuel, not for any reward." He changed the subject away from money. "What did you think of Montezinos?"

"A tale to inspire the messianists and useful for serious men of business. It may motivate the English Parliament to pass laws allowing Jews to live in England as citizens free to worship in synagogues and thrive in all endeavors."

The servant arrived, poured tea, and opened a porcelain jar containing tobacco. Santcroos urged Rocamora to sample the array of cheeses and lit his pipe. "I believe those Indians Montezinos encountered were descendants of *converso conquistadores* and not of any Lost Tribe of Israel. What is your opinion of Montezinos, Don Isaac?"

"I had the same thought."

"I fear the congregation might someday accept any charlatan who claims to be the Anointed One, especially if our rabbis tell them he is the true messiah."

Rocamora sipped the tea delighted his friend was no messianist. "Menasseh is Montezinos greatest supporter."

"Every great man has flaws." Santcroos sliced a wedge of cheese with a gold paring knife and offered it to Rocamora. "Do you still intend to matriculate at Leyden?"

"I do."

"I have better plans for you, Don Isaac. Wed my eldest daughter Lea, and I will take you into my business."

Santcroos' offer stunned Rocamora. "Why … why, she is but a child."

"Lea is fifteen and nubile. She is agreeable to marrying you and would be a devoted wife."

"I have neither the desire nor the talent to be successful in trade."

"You have no interest in business? Fine. Give me grandsons, and you will never have to work a day in your life."

"Again, I must decline your generous offer, Don Samuel. My destiny is to be a physician, but I am honored you have thought of me as a son-in-law."

"Think it over. In the meantime, will you perform another service for me? I am sending a large shipment of silver bullion to Parliament in support of their efforts to defeat King Charles. I would go myself, Don Isaac, but for my current duties and obligations to my family and the congregation. Would you be willing to accompany the silver to London? I have heard you are skilled with sword and pistol, that you are resourceful, and most important of all, I trust you. I will pay you well, of course."

"Our plans coincide, Don Samuel. I came here to ask if you could find me a berth on one of your ships going to England because I want to meet their physicians and learn what I can from them."

"Excellent."

"May I assume you do not expect me to walk into Parliament and dump the silver on their laps?"

"That would be a sight worth seeing. I have prepared and signed a letter of introduction to my factor in London, António Fernández Carvajal. He will arrange the delivery to Parliament."

Rocamora had read the Carvajal family dossier amongst many others accumulated by the Holy Office. Several men and women from that family had burned at the *quemadero*. A Portuguese born new-Christian, Carvajal earned a fortune in Madeira. He later made London his headquarters and imported Spanish silver bars to exchange for goods of English manufacture.

Rocamora calculated how long he might be away. It was late September, and he could not matriculate at Leyden Medical School until August of next year. "I thank you for your faith in my abilities and your trust. I accept your offer provided I can leave before the weather worsens and return by late spring."

"One of my ships leaves Rotterdam for England in five days. It will be captained by one you have met, Gaspar Hendrijks."

"I thought Hendrijks would be looting Cartagena or some other Spanish port."

"At the last moment, our plans changed, and for this short journey, it is essential you address him as Captain Enríquez. In England, Spaniards are more in favor than the Dutch."

"You are not planning to have that pirate head south to the Atlantic and take me to the Americas for other purposes?"

"A delicious thought, but no, my friend, I promise you. The ship will sail directly to England."

Vrouw Cornelia stood in the doorway of Rocamora's room. "Not again? And so soon."

"Yes, I shall be gone for several months, but this time I am taking everything with me."

Cornelia frowned. "I fear you will not return. I cannot understand your wanderlust."

"I must cure myself of that affliction before I settle in Amsterdam once and for all." Rocamora heard Hombrecillo meowing. The cat lay atop of one of his trunks and dug its claws into the edge as if to prevent him from leaving. He swept Hombrecillo into his arms and stroked his head. "So, my little friend, you do not want me to go. I wonder ... have you a desire for adventure?" Rocamora turned to Cornelia. "I will take him with me if you have no objections."

"I shall be more than pleased if you do. While you were away, he meowed without cessation every night, driving all of us to madness."

Rocamora made a place for Hombrecillo in his satchel when Santcroos' men came for his trunks, one filled with changes of clothes, disguises, and other necessities for his journey to England. The other containing his most valuable possessions would go to Santcroos who promised to store it in a secure place.

"*Ga met God*, Mynheer Isaacus."

"And you, Vrouw Cornelia."

23.
Turbulent Waters

Rocamora stood with Santcroos at the gangplank of *The Baltic Queen*, a three-mast fluyt designed similar to galleons but smaller in size. Seabirds screeched above them. Nearby, aggressive fishwives called at prospective customers and screamed curses at those who did not buy their husbands' catches. Along the docks, sailors in colorful tops and pantaloons worked on riggings, loaded and unloaded cargo, and added their yells and curses to the cacophony.

Rocamora pointed his walking stick at the topmost mast. "Don Samuel, why are you flying the standard of Poland?"

"We dare not display the flags of Holland and Amsterdam, for we are England's great rival in trade and the acquisition of colonies throughout the world. They forbid entry to our ships. The Polish banner is appropriate because much of our cargo is grain from Poland and goods accumulated at other Baltic seaports. The rest are exports of Dutch manufacture. The fluyt can carry more freight with less crew than most other merchant ships, which is why we can offer rates of half or less than our rivals."

Rocamora frowned when a family with two small children, a pair of dour preachers, and a couple boarded the fluyt. "I supposed I would be the lone passenger."

"They make a good cover for our important merchandise especially that newly married pair. Remember to address our friend Hendrijks as Captain Enríquez, his true surname. And now I bid you a safe and successful journey."

Rocamora said farewell to Santcroos and ascended the gangplank. On deck, the preachers and the couple conferred with a weathered sailor, whose braided blond beard had been tied with colorful ribbons. They lowered their voices when he passed. Rocamora did not trust them and the other passengers, not with so much silver aboard. He intended to carry his weapons at all times.

No Turkish costume this day, Gaspar wore a sleeveless leather vest over his white linen shirt with scimitar, dagger, and two pistols attached to a green silk sash tied around his waist. He supervised the loading of freight into a hold and touched the brim of his plumed hat when he saw Rocamora.

"Don Isaac, I have no time to chat now. My First Mate will see you to your quarters. Krogh."

Braided Beard ran to him "Captain?"

"Gustav Krogh is my First Mate. He will escort you to your cabin."

"Aye, Aye, Captain. Mynheer, please allow me the honor of showing you to your quarters."

Rocamora did not trust the unctuous rogue, whose eyes did not meet his. He followed Krogh below deck to a narrow cabin with a hammock. A seaman brought his trunk and set it on the floor. Rocamora placed his satchel on its top and reached inside to stroke Hombrecillo. The cat had not stopped trembling and whining from the moment they boarded.

Krogh touched the netting. "You might be better off sleeping on the floor. The ship's motion will cause your hammock to swing against the walls. No body of water is rougher than this part of the North Sea."

"Thank you. I shall heed your advice." *And not turn my back to you.*

Rocamora returned to the deck when the fluyt left the Rotterdam docks. He enjoyed the fresh breeze and sights along the conjoining mouths of the Maas and Rhine Rivers during the sail toward the North Sea. Gaspar did not summon him to the bridge, and he went to his cabin after the fluyt passed the last piece of land, Hoek van Holland, Corner of Holland.

Rocamora stroked Hombrecillo still trembling and meowing in the satchel. "You will soon have your sea legs, little friend. Perhaps a rat will appear for you to chase."

He climbed onto the hammock for a late afternoon siesta. He had ingested a good amount of marjoram tea earlier in the day and chewed more leafs even though the ship's motion bothered him less so far than his ride in Santcroos' carriage on the rutted roads to Rotterdam.

They had stopped for a day at The Hague so Don Samuel could confer with the Stadhouder. Rocamora had looked forward to seeing van Noordwijk, but Frederick Hendrick sent him and his father on a diplomatic mission to King Charles. He thought it likely they would meet somewhere in England.

Rocamora settled deeper into his hammock, and like a baby gently rocked in a cradle, he fell asleep. He did not know for how long when the fluyt's motion sent him hard against the walls. He staggered to his feet and peered into the satchel where Hombrecillo had burrowed deeper.

"I would join you if I could fit."

Rocamora went on deck hatless and stepped into a fierce wind. The North Sea churned and roiled. Splashes of water exploded over the railing. No moon or stars above on this overcast night, faint light blinked from lamps on bridge, bow, and stern.

Rocamora gripped a rail for balance and imagined how difficult it must have been to sail centuries earlier without a compass. He breathed deeply to clear his head until a roar came from someone behind him, and he felt something warm, wet and rancid hit the back of his head. Rocamora turned and saw one of the preachers on his knees vomiting, a dagger on the deck beside him. He picked up the blade, seized the groaning man's hair, and threatened to slash his throat.

"Assassin, who sent you? Who are you? Where is your companion?"

The assailant retched again, his eyes focusing on the bridge. Rocamora kicked at the man's jaw rendering him unconscious. He hurried toward the bridge, ricocheting from mast to mast and gripping rigging and railing between. At the foot of the stairs he caught the second preacher and another man ascending to the bridge, both armed with pistols. Rocamora called a warning to Gaspar, plunged the dagger into the preacher's back, and threw him from the stairs.

Gaspar reacted in time to disarm and subdue the other assassin. He looked at the dead preacher. "Well done, Don Isaac, which proves the truth of what they say about you Valencians and knives. You saved my life."

"And seasickness my own. Now we must find the woman."

Gaspar tossed the assassin into the arms of several crewmen below the bridge. "Put this scum in irons and that one too lying over there in his own vomit. Search this dead vermin and then throw him overboard. Helmsman, maintain a steady course. Now, let us deal with the other mutineers. Krogh, you come with us." Gaspar removed two pistols from his sash and offered one to Rocamora who refused and brandished his wheel lock.

"I have my own."

Below deck, Rocamora heard masculine cursing and Hombrecillo's angry screeches coming from his cabin. Gaspar and Krogh followed him inside. The cat leaped from the intruder's head into Rocamora's arms. The false wife held gloves to his bloodied face and moaned. Furrows made by Hombrecillo's claws oozed crimson rivulets down the man's forehead and cheeks close to his eyes.

Gaspar prevented his First Mate from slitting their captive's throat. "Krogh, are you a fool? We want information from him."

Rocamora read Krogh's expression and wrested the weapon from his hand. "He is one of them. These matones would have needed someone to captain your ship had they succeeded."

Gaspar stared into his First Mate's eyes. "By Neptune's balls, you are right. Mutinous swine. I always treated you fairly, Krogh." He opened the door and beckoned his crew in the corridor. "Men, take them below … yes, Krogh too. Do not be gentle. Give them berths beside their companions."

After Rocamora and Gaspar confirmed that the parents and children were not involved in the mutiny, they searched the conspirators' possessions and found more than three hundred Carolus guilders.

"This must be the fee someone paid them for our lives, Don Isaac."

"I am insulted our death was assessed at so cheap a price."

"Well said, *amigo*."

In the damp hold, Gaspar held a lamp to each prisoner satisfied their chains were secure. Rocamora had seen instances when fear of torture worked better than its application in the dungeons of the Inquisition. He faced the man who failed to kill him and affected a menacing rasp. "We could catch a rat, place it in a pan against your belly and heat the metal, forcing the creature to eat its way out. Other methods can make each second seem an eternity."

The seasick assailant moaned. Spittle decorated his lips and jaw. "Please, will you spare our lives if we tell all?"

Gaspar forced one of the most insincere smiles Rocamora had ever seen. "Of course we will if you tell us who hired you."

The prisoner inclined his head to the left. "He knows."

Gaspar placed the tip of his pistol against the false wife's genitals. "I can easily turn you into the woman you pretended to be. If you cannot give us his name, describe him, and you had best tell the truth."

"Your First Mate … he told us about the cargo of bullion. We were to take control of your ship, pay other members of your crew to join us or kill them, and Krogh would sail us to Hamburg."

Gaspar confronted his First Mate and twisted his scrotum. "It will go easier if you answer all questions. Who bribed you, Krogh? Is he someone close to Santcroos?"

"I do not know. He never gave his name."

"Describe him."

After the First Mate finished, Gaspar turned to Rocamora. "I know the swine's identity. Don Samuel will deal severely with him after I return. Now, what shall we do with our failed assassins?"

Rocamora did not reply to the rhetorical question. There could be but one answer.

Gaspar struck his First Mate. "You sailed with me for more than ten years. Until now, you had been my most loyal crewman. You have done far worse than betraying my trust and generosity. You have desecrated my ship. You attempted mutiny. You tried to murder me, and Don Isaac. For that, for all you swine, I shall enforce the Law of the Sea." He ignored their pleading and faced his Second Mate. "Tell my crew that for their loyalty I shall distribute equally all the gold coins and belongings of these mutineers. Now, bring out the plank and let us see how well they walk it. You approve, Don Isaac?"

"They would have murdered us. Yes, I approve."

After they dealt justice to the mutineers, Rocamora washed vomit from his hair and joined Gaspar on the bridge. "Will the sea be this violent all the way to England?"

"Most likely. You are not seasick?"

"To the contrary, I have a sudden appetite." Rocamora intended to chew on more marjoram if necessary.

"Then, let us enjoy food and drink."

In the captain's quarters, the ship's cook served a meal of stew, cheeses, biscuits, and strong wine. Rocamora gripped the cup to prevent spillage. He pressed his boots hard against the floor and buttocks on the seat to prevent his sliding off the chair at each rock of the fluyt.

"Why have you brought your bag to my cabin?"

Rocamora coaxed Hombrecillo's head out of his satchel with morsels of food. "My *amigo* deserves a reward for protecting me."

"A unique weapon to be sure." He raised his glass in a salute to Rocamora. "Don Isaac, I owe you my life and offer my eternal friendship. I wish you would sail with me to pirate against Spain and Portugal and seize prizes beyond dreams of wealth."

"Friendship with you is prize enough for me, *Capitán* Gaspar, and as you know, I have decided to be a physician. When do you plan to sail next to raid and plunder the Spanish colonies?"

"In December. The North Atlantic Ocean may have its storms, but they are mild when compared with what the natives call *huricanos*. Those winds are stronger than any we see here in Europe. They appear with little or no warning and are most violent during our months of June through November. Because of Neptune's avarice, more gold, silver, and precious gems may lay at the bottom of the Atlantic than all the prizes taken by pirates and privateers."

"The greed of gods has been well documented throughout the ages, Don Gaspar."

Gaspar guffawed when Hombrecillo leaped onto the table and lapped the stew. "And that of cats."

24.
Return

Rocamora arrived in Rotterdam at the end of July 1645 on the same ship with van Noordwijk, who completed his mission to King Charles. They parted at The Hague. Van Noordwijk left to report to the *Stadhouder* and propose marriage to Princess Royal Mary's lady in waiting, Arabella Douglas.

Upon his return to Amsterdam, Rocamora gave Santcroos letters from Carvajal at his dockside warehouse. Don Samuel told him a nephew he hired to appease his sister paid for the attempted mutiny. The temptation of so much silver bullion had been too much for the wastrel to resist. Gaspar found the fool a berth aboard *The Avenger* bound for Recife and guaranteed he would be lost at sea, a drunk who fell overboard during rough weather.

Santcroos had much news from Spain of interest to Rocamora. Queen Isabel died of fever at age forty-one. Rocamora had fond memories of the lively woman who enjoyed plays and pranks. He respected Isabel for the way she wrested control of the government from Olivares. Rocamora never forgot the day Isabel advised him to leave Spain, which saved his life.

He almost crossed himself. "May she rest in peace."

"I have more to tell you, my friend. King Philip has appointed your kinsman, Tomás de Rocamora, Bishop and Viceroy of Mallorca."

"And the even more bigoted Diego Arce y Reynoso is still Inquisitor General?"

"Unfortunately, and that is not all. Familiars of the Holy Office arrested one of your strongest supporters, Jerónimo de Villanueva, *Protonotario*, Secretary of State, for the Kingdom of Aragón."

"I am not surprised. The Holy Office had long suspected Villanueva of being a Judaizer."

"They had no proof of that. Instead, they accused him of participating in sorcery years earlier at the notorious Convent of San Plácido. After the *Protonotario* reconciled with the Church, they banished him from Madrid."

"Villanueva would be wise to leave Spain."

That evening Rocamora soaked in a tub provided by Vrouw Cornelia. He reached to pet Hombrecillo, but the cat avoided his wet hand. "Ay, my loyal companion, you can be assured that I have had my fill of traveling."

The time had come to set a structured course for the rest of his life however long or short it might be. While Rocamora was in England, Abigail's image came to mind often during the day, and at night, she haunted his dreams. So did Moraíma's prophecy he would have three loves and children with the last.

Rocamora had never considered marriage in Spain because the Church forbade it. If he successfully wore the masks of piety and rectitude while a Dominican for twenty-six years, surely pretending to be an observant Jew in Vlooienburg should be less burdensome. Rocamora laughed at himself for being so presumptuous. He did not know for certain Abigail's mind in regards to their marrying.

Early the following morning, Rocamora timed his arrival at the synagogue so he would encounter Abigail's uncle and guardian after morning prayers. "Don Judah."

"Don Isaac, a pleasant surprise to see you. I heard you were in England."

"I returned yesterday."

"We are well met. There is an issue of great importance that I have to discuss with you. It concerns my niece, Abigail."

Rocamora strained every facial muscle to prevent himself from smiling. "How so?"

"Don Isaac, I am in a most difficult position. I do not wish to offend you. Yet, I must know your intentions regarding our community, for if you were to become a *relapso* and return to your previous faith, or be tempted by the Dutch Church, or even secularism …."

"What are you trying to say? Can you not be more direct?"

"Yes, of course, forgive me. I love my niece as if she were my own daughter. I would do anything for Abigail, anything and everything to ensure she marries well. To my great distress, she has refused offers any other young woman would have accepted. She has twice rejected the esteemed Don Abraham da Mexia."

"May I ask when Mexia proposed marriage to her?"

"A strange question."

"Please continue."

"Mexia never proposed to her directly. His cousin, the respected physician Ephraim de Bueno, spoke to me on Mexia's behalf, the first time shortly before you arrived in 1643, and again early last year. Mexia was enraged when he heard that Abigail refused his offer and told Bueno she will marry you or no one."

"She said that?"

"Yes, my niece wants you for her husband."

"Don Judah, I will speak the truth. We did not meet by accident. I have sought you to discuss the possibility of my marrying Abigail."

"Is it true?"

"Yes."

"Then my prayers have been answered. I give you permission to wed."

Even if Judah had accurately described his niece's determination to marry him or no one, Rocamora preferred to hear it from Abigail. "I am grateful to you for that, Don Judah, but I have not yet asked Abigail to be my wife. We must not leap too far ahead. Abigail and you should know that I first must make my place in Amsterdam as a physician before I can marry. I have two years of medical school ahead of me before I obtain my license to practice."

"She will wait for you."

"If what you have said about Abigail's affection for me is true, I need to establish a place and time where I may speak with her alone. Preferably today."

"You have made me the happiest of men, Don Isaac. Our family will be honored to have one from so esteemed a lineage wed our Abigail."

Rocamora next visited Velde where he received a warm welcome from Johanna and her daughters. He found the surgeon in the basement giving anatomy lessons to his son Peter. A cadaver of a young man lay on a table. Rocamora admired Velde's skills with tools, knowledge of the human body, and his patience teaching Peter.

"Isaacus, you have returned. Welcome back, my friend. I greatly missed your company. You must share our midday meal, and tell me everything about your adventures in England."

"I shall, but please, Jacobus, do not interrupt your lesson on my account."

"As you can see, this unfortunate fellow's throat has been slit, yet another sailor who lost a brawl over some doxy. Peter, show your *Oom* Isaacus how I taught you to remove the appendix."

Rocamora smiled every time he heard that peculiar Dutch word for uncle. The ten year old impressed him when he made a neat incision with a steady hand and swiftly removed the appendix.

"He has his father's skills."

"Peter is a quick learner. Now, son, demonstrate your sewing abilities."

The boy stitched the incision. "Did I do well, Father?"

Velde tousled Peter's curly blond hair. "I could have done no better. Your stitching would have left no significant scarring on a live patient. After we sup, you may open the torso. Later, I will test your ability to identify the organs, bones, and muscles."

Velde removed his leather apron, washed his hands in a basin, and made sure Peter did the same. That was why Rocamora respected him. He would never work with a surgeon who operated with filthy hands and instruments.

Velde offered to shave Rocamora's face and trim his hair, mustache, and beard. "I am most curious to know everything you have been doing these past months."

"Jacobus, the time I spent in England cured me of any desire to live there. It is a lush and green country, but too damp, foggy, and chilly for me, more so than Amsterdam, and London is a filthy city."

"And how did you find their wenches?"

"Nearly all I met needed a good sponging fore, aft, and under the arms."

"My unfortunate fastidious friend. Now tell me about William Harvey. Did you meet him?"

"When I arrived in London, he was in the field with King Charles serving as His Majesty's regular physician, Physician in Ordinary the English call it. I had access to the royalist camp because van Noordwijk introduced me as a courier who brought him several messages from the *Stadhouder*. I found Harvey to be courteous, modest, and charming, and our first meeting was instructive. He suffers from gout and treats himself in an efficacious manner I had not seen before. Although it was bitter winter, Harvey immersed his afflicted foot in a pail of cold water. After it became numb, he placed it close to a furnace. The pain ceased and he could function normally until the next attack."

"Interesting. Tell me more."

"Unfortunately, Harvey has yet to discover how blood passes from the arterial to the venous system or why the heart beats. One day, he or others like him will provide the answers. I hope we live long enough to see them."

"Amen to that. Did King Charles recognize you?"

"Not at all. Twenty-two years have passed since we saw each other. He did not condescend to notice me. Even if he had, my mustache, beard, long hair, and clothes were not the robe, tonsure, and clean shaven face I had at the time he wooed the Infanta."

"I have heard that at The Hague men are imitating the current French fashion of a clean shaven face. A good business for all barber-surgeons." Velde held his razor close to Rocamora's mustache. "Do you wish to follow the trend and be fashionable, my friend?"

"No, Jacobus, for such trends are transient. A well-trimmed mustachio and chin beard suits me best."

25.
Confessions of a Confessor

Midafternoon, Rocamora ambled along the Houtgracht besides its narrow canal and bore the humid late July Amsterdam summer heat better than when he had to wear woolen Dominican robes in Madrid. Progress was slow because shoppers filled the streets lined with vegetable markets and stalls of fragrant flowers where he purchased a colorful bouquet. Clusters of citizens gossiped and repeated rumors, which reminded him of the *mentideros*, lie-parlors, of Madrid.

Abigail and Doña Ribcá arrived at Dam Square as Rocamora prearranged with Judah. Vlooienburg, where all would stare and gossip, was the last place he wanted to meet them. Rocamora greeted Ribcá and handed Abigail the flowers. She wore a modest dress with plain linen collar and cuffs and a cap that covered her hair but not her loveliness. Ribcá, acting as chaperone, followed at a distance out of hearing if they spoke softly.

Rocamora and Abigail walked in silence, and he imagined, for that was all he could do, what life might be like as her husband and father of their children. Would their true temperaments be in harmony or conflict?

Here in Amsterdam money was all. He had enough guilders to establish a household even after several years of medical training if he were to be more frugal, but after that, a regular income would be needed to feed and clothe his wife and any children they might have.

Rocamora did not doubt his abilities, but how long would it take to establish himself as a successful physician? He also considered their difference in age. Abigail had celebrated her twenty-third birthday, and he had reached his forty-fourth, a gap of twenty-one years. Yet, men commonly wed brides much younger.

"Doña Abigail."

"Yes, *Capitán*?"

"Your uncle, Don Judah, and I had an extended conversation." Abigail did not respond with words or change of expression. "Did he speak of the subject to you?"

"No, he did not."

"Is it true you have told him you will marry me or no one?"

"From that time I first saw you in Antwerp when but a girl of eleven, through the day of your *berit milah*, until this moment, I have said and I say to you … I shall be your wife or never wed at all."

Abigail's unique serenity impressed Rocamora. "May I ask why I am the object of so great an honor?"

"Honor? Yes, I suppose you would say that to be polite, but I do more than honor you, *Capitán*. I love you. Regardless of your feelings for me, I love you. I shall always love you even if you never return my love."

"I can understand why you may believe I do not love you. From the day I arrived in Amsterdam, I have not sought your company. In truth, I have avoided seeing you and courting you for reasons I shall explain. I believe I know when the seeds of my love for you were sown. It was the day I saw you bruting diamonds. After that, you came into my thoughts often, unbidden, and I found the images and memories of you to be pleasurable. And now, in your presence, know this. I have come to love you, Abigail. I do love you above all others, more than anyone who came before you."

"Do you? I had hoped … but do you truly love me?"

"Yes, I confess I do, but will you tell me how I have earned your love without trying, without any token of courtship until now?"

Abigail stopped, waved at *Tía* Ribcá to keep her distance, and faced Rocamora. "It is what it is, what it always has been, what it always shall be."

"The difference in our ages …."

"You have more vitality than men in their twenties."

"Then I declare my love and desire to wed you."

"*Mi Capitán* …."

"Unfortunately, our marriage must wait until I have my license to practice medicine. I cannot guarantee that I will be able to earn much as a physician."

"I am resourceful and can earn money polishing diamonds."

"I hope it will not be necessary, Doña Abigail. There is something else. I do not know if I can give you children."

"Nor do I know if I can bear them. The affliction of barrenness knows no age, nor does the ability to procreate."

Rocamora appreciated her wisdom. "Doña Abigail, I wish we were in a more romantic place, a fragrant bower or a patio on a moonlit night, instead of a street along this reeking canal with the hurly-burly of commercial activity surrounding us and your *duenna* spying on us."

"I see you and no one else, my handsome *Capitán*. I hear you and nothing else. I love you above all."

"I love you no less, for you are the most desirable woman I have ever encountered, so comely and graceful, and you may be more intelligent than I."

"I doubt that, but perhaps I am wiser in some areas."

"Of that I am certain."

"Before we wed, you will have to join the congregation and conform to the community."

"And if I were to choose to live a different life for us?"

"I would still wed you."

"And forsake your family?"

"Yes."

Abigail's eyes expressed contrary feelings she could not hide, and Rocamora understood so radical a break from family and tradition would be painful if not impossible for her. "It may not come to that, but you should understand this about me. Although I would have to accept and never speak against the foundations of your beliefs ... that the Torah is God's revelation to the Jews, that the soul exists after death, and that God rewards the good and punishes the evil ... all that I do not believe."

"You would not be the first to conform without belief to the requirements of our congregation and yet live and thrive here."

"No different from Spain and the clergy, it seems."

"I am not as worldly as you, but I do know this. Everyone conforms to some degree. One must to survive."

"You know nothing of my history, the things I have done, the sins I have committed."

"Are you going to say you are unworthy of me?"

"Perhaps I am, but I cannot lie to you because the sins of one's past often become known. That is why I must tell you everything."

Rocamora recalled that day at the well of rich water outside Orihuela when he told Ramón he was not meant for the clergy and recited all his sins. He heard himself speaking the identical words. "I have broken most of the Ten Commandments."

"I do not wish to hear ...."

"But I must confess all to you. I have lain with many women." Rocamora first mentioned his sister-in-law Violante who drugged and raped him to bear his daughter Brianda, his passion for Moraíma and lesser women he used to satisfy his needs, Catalina his lusty mistress, and his worship of Infanta María.

"How could it have been otherwise? You are a man."

He next described his act of revenge against Anglesola, who murdered his father, the duel when he fatally wounded Inquisitor General Arce's cousin Lograno, whom he prevented from raping Moraíma, the two Anglesolas he shot to protect Brianda, the assassins he had killed in self-defense, and his participation in the slaughter of Swedes at the Battle of Nördlingen. He concluded with the story of his final act of vengeance against Jacinto.

"That was another life. Now you shall become a healer, a saver of lives."

"I have sworn oaths falsely to God, to the Church, and I shall again were I to become a member of your congregation, taking the name of God in vain."

He studied Abigail's features. Was she struggling not to smile? Did she disbelieve all he said?

"Have you completed your confession, *Capitán*?"

"Yes, I have confessed all."

"May I presume you have recounted your sins not to discourage me but to know if I would still love you and still wish to be your wife and mother of your children in spite of all?"

"Yes, but there is one more thing. I may be cursed. Those whom I have loved and who loved me are dead, all taken before their time. My parents, my beloved daughter, my dearest friends."

"Then we shall be the best of friends and create more lives together."

He felt stirrings of tumescence and worried if he could be faithful to Abigail for the two years until they wed.

"Regarding all your sins, *mi Capitán*, be assured, the *mikvah* will cleanse them."

"*Mikvah?*"

"Our ritual bath that washes away the past and cleanses one spiritually."

The same as baptism.

"How soon must you leave for Leyden?"

"In two weeks. It is but a short distance. I shall visit you whenever I can. One more thing. Here is but a small symbol to represent my great love for you, *mi querida,* my darling, and desire to make you my wife." Rocamora took Abigail's left hand and placed a diamond ring on her smallest finger.

She gasped and her face reddened. "I can barely speak."

"I would take you in my arms and kiss you here and now."

"I shall not resist."

Tía Ribcá separated them. "Have you no shame? What will people think?"

"That Doña Abigail and I love each other."

26.
Fiat Scientia

Instead of suffering an uncomfortable carriage ride along rutted roads through mosquito-infested marshlands to Leyden, Rocamora chose to take the new and larger bright orange and sky blue public *trekschuit*, horse drawn water carriage. It left every hour from sunrise to sunset and traveled along a canal dug in a straight line for the six miles between Amsterdam and Haarlem. At the City of Flowers, he would transfer to a boat going south to Leyden.

Rocamora stood on a grassy canal bank amidst lively passengers waiting to board. Many had come with family and friends. Abigail had not yet arrived, and he walked to the edge of the embankment where a powerful horse stood harnessed to ropes attached to the water carriage. It fed from an ample mix of crushed oats, hay, and barley provided by the boatman.

"You have but one horse to tow your boat?"

The boatman added more feed. "Mynheer, that is all we need. The lack of friction on the water enables these beasts to pull a hundred times the weight of a cart or carriage on the roads even if we have a full load of fifty passengers and their baggage. Be assured we do not abuse them, for they are valuable animals. Our livelihood depends on their well-being. That is why we change horses at Halfweg, exactly three miles between Amsterdam and Haarlem."

"I thank you for the information." Rocamora left the boatman when he saw Abigail approaching alone. She handed him an open basket filled with bread, cheeses, hardboiled eggs, and fruit. "I prepared this for your journey to Leyden, *mi Capitán*."

"I remember you doing the same when I departed from your home in Antwerp during the winter of 1635. As I did that day, I thank you." He placed the basket, his satchel and walking stick on the grass so they could embrace and kiss. "I feared you might not come."

"*Tío* Judah wanted to accompany me, but he had not finished his morning prayers at Talmud Torah. I could no longer wait for him."

"I prefer it you came without him." The boatman rang a hand-held bell to begin the boarding. Rocamora lingered with Abigail. "May time pass quickly for us."

"I fear it shall not, *mi Capitán*." Abigail saw Hombrecillo peering at her from Rocamora's satchel. "I envy your cat, for it will be with you every day and night."

"And you, my love, are continually in my heart and mind."

At the second bell, Rocamora kissed Abigail a last time and boarded the ferry. The steering master signaled he was ready. The boatman rang his bell a last time, and precisely at the hour, he mounted and rode the horse along the edge of the embankment on a worn path towing the water carriage.

Rocamora waved to Abigail until she was no longer in sight. The summer heat had given him a mighty thirst, and he went inside the clean spacious cabin and part tavern above deck. After Rocamora ordered a single beer, he sat on one of the varnished benches between a clerk balancing his accounts and an avuncular elderly academic he recognized. "Professor Poons."

"Mynheer Isaacus? A most delightful coincidence. May I assume you are going to Leyden?"

"Yes, to matriculate at your medical school."

"A wise decision. Last year, I received a letter from my friend, Professor Hagedorn, whom you met. He praised your medical knowledge and expressed his disappointment that you chose not to enroll at Franeker."

"It was a near thing."

"His loss, our gain. Have you arranged for lodgings in Leyden?"

"I will stay at an inn for a day or two until I find a suitable room."

"Let me make you an offer. My home is large, and we can accommodate you in comfort."

"At what cost?"

"I am no businessman, Mynheer Isaacus, and I truly would be honored to have your company and friendship. I can reduce the cost to … let us say a minimal amount to cover expenses for the food and drink you consume."

Rocamora stroked Hombrecillo. "My cat and I are inseparable."

"Is it a good mouser?"

"He is a master hunter."

"Then it is welcome too."

"Have you a tub I can use for bathing?"

"We are like-minded, for there is nothing more gratifying than a warm soaking by the kitchen fire on cold winter nights."

"Then I accept your hospitality." Rocamora offered Poons his choice from the basket of food Abigail had prepared. He smiled when the professor selected a hardboiled egg. Rocamora had yet to tell Abigail why he never ate them.

Poons' typically narrow three story home on Heerensteeg near the university was of modest size. Robust and decades younger, his wife Roosjie welcomed Rocamora. "My husband has spoken of you, and I … She stepped back when Hombrecillo meowed, leaped from Rocamora's satchel, and ran to the basement. "… but what was that?"

"Do not be surprised, Mevrouw, if my cat returns with a rodent."

Roosjie regained her composure. "Please consider our home to be yours."

"Perhaps after Mynheer Isaacus is more settled, he will describe for us what life is like at the Spanish court."

So everyone I meet wants to know.

"Please, come with me."

Rocamora followed Poons to a bright immaculate room on the third floor and placed his satchel on a bed softer and wider than the one Vrouw Cornelia provided. "I shall sleep well here, Professor?"

"It was my son's room. He no longer has the time to visit."

They next went to the kitchen where Hombrecillo lapped cream from a bowl at Roosjie's feet. "Mynheer, your cat caught two mice, and I am rewarding it."

"He enjoys herring no less."

"We have plenty of that in Leyden." Poons invited Rocamora to join him for beer and a smoke in his study filled with anatomy charts and volumes on medicine. "Although our university has a comprehensive library, feel free to avail yourself of everything you see here."

"I shall, and I thank you and your lovely wife for your generous hospitality."

Poons lit his pipe. "I imagine you are surprised Roosjie is so young. She is my third wife. My first died in childbirth a year after we wed. So did the infant. My second went to her reward two years ago after thirty-seven years of marriage and four children. Two of them passed away too young. My son and three grandchildren are in Gouda. His wife comes from a family of prosperous cheese makers, and he now heads the business. My daughter is …."

Rocamora never failed to be amazed that his austere Spanish reserve provided no barrier against the loquacious Dutch who spoke freely about their lives and asked his opinion on the most personal of matters.

"… and Roosjie is a gift from God, an efficient housekeeper, excellent cook, and more pleasing than the finest copper bed warmer. Let me tell you how we met. It happened …."

Poons accompanied Rocamora for his first visit to the university situated on Rapenburgstraat and brought him to a small room where a man bent over a ledger and wrote.

"Mynheer Nikolaes Lertsma is our *Pedel*, both registrar and factotum. He combines the functions of university bailiff, ceremonial mace-bearer, and secretary. Klaes, I am honored to present the esteemed Isaacus de Rocamora who wishes to enroll as a student of medicine. He was the Dominican confessor for Empress Maria when she was Infanta of Spain."

Lertsma frowned and peered at Rocamora above his thick spectacles. "A Spaniard and a Catholic?"

"I am no longer Catholic, Mynheer."

But forever Spanish.

"I vouch for him, Klaes."

"Your word is enough for me. Mynheer, have you the registration fee?" The *Pedel* bit Rocamora's coins, dropped them in a metal box, and opened another ledger. He dipped his quill in ink. "Name."

"Don Isaac de Rocamora."

Lertsma spoke each letter aloud that he wrote in the ledger, "I-s-h-a-k d-e R-o-k-a-m-o-r-a. City of birth."

"Valencia."

The Pedel continued to speak and write laboriously. "V-a-l-e-n-c-i-a, H-i-s-p-a-n-u-s. Year of birth?"

Fearing the *Pedel* might reject a man in his forties or even late thirties, Rocamora relied on Lertsma's poor eyesight and made himself fourteen years younger. "1615."

The *Pedel* entered the date, closed the ledger, and wrote on a small piece of paper. "Here is your receipt. Enrolment confers upon you the right to walk the streets of Leyden in dressing gown and slippers provided you also wear a wig and hat."

Rocamora restrained an urge to laugh aloud at the image of himself or any Spaniard garbed so absurdly on the streets and plazas of Madrid.

Poons interrupted Rocamora's thoughts. "Welcome to the University of Leyden. *Fiat Scientia*, let there be knowledge."

27.
Medical Student

Rocamora settled into his routine. Each professor delivered lectures in Latin or Greek between two to five hours a week interspersed with disputations, sessions of observation at the botanical gardens, and lessons in the teaching hospital. Examinations for a degree were not written; instead, the candidate defended a thesis of his choosing against arguments posed by professors in June or July in the presence of students, local magistrates and the general populace.

The students, who came from many kingdoms and principalities, resided, ate, and studied in groups separated by nationality and the Dutch by provinces. Because most were more than half Rocamora's age, he hoped to dine and study alone, but at breakfast, he had to share with three others a loaf of bread and a pound of butter.

The university provided ample beer and ale at all meals. At midday, the students ate soup, bread, butter, cheese, and depending upon the day of the week, hashed meat with cabbage, a hutspot, haricot beans, and fresh or smoked fish. Sundays after church services, the young men consumed a hutspot and hot meat, and for dinner more bread and butter with a huge portion of cow's cheese.

At first, the students assumed Rocamora was a professor because of his age and knowledge. Soon they vied for seats next to him at meals and asked for help in Latin and their studies. Many sought his advice for their personal problems. After word spread throughout the university that Rocamora had been Empress María's confessor, Catholics came to him for confession in the belief that if a Dominican had not been defrocked or excommunicated he was still a friar.

More than the meals, the life of a student at Leyden Medical School contrasted sharply with the four years Rocamora experienced in the austere and regimented College of Confessors of Santo Domingo in Orihuela. The casual relations between professors and students surprised him most. They drank prodigious amounts of beer together at *The Fir Cone*, *The Fighting Lion*, and other popular taverns. They brawled together as well.

On the third day of October, the university closed so students and professors could join the populace in the annual celebration of Leyden's lifting of the long Spanish siege in 1575. That was when the Dutch opened their dikes to flood the lands surrounding the city and forced the enemy to withdraw.

Militias paraded through the streets, and all used the holiday as an excuse to wallow in *overvloed*. In particular, the populace consumed enormous portions of the same hutspot mix of herring, eels, carrots, and potatoes that fed the starving citizens of Leyden after the siege ended.

Rocamora sat with Poons and several students at *The Fighting Lion*. He alone chose not to wear the dressing gown and slippers that differentiated them from the locals. The Dutch and Protestant students from England, the Germanys, Denmark, and Sweden celebrated more than the liberation of Leyden. Bulletins posted earlier in the day announced their hated enemy, the Count-Duke de Olivares, had passed away the twenty-second day of July.

Amidst the carousing, Rocamora mourned the death of the greatest man in Spain, whom he served for more than twenty years. He reminisced about the past and what might have been. A word from the Count-Duke or King Philip, and he would have become Inquisitor General.

Poons interrupted Rocamora's reveries. "You must have encountered Olivares when you lived at the Spanish Court."

"We met on occasion."

"Do you believe he died a madman?"

"I do not trust those reports. The Count-Duke's enemies in Spain hated him even more than the Dutch. They tried everything possible to defame Olivares and tarnish his reputation. Not mad, he was given to extreme …."

A commotion at an adjacent table interrupted Rocamora. Rowdy students well into their cups were kissing and fondling agreeable girls to the chagrin of several putative local beaux. The girls preferred to stay with the students, and the townsmen left promising retribution.

Poons leaned closer to Rocamora. "There will be the usual trouble this night. Brawls between students and townsmen are common."

"So I have observed. Too much drink leads to both lack of judgment and aggression, a dangerous combination. I am well out of such folly." Rocamora stood. "Professor, Mynheeren."

"Surely you are not leaving so early."

"My studies come before all else, Professor." Rocamora bade good night to Poons and the students and stepped outside into a dense fog. Alert to the slightest sound, he heard whispering.

"He is one of them."

"Then let us teach him a lesson he could never learn at the university."

Rocamora drew the sword from his walking stick, turned, and confronted the same two young men who had lost their girls to the students. Because they held hammers, he assumed they apprenticed to a carpenter.

Rocamora slashed the mist with his sword. "Mynheeren, you do not wish this to be the last night of your lives. I am not interested in your girls and have no quarrel with you."

The young men conferred, and one spoke for both. "Mynheer, we can see now that we have made a mistake. Please continue on your way."

"For your courtesy, I offer you some sound advice. Find yourselves young women who have a greater sense of loyalty."

By the arrival of spring 1646, Rocamora began his thesis on the causes, prevention, and treatment of tertian and quartan fevers, commonly called ague, which caused the death of so many beloved friends in Spain. He believed he had learned enough to practice medicine. If he completed the dissertation over the summer, his professors might allow him to defend it when he returned in August and give him a license to practice.

Ague came from the Latin word for sharp or pointed, *acutus*, and manifested itself by chills, fever, and sweating. The most popular treatments were failed remedies recommended by Galen: amputation, trepanning, bloodletting to rid the body of corrupt humors, and purging to expel poisons, which further weakened the patient.

While in England, Rocamora had seen physicians and apothecaries prescribe herbs named pennyroyal, creeping cinquefoil, yarrow, and bogbean, which they called fever herb, wormwood, and sea wormwood. Much of the population in the United Provinces believed tobacco smoke was a preventative. Some added opium extracted from locally grown poppies to beer and wine in the belief it was a curative.

More than a few quacks asserted that comets and the alignment of planets caused ague. Rocamora did not yet understand one anomaly: The poor who could not afford physicians were more likely to survive even though they sought the advice of *curanderas*, self-styled healers, and ingested potions that included insects, urine, cat's blood, and pepper in brandy.

In June shortly before Rocamora returned to Amsterdam for a summer respite between the school years, he read a bulletin that distressed him. Empress María died the thirteenth day of May from food poisoning three months short of her fortieth birthday.

He walked alone along the canals remembering his first appearance before the unattainable golden Infanta and the hours in the Casa de Campo when they sat on the bench beneath the elms amidst spring flowers and María confessed her most intimate thoughts. He recalled their scheming to prevent her marriage to Prince Charles, and most of all, that night they met in the secret passage outside her suite before she left Spain forever.

Rocamora had left the trunk containing his most valuable possessions with Santcroos. Fearing someone might break into it not to steal but to snoop, he had brought with him to Leyden mementos even Abigail must never see. Rocamora would always keep the ruby ring María had given him. He took from a small box a lock of her golden hair, dropped it into the water of the canal, and watched the curl float with the current until out of sight. That night he wrote his first poem for Abigail:

>As Adam and Eve
>So shall we abide
>In a Garden of Eden
>Created by our love
>Where you shall be Queen
>And I King of our domain
>
>Above all, the glory of your beauty
>Shall shine and illuminate
>Our own Tree of Knowledge
>From which shall blossom
>Fragrant flowers and sweet fruit
>Of our union sanctified by God.

Rocamora wanted to substitute Destiny, Fate or Kismet for God, but thought it best to mention the Deity in whom Abigail believed.

28.
Menasseh Instructs

Throughout the late spring and midsummer in Amsterdam, Rocamora saw Abigail daily and dined regularly at the homes of her Touro relations. Whenever they attempted to be alone, her uncles, aunts, and cousins seemed to infest every nook and cranny of Vlooienburg.

Rocamora was most uncomfortable when Abigail's *Tío* Eliahu came from Rotterdam for monthly visits to discuss business with his brother Judah and to seek a husband for Sara, his twenty year old daughter. Sara stared at him unblinking as a hungry bird of prey. He chose not to mention it to Abigail because she enjoyed the company of her cousin.

Rocamora pitied Eliahu and Sara. Because few eligible men were available in the United Provinces, finding a husband for the young woman would be a formidable task. Well formed with a pleasing face in repose, Sara's sour disposition distorted her features to suggest a young crone.

Despite the intrusion of others, Rocamora looked forward to each moment he could be with Abigail. In her presence, he experienced a unique comfort and well-being. And desire. Abigail's facial expression when she saw him and the light in her eyes never failed to stir him to tumescence. If they did not wed soon, he would be driven mad with desire for her. Apart and alone in his room at night, he wrote odes and sonnets to his intended and read them to Hombrecillo.

Abigail spent much of the day polishing diamonds. Rocamora occupied his by refining the dissertation, observing Velde in his surgery, studying further the application of herbal cures, and discussing with any physician who would give him the time the latest discoveries and theories regarding medicine.

To please Abigail and her family, Rocamora agreed to meet with Menasseh in the rabbi's office at Talmud Torah for instructions in the restrictive *mitzvoths,* God's 613 commandments from Leviticus, and secular laws governing the civil, moral, and daily life of the community.

"Don Isaac, many new arrivals from Portugal and Spain resist our ways and consider them oppressive. I hope you do not. Be assured, Judaism is based on what one does rather than what one believes, which is why certain practices and actions are required. Who can know what a person truly thinks anyway? As an example, helping the poor and unfortunate is a sign of the truly observant Jew. If you have a strong belief in God and can afford to give to the poor but fail to do so, you are not as good a Jew as the Jew who does not believe in God but gives to charity."

"I have always judged men by their actions rather than attempt to guess what they truly believe."

"Good."

Menasseh pointed to specific passages in the Torah and Talmud and taught Rocamora the rituals that reminded Jews of their history and essential foundations of faith, such as the observance of the Sabbath, the celebration of Passover, and the affixing of a mezuzah on the doorpost.

Rocamora would not follow the dietary laws called *Kashrut* when he ate at taverns or in the homes of Christian friends like Velde. He did not understand why wearing clothes containing a combination of wool and linen was prohibited. Most intrusive of all were the external rituals of wearing phylacteries, *tefillin*, on the head and arms first thing in the morning while reciting prayers, and the tallith, prayer shawl with its *tzitzit*, fringed knotted loops that spelled YKVK, the name of God. Rocamora thought them all to be unnecessary nuisances.

"As a member of our community, you will be subject to three taxes."

Rocamora never paid taxes and tolls in Spain because he was of the clergy. No one in Amsterdam must know how much secret wealth he had accumulated. The security and comfort of Abigail and their children would come before the needs of the community.

"The first tax is the *finta* based on one's property holdings."

"I have no holdings."

"The second is the *imposta*, a business tax determined by the volume of one's imports and exports."

"That is another I shall not have to pay."

"The third is the *promessa*, pledges of donations one makes in honor of special occasions and religious events. *Promessas* also give aid to poor widows, orphans, impecunious new arrivals, and to the *dotar*, dowries for brides whose families cannot afford them."

"That seems reasonable. How often must one pay these taxes?"

"Every six months after the *fintadores* calculate the tax for each member, the treasurer collects the payments due and balances accounts."

"He knocks on doors?"

"We prefer our members to come to his office."

"These taxes are in addition to what the municipal government collects?"

"Yes."

"I will help the less fortunate with my services and with florins."

Menasseh opened another book bound in shiny leather adorned with letters of gold. "I am delighted you said that because the *Bet Din*, our rabbinical court, supervises the behavior of each physician according to the writings of Maimonides and our traditional laws. If necessary, we can compel you to make yourself available to the poor. Thus, the burden of providing care is shared equitably by all physicians."

"And if a patient needs to be treated on the Sabbath or the holy days?"

"A physician can violate the Sabbath so the patient may regain his health and by doing so enjoy many more Sabbaths. Yes, the Sabbath and other laws and rituals can be suspended to prolong life, the most precious of all gifts from God." Menasseh opened his copy of the Talmud and recited from a passage: "Said the Holy One, blessed be He, there is no affliction for which there does not exist a cure."

"If only that were so."

"The therapy and medicament for every affliction is discernible. The study of Torah is a therapy for the entire body."

"Physicians also provide efficacious cures."

"Of course, but as you know, alleviation of physical pain is often beyond a physician's abilities and knowledge. The easing of mental anguish is within the power of all. A patient's mind can affect the pace of his recuperation. A caring physician can strengthen his will to live."

Rocamora could not argue that point. In Spain, he had visited many seriously ill and dying penitents to perform last rites, but after giving several a sympathetic hearing, whatever he had said somehow contributed to their recoveries.

Rocamora conceded that perhaps Torah and Talmud contained more wisdom than he had previously credited those holy writings.

29.
A Fortuitous Cure

After one of his sessions with Menasseh, Rocamora encountered Santcroos outside the synagogue. He had not seen his friend in more than a week, and Don Samuel appeared uncharacteristically disheveled and drawn with the bloodshot eyes of a man who had not slept.

"Don Isaac, do you have your license to practice medicine?"

"Unfortunately, I have one more year of study, but why do you ask? Are you ill?"

"It is my son David. My brilliant eldest is dying of fever."

"Typhoid?"

"The physicians Bueno and Barossa have diagnosed it as ague."

My dissertation.

"What cures did they prescribe?"

"Liquids. Eau de Vie and wine to drive away my son's chills. Tea and something called the sweet-flag …."

"*Acorus calamus.*"

"… which they mixed into brandy and tea. Barossa also recommended Haarlemmer oil."

"A mix of linseed-oil and turpentine. Yes, some physicians believe it to be one of the most effective remedies against intermittent fevers."

"And you do not if I hear you correctly."

"No one has yet discovered a definitive cure."

"Please, Don Isaac, step into my carriage with me. Come to my home and look at my son."

Inside Rocamora sat opposite Santcroos. "I would suffer great penalties if it were proven I practiced medicine without a license."

"You have my word. No one except the two of us will know."

"And were I to fail?"

"My beloved son will die anyway."

"Have you any idea how he acquired the fever? Did he eat or drink anything out of the ordinary? Did he travel beyond Amsterdam?"

"I sent him to The Hague on business at the beginning of July."

"Did he travel on roads through the marshes?"

"Is that significant?"

"It is summer. He may have been exposed to *mal aria*, bad air."

"If you suspect that to be the cause of my son's ague, do you know the cure? Does anyone survive?"

"A friend of mine survived the fever of 1638 when his sister, niece and so many others did not. It has always confounded me why."

"Perhaps you can help my David to be a similar exception."

They arrived at Santcroos' home, and he brought Rocamora into the room where his wife wept at David's bedside. "You must swear an oath never to mention that Don Isaac was here this day."

"Can he save David?"

"If Don Isaac cannot, no one can."

Rocamora spoke with Doña Rachael and within minutes calmed her. After she left the room, he stood over David. The fifteen year old was soaked in sweat.

"Don Isaac, can you do anything?

"Have you heard of a bark found in Peru called Chinchona?"

"Yes, I have been importing it under another name for the Vatican and certain Catholic rulers, but Bueno and Barossa called it Jesuit powder and said it was of no use. You have a contrary opinion?"

"It is a recent discovery and does not always work because no reliable prescription exists, but anything, even doing nothing, is better to try than bleeding, purging, quackery, and worse."

"I give you permission to experiment with the bark on my son. A shipment of Chinchona arrived yesterday. I have not yet dispatched it to my buyers."

Rocamora thought for several moments about how best to mix powder of Chinchona with a liquid. Should it be water, beer, wine, milk, or brandy? "Fetch enough bark for me to grind into a fine powder, and I will also need red wine."

"For a potion."

"A medicine. Bring it with an apothecary's mortar and pestle. No one but you and I must know what we are doing or else I shall be ruined and branded a criminal for practicing medicine without a license."

Rocamora paced the floor in front of David's bed and calculated measurements in his head. How much powdered Chinchona should he use per glass of wine? Too little would be of no use, too much could bring about death. Rocamora also factored in the boy's weight and age, and by the time Santcroos returned with the bark, mortar, and pestle, he had made a rough estimate of the ratio.

Rocamora ground the bark into a fine powder. Next, he spooned a measured amount into a tumbler, added wine, and stirred the mixture. He tasted it and handed the glass to Santcroos. "Give this to your son. Force it into his mouth if necessary. If it has no effect, I shall increase the dosage. If there is a negative reaction, I shall reduce it."

Santcroos followed Rocamora's directions. Several hours later, the fever broke, and they gave the boy another dose of powdered bark and wine.

"Don Samuel, I do not know all the properties of Chinchona, so I suggest you always keep a fresh supply in your home and later teach your son how to use it should ague reoccur, or, if it strikes another in your family."

Santcroos kissed Rocamora's hand in gratitude. "After you have your license, you shall be our family physician. You saved my David's life. Name your price."

This time, Rocamora did exactly that.

30.
Change of Plans

Rocamora returned to Leyden for his second year of medical school impatient to obtain his degree and license to practice so he could wed Abigail. Upon his arrival, he informed the faculty he was ready to defend his dissertation. The Academic Senate said it would consider Rocamora's unusual request, but by the middle of March, 1647, they had not responded. By then, everyone was more concerned about the future of the Republic.

Frederick Hendrick died on the fourteenth of March,, and Willem II became *Stadhouder*. Rocamora saw a similarity between the House of Orange and the Spain of 1621 when Philip IV became King at sixteen with a seventeen year old wife, and his former tutor, the Count-Duke de Olivares, became the de facto ruler of Spain. At age twenty, Prince Willem II had a fifteen year old wife and a domineering mother, Princess Amalia, who intended to dictate domestic and foreign policy.

Rocamora also saw differences between the houses of Orange and the Habsburgs. Unlike Philip of Spain, Willem II was impetuous and sought military glory, a dangerous combination. Spain had no republicans, and the war weary Dutch who believed peace led to prosperity trusted their provincial and national Estates to curb the dynastic ambitions of Amalia and Willem.

The following week, the Pedel notified Rocamora that he would have to wait until June to defend his dissertation and pay a fee for the license much higher than stated the day he enrolled. That same day, Poons invited Rocamora to walk with him in the botanical gardens.

"I am as disappointed, frustrated, and angry as you, if that can be possible. I have it on good authority that you will not obtain your degree regardless of the range and depth of your knowledge of medicine. Two professors who will be examining you have decided to reject your thesis regardless of its unquestionable merit."

"Because I am a Jew?"

"If it were that, we could do something about it. They envy your knowledge and resent it that the students defer to you more than to them."

Making enemies without trying is too easy in this world.

"Then I must go to Franeker. I should have accepted Professor Hagedorn's offer when I visited there two years ago."

"I have already prepared a letter to my good friend. It describes your worthiness to be a physician should you well defend your thesis."

"That I can do. Professor, I cannot express my gratitude …."

"It is not necessary. I suggest you leave immediately for Franeker."

Rocamora paid a fee at Franeker less than Leyden would have charged, and Hagedorn arranged for him to defend his thesis on causes, prevention, and cures for ague that same day. Rocamora stood in the center of the university amphitheater before seven members of the Academic Senate capped and gowned in robes with piping and tassels of vivid colors identifying their rank. Behind them sat the faculty numbering several dozen.

Rocamora faced the academics with all the confidence of a seasoned theatrical performer. In Madrid, he had been renowned for his eloquence. Rocamora's audience at Franeker was small compared to the hundreds he sermonized in cathedrals and thousands when he harangued at *autos de fé*. Despite his need to convince these men they should give him his license to practice medicine, Rocamora thought them to be considerably less intimidating than the Spanish royal family and inquisitors who heard his preaching.

He thanked Hagedorn, the Academic Senate, and members of the faculty for allowing him to present his dissertation on such short notice. His deep voice silenced the slightest murmuring, and he enthralled all with a vigorous defense in Latin on the causes, cures, and prevention of ague.

Rocamora added anecdotes from his observations of tertian and quartan fevers suffered by Philip IV who survived, and Ramón, Moraíma and her daughter who did not. He asserted that the bad air from marshes in summer caused ague and described commonly used preventatives from all continents:

Smoke from tobacco.

Tea made from the seeds and leaves of the fenugreek plant found along the Mediterranean, which produced an odor similar to curry that seeped through the drinker's pores and repelled insects.

Mashed root of goldenseal mixed with bear fat the Cherokees of North America smeared on their bodies.

And the recently discovered chinchona bark as perhaps the best cure of all.

After Rocamora finished, the three senior members of the Academic Senate fired a salvo of questions. He responded to each without hesitation.

Hagedorn took over.

"You mentioned that insect bites in the marshes contribute to fever. How so?"

"I cannot say, but it seems their bites presage ague. I have never encountered a patient who has not been bitten."

"What is the best insect repellant?"

"Oil of citronella from Java and Ceylon."

"And you are convinced chinchona is a cure for ague caused by bad air?"

"Yes, but we need to experiment more to find the most effective dosage and how best to deliver it. Too weak and too late, chinchona will have no effect. Too strong, it may kill the patient."

Hagedorn and his colleagues conferred in front of Rocamora for no more than a few minutes and the Professor beckoned him to come closer. "It is our great pleasure to bestow upon you your doctorate and license to practice medicine. Congratulations Dr. de Rocamora."

On the first day of April 1647, shortly before his forty-sixth birthday, Rocamora studied the documents. He had at last become a physician. Pride in his accomplishment gave way to sadness.

Rocamora wished a heaven existed from where his mentor Don Lope could look upon him with pride. And if there were an afterlife, what must his beloved parents be thinking?

The day of his return to Amsterdam, Rocamora first went to register as required at the *Collegium Medicum*, the professional guild of Amsterdam physicians. When he produced his diploma, the clerk read it and frowned.

"Your name, you are a Jew?"

"I am."

"As you know, the Estates recently issued a *Patenta Honorossa* that declared Holland's Jews to be Dutch subjects and no longer mere residents. You are now entitled to nearly all the same rights and protections as the burgher class, but still not citizens with few exceptions. Therefore, being a Jew, you may register with us but cannot become a full member of our *Collegium* or a medical inspector. You cannot attend our banquets. However, you may treat Christian patients, and it is not impossible to achieve full membership for one of your faith. Both the physicians Bueno, father and son, have been granted *poorterschap*, citizenship, and membership in the *Collegium*."

The clerk wrote his name in the registry as Ishak Israël Rokamora.

Ishak, Isaacus, Yitzak. From this day, I must try to think of myself as Isaac, the physician, and forget Rocamora, the Valencian caballero and royal confessor. But can I?

Rocamora estimated that the small Sephardic community had about fifteen hundred residents and a sufficient number of physicians. He intended to broaden his practice beyond Vlooienburg to the greater Amsterdam population. His fluency in Dutch and friendship with Velde and van Noordwijk should help him.

First, he intended to wed Abigail.

31.
A Surprise for Abigail

On the tenth day of April at the Amsterdam Town Hall, Rocamora and Abigail stood before the municipal clerk who formalized the banns. He wrote their names in the Municipal Register, his as Ysaak Israel Rokamora born in Valencia, doctor of Medicine, age thirty-eight, and hers as Abigael Toura, born in Antwerp, age twenty-five, with her *Tío* standing beside them as witness. They would have to wait another ninety-one days before their wedding according to Jewish law to ensure the bride would not be pregnant with another man's child.

After they left the Town Hall, Judah cleared his throat. "Don Isaac, after you and Abigail wed, you may live in one of the rooms at my home if you cannot afford your own place. I assure you the rent will be reasonable."

"I thank you for your generous offer, Judah, but that will not be necessary."

"You have found a residence? Where is it? I hope you are not taking my niece to live with you in that small room you rent amongst the gentiles."

"Patience, Don Judah, I shall now take Abigail and you to our future domicile."

Rocamora appreciated Abigail's wisdom to say nothing even though he sensed her excitement and curiosity surpassed even that of her uncle. They approached a row of brick façade houses along St. Anthony's Lock facing the bridge to Vlooienburg and the Breestraat, none more than twenty feet wide. Some leaned to one side; others appeared to be sinking because they lay on marshland that Amsterdam had reclaimed. Everywhere, the city filled marshy land with soft sand and sod to accommodate its growing population. The foundations often became waterlogged, which resulted in those crooked, deranged houses. Inside, plasters cracked, doors did not close properly, and contractors did a good business raising and leveling the houses anew.

Rocamora stopped in front of a sturdy four-story house with a basement and attic. "Doña Abigail, *mi querida*, here is where we shall reside and raise our family."

Her eyes misted. "Our home."

Judah confronted Rocamora. "Its size … we … I thought you were near destitute."

"My finances are no one's business."

"But why did you not select a house on the other side of the bridge in Vlooienburg and closer to the synagogue and our family?"

"This is near enough, and I could not ignore so attractive a lease."

Judah would never know that after he saved the life of Santcroos' son, the merchant told him to name his price. Rocamora asked for a low cost lease on a home. Santcroos offered one of the houses he owned free of rent for the lifetime of Rocamora and his children with the freedom to add to the structure and deal with the interior as he saw fit.

Rocamora chose this particular house because he wanted to be as far away as possible from the prying and spying within the narrow Iberian community and still be close enough to Abigail's family and the synagogue he would be required to attend.

"How much rent are you paying?"

"*Tío.*"

"Yes, forgive me, Abigail, Don Isaac. It is not for me to know. I am delighted my niece will have her own home."

"Now, let me show you the interior." Rocamora led them to the door front door where he ostentatiously touched the mezuzah on the post kissed his fingers. "This is the one change I have made so far."

Inside the vestibule, Rocamora did not tell them that Santcroos' contractors had repaired the plaster on the walls and realigned most of the doors during the past year. He took them to the basement. "The front room will be my laboratory where I shall store and mix my medicines."

Rocamora led Abigail and Judah into a narrow hallway. "The cooking kitchen and scullery are here at the rear with a small room where wash can be hung. The foundation is solid. *Mi querida,* I leave to you the choices for color of paint and furnishings except that I want tiles of aqua blue and the color of sand to remind me of my lost fragrant coast of Valencia."

"Yes, *mi Capitán.*"

Rocamora next guided them into the front room on the ground floor. "This will be my study and where I shall consult with my patients. Behind it is the serving kitchen, and at the rear a room where we can take our meals."

In the front room on the second floor, Abigail went to the window. "So much light in here."

"This will be our private parlor where we can sit and tell each other of the day's events." Rocamora guided them through the adjacent reception hall and into the great hall to a bed attached to the brick and timber wall near the hearth. "I shall never become used to sleeping in a sitting position and in a room where we will be entertaining guests."

"Our bed will have curtains around it for privacy."

"Even so, *mi querida,* I prefer a Spanish bed."

Abigail blushed, bent, and pulled a set of drawers from under the bed, which the Dutch called *rolkoetsen,* rolling coaches. "This is where our newborns will sleep."

"May the Lord, Blessed be He, grant you many children."

"Thank you, Don Judah."

On the third floor, Rocamora showed them more fixed beds for their children after they become too large for the *rolkoetsen.* "The back room can serve as servant's quarters. We have a privy in the yard, but I shall have a withdrawal room constructed inside our home."

"Withdrawal room?"

"Yes, *mi querida,* the royal family had one at the Alcazar, which makes sense given how freezing and stormy Amsterdam winters can be."

Abigail went to the front windows on the fourth floor and took in the view of the bridge and Jodenbreestraat. "I can polish diamonds here."

"I intend to earn enough money to ensure that will not be necessary. Although there are fireplaces, I will want a brazier for each room. My blood has not thickened sufficiently to bear the Amsterdam winters in comfort."

"Your house is much larger than mine. You can accommodate guests such as my brother Eliahu and niece Sara better than I."

"That may be true, Don Judah, and I do not want to seem uncharitable, but Doña Abigail and I will want our privacy for the first years of our marriage."

"*Capitán,* these rooms will be perfect for our children and their spouses after they marry."

"May we both live to see that day, *mi querida.* There is also an attic we can use for storage." Rocamora heard meowing, coaxed Hombrecillo from the fireplace, and cradled the cat in his arms. "Don Judah, allow me to introduce you to Don Hombrecillo, my inseparable companion.."

"You must rid yourself of that creature."

"Why do you say that?"

"They smother newborns."

Abigail took the Chartreaux from Rocamora. It purred against her bosom. "I have heard the same from my aunts and cousins. Is that true, *Capitán?*"

"It is superstition."

"Then I am content to keep him."

"He is a superb mouser."

Abigail stroked its back. "I shall make ours the cleanest and most comfortable home in Amsterdam."

"A house filled with love and laughter too."

"I promise you that, *mi Capitán*. Why are you smiling?"

"The *señorio* where I was born and lived for my first fifteen years, the homes of my kin and most others in Spain from the poorest to the most grand *palacios* ...." Rocamora pointed his stick side to side and up and down. "... there we lived horizontally. Here in Amsterdam, I must become used to living vertically."

32.
Marital Instructions

Yet again, as he had done so often in Spain, Rocamora donned his mask of conformity during instructions from Menasseh regarding the marriage bed. He sat beside the rabbi at a table in the synagogue covered with scrolls and volumes containing Jewish law, commentary, and traditions.

Menasseh opened a scroll and pointed to a specific line. "The word used here in the Torah for intimacy between husband and wife comes from the root *yod-dalet-ayin*. Knowledge. Knowing one's wife goes beyond mere physical pleasure and procreation. The husband has an obligation to satisfy her carnal needs before his own, unlike Catholic and Calvinist teachings, which consider relations between man and woman to be a necessary sin to produce children."

In some instances, Rocamora struggled to avoid laughing when he read in the Babylonian Talmud instructions for making love: each day for a man of independent means, twice a week for a laborer, for sailors once in six months, ass drivers once a week, and camel drivers once in thirty days.

I doubt if I will see any camel drivers here in Vlooienburg

Rocamora did agree with other dicta based upon common sense. Physical pleasure was one of the wife's three basic rights, the others being food and clothing, none of which a husband might withhold or reduce. The couple should know each other during moments of happiness, never when drunk or angry, and neither should withhold intercourse to punish or manipulate a spouse. A man had a duty to know his wife regularly, ensure she was pleasured, recognize signals that she wanted intercourse, and to offer it without her having to ask.

He read more centuries-old advice:

Begin with words to draw her heart to you, which will settle her mind and make her happy.

Tell her things that will arouse her desire, attachment, love, willingness and passion.

Win her heart with words of charm and seduction.

Never know your wife when she is sleepy, for your minds will not be unified.

Never hasten to arouse her desire. Begin in a pleasing manner of love so that she will achieve satisfaction before you.

If a man cleaves to his wife in holiness, the divine presence is manifested. In the mystery of man and woman, there is God. But if they are merely aroused, the divine presence will leave them and it will become fire.

Much of what Rocamora read reminded him of the heretical *alumbrados* and their rites of sexual union in the belief a couple became one with God while experiencing climax.

"Don Isaac, scripture, as interpreted by the rabbis, considers it preferable for the wife to let her husband know she desires him to make love although she must not appear to be too bold."

Rocamora imagined his former Dominican brothers reacting in horror when he read how Jewish Law included rules for intercourse between husband and wife. The Talmud recommended it should be enhanced by nudity. If one of the partners refused to make love in the nude, it was considered grounds for divorce. Furthermore, the Talmud forbade making love during the day or by the light of a lamp. Midnight was considered the ideal time.

"Why must it be always in the dark, Rabbi? Surely desire for one another may come upon us at any time."

"It is the rare marriage that is not arranged. In the light, a man may see his wife's blemishes and observe something repulsive in her, thus making her undesirable and perhaps even loathsome to him."

Rocamora had speculated often about Abigail's body always hidden beneath her appropriately modest garments.

"There are exceptions, Don Isaac. The Talmud also states that if one or both are inclined to sleep through the night, the couple may have intercourse during the day provided it is done modestly with love and is not forced. There must always be joy in carnal union, for that is our rabbinic tradition, but it must be in the approved positions."

"Approved? Your laws are that detailed?"

"Indeed they are. A man may lay with his wife whenever he wishes, kiss her on whatever part of her body he wants, have natural or unnatural intercourse, provided he does not bring forth seed in vain, for the purpose of it all is procreation. Unnatural relations are those in which a man plants his seed outside the … ah … traditional place."

"Mouth and anus."

Menasseh's face reddened at Rocamora's bluntness. "Yes, and that also includes premature withdrawal. Yet, it is permissible if it is occasional and not exclusive and if the intent is mutual pleasure. I want to emphasize this. Both husband and wife must agree upon any unnatural relations. Jewish law forbids a man from forcing his wife into any act against her will."

"The Talmud is thorough."

"Yes, it is. It prohibits a man from getting his wife drunk so they can have unnatural relations."

"Am I reading correctly, Rabbi, that a man is forbidden to compel his wife to have marital relations, and yet a wife has the right to compel her husband?"

"Whomsoever knows his wife to be a God fearing woman and does not duly visit her is called a sinner. If a husband refuses to perform his marital obligation in a loving, romantic, and physically pleasing way, his wife has the right to demand a divorce and to take back her *ketubah*, her marriage contract settlement. I should add, however, although it is the woman's right, she may not refrain from intercourse to punish her husband, and if she does, the husband may divorce her without paying the substantial divorce settlement provided for in the *ketubah*. 'Thou shall not commit adultery' also implies, thou shall not practice masturbation either with hand or with foot."

"Or with any foreign object, I presume."

"That is correct, and so, Don Isaac, the primary purpose of making love is to reinforce the loving marital bond between husband and wife. The first and foremost purpose of marriage is companionship, and knowing each other plays an important role. Procreation is a reason for making love, but it is not the sole reason. Carnal relations between husband and wife are permitted, even recommended, at times when conception is impossible, such as when the woman is pregnant and after she is past childbearing. Now, tell me if you wish, Don Isaac, when you were a Dominican in Spain, did you give advice to those about to marry?"

"It was more general and less specific."

Was Abigail receiving similar instructions?

Rocamora had a final session with Menasseh before the wedding regarding the *mikvah*. "Meaning no disrespect, Rabbi, it appears to be no different from baptism."

"Appearances are deceiving. The *mikvah*, our symbolic ritual bath of purification existed long before the Christian practice of baptism. It is as old as the creation of man. In the beginning there was water, the primary source of life and purification of our bodies and spiritual selves. Even the gentile convert who immerses himself in the *mikvah* emerges as a Jew, and each groom must undergo immersion on his wedding day. The waters must cover each and every part of your body and each hair, otherwise the ritual lacks validity."

"And each bride?"

"Yes, but you also should know that the most important and general usage of *mikvah* is for purification of menstruant women, which is part of the laws of family purity."

Rocamora remembered confessing unprepared hysterical girls who believed they had sinned when their first bleeding arrived.

"Obviously, the wedding date should take into consideration your bride's monthly cycle, so she can be immersed in the *mikvah* before the nuptial, which also draws God and His blessing into your marriage. You must also be separated from her at the beginning of her first bleeding."

"About four or five days?"

"No, it is a minimum of twelve days. A man may not touch his wife or sleep in the same bed with her during this time."

That dictum appalled Rocamora. "For twelve days?"

"A two-week period of abstention every month forces a couple to build a non-carnal bond, which also increases desire for one another, thus making intercourse during the remaining two weeks more special. Family purity is based on the woman's monthly cycle. Therefore, you both should avoid actions and behaviors you normally find to be arousing such as direct physical contact and all forms of affection. You may not engage in sexual relations from the onset of her menstruation until after nightfall of the seventh day after its end and after your wife has immersed herself in the *mikvah*. As a physician, Don Isaac, surely you know that each month a woman's body prepares for the possibility of conception. Menstruation ends the possibility of conception."

"Of course I do."

"The Torah teaches that the presence of potential life within fills a woman's body with holiness and purity. Menses places the woman in a state of impurity. Immersion in the *mikvah* can return her to purity."

"Half a month."

"Yes, but think on this, Don Isaac. Those twelve days of waiting increase desire, and when next husband wife unite, it is the same as the first time, so that she will be as beloved as on the day of her marriage. And as pure."

Menasseh changed the subject and explained that unlike Catholicism Judaism allowed birth control if the married couple eventually fulfilled the commandment to be fruitful and multiply, the minimum requirement being to have two children, one of each gender.

Rocamora held his tongue. To abstain from affection during the days of his wife's menses and seven days after was a matter he and Abigail would decide for themselves.

"Don Isaac, Judaism also permits abortion even though an unborn child has the status of potential human life, which we consider valuable and may not be terminated casually. The Talmud says if the fetus threatens the life of the mother, you may even sever it within her body and remove it limb by limb if necessary because its life is not as valuable as hers. But once the greater part of the infant has emerged, you cannot take its life to save the mother's because you cannot choose between one human life and another."

Yet again, Rocamora remembered and mourned the death of Brianda and her stillborn child. He would have sacrificed the baby to save his daughter.

Rocamora thanked Menasseh for his instructions. "One last thing, Rabbi. Will you officiate at our marriage?"

"I shall be honored to do so. On certain occasions, we marry a couple outside our synagogue. Would you have any objections to that?"

"Of course not if Doña Abigail agrees. May I ask why?"

"You are an ornament of our community, and we want to proclaim to the world that you are one of us."

33.
Wedding

During the required interminable three months before their wedding day, Rocamora and Abigail shared a near unbearable impatience for the day of their nuptials so they could at last cohabit. Regardless of their frustrations, each made great use of their time living apart.

Rocamora's practice grew because of recommendations from Santcroos and Velde and word of mouth from satisfied patients. Many came to him out of curiosity at first because of his fame as Empress Maria's confessor.

Between diagnosing ailments and prescribing treatments and cures, Rocamora selected shelving and tables for the basement, stocked it with medicines, herbs, and spices, and ordered comfortable chairs for his study. He let Abigail handle their finances. Far better than he, she understood how to keep accounts and had a natural ability to be charming while she haggled mercilessly with shopkeepers.

Abigail supervised the reconstruction of their future home, and it soon became livable with polished tile floors the colors of aqua and sand Rocamora requested. Fresh linens and bedding awaited their wedding night, and in the vestibule, a cabinet contained slippers for Rocamora, Abigail, and their guests to wear inside the house.

When Hombrecillo was not stalking and catching the occasional foolish rodent to trespass into his domain, he watched the activities from atop furniture and fireplace mantles and hissed whenever Abigail's kin came near.

Several weeks before their nuptials, Rocamora stood with Abigail and two of her aunts in the cooking kitchen. Shiny copper and brass cooking utensils, pots, and pans hung from the ceiling and on the walls. The copper sink had a hand pump. Cupboards held plates, silver, and table linens from Abigail's dowry.

"Your ability to organize rivals that of the best generals, *querida*."

"Thank you, *Capitán*, but why are you holding that guitar? Have you come to entertain us?"

"A patient lacked sufficient coin to pay for my services and offered this instrument instead. I had not played in many years and missed strumming my favorite airs."

"And did you serenade your Infanta and other ladies you confessed with songs of love?"

He enjoyed the shocked reaction of Abigail's aunts and her mischievous expression. "*Querida,* I was but a humble friar of the false faith with a reputation for piety, and every December, I sang songs of the Nativity."

Abigail smiled at her aunts. "Do not look so horrified. I am sure my future husband will change the lyrics when our sons are born."

"I shall teach them to play, our daughters too, for a house without music, joy, and laughter is merely a structure and not a home. Perhaps one day we can afford a harpsichord."

Rocamora strummed the five strings and depressed several to achieve the desired sounds.

He sang in Portuguese:

> *Isaacc um bom trovador,*
> *Mas também sabe bailar.*
> *Na guitara é um primor,*
> *Rouxinol no seu cantar.*
> *Numa festa de Purim*
> *Isaac falou a Abigail,*
> *Cantou, dançou é no fim*
> *Dela foi s'enamorar.*

> Isaac was a good troubadour,
> But he also knew how to dance.
> At the guitar he was the best,
> And sang better than any nightingale.
> At the Purim Festival,
> Isaac spoke to Abigail,
> He danced, he sang, and at the end,
> He fell in love with her ....

Rocamora sang the travails of Isaac and Abigail until they convinced her father and the rabbi they should wed. "And so it shall be with us, *querida.*

The morning of their nuptials, Rocamora emerged from the *mikvah* at the synagogue and dried himself. After he donned his finest doublet and breeches, boots, cape, and plumed hat, he went to the synagogue office where Abigail and her uncles, Judah and Daniel Touro, stood beside Menasseh.

Rocamora had never before experienced so intense and sustained a feeling of love and well-being, and he thought Abigail could not have been more beautiful on this auspicious day. His bride wore no veil or covering for plaited hair held in place by fine bands of gold. Her wedding dress of white linen had a surprising décolletage, with delicate lace covering cleavage to her throat. Gold thread in curvilinear swirls decorated her billowing sleeves. Two necklaces hung from her neck, one of pearls, the other of three small gold encased diamonds. Abigail's expression was demure, the light in her eyes lively.

She will be mine for the remainder of my life, and I shall be hers.

Menasseh removed from a silver tube etched with curvilinear swirls and flowers a parchment as beautifully illustrated with plants and scenes from nature as any Catholic illuminated manuscript. "As you have been instructed regarding this *ketubah*, your marriage contract, it must be read in the presence of the bride, the groom, and these two witnesses who will sign it."

Rocamora studied the document. "The letters are of the Hebrew alphabet, but I do not understand the words."

"They are Aramaic, and because you have answered certain questions, your ancestors and the communities both you and your bride have come from are mentioned. It also specifies that Doña Abigail is marrying for the first time and is not divorced, a widow, or a convert. The *ketubah* also lists the contents of her dowry: two diamond mills, silver service and decorative pieces, several necklaces, rings, and bracelets of gold with precious gems, and close to a thousand Carolus guilders, all of which are to be returned to her should you divorce."

After Abigail's uncles signed the *ketubah* as witnesses, the rabbi took the contract and led the party outside Talmud Torah to the *huppah*, a canopy decorated with colorful summer flowers held by four men at the bottom of the steps: Santcroos, his son David, Eliahu Touro, and Eliahu's son, Solomon. Petals had been strewn on the steps and cobblestones in front of the synagogue where men, women, and children of the community had gathered. Across the street, others stood on balconies or watched from open windows.

Abigail's auburn hair shone in the sunlight as if woven in copper threads. Rocamora believed the most gifted artists in Spain and Holland could never paint or sculpt so great a beauty as his bride, and he imagined how family and friends in Spain might have reacted to Abigail. He saw his parents welcoming his beloved as the daughter they never had and Brianda accepting her as a sister. Don Lope would have been no less pleased, of that Rocamora was certain. He pictured Ramón wishing them well with many toasts, Moraíma being delighted to see her prophecy fulfilled, and Pablo, Yusef, and Koitalel, his *pícaro* companions, offering bawdy advice. He did not dwell on how María might have reacted.

Rocamora fought tears at so many memories and concentrated on the present. He recognized throughout the crowd Abigail's many Touro relations, including small children who inspected and touched her garments, Santcroos and his family, Velde and his son Peter, Vrouw Cornelia, Professor Poons, and Van Noordwijk, whom he had not seen in the two years after they returned from London. Rocamora avoided eye contact with Abigail's cousin Sara Eliahu Toura, who stood beside her and stared at him as she always did, hungrily, unblinking.

Menasseh began the betrothal ceremony with blessings over wine. After Rocamora and Abigail drank from the same glass, the rabbi spoke for all to hear. "Don Isaac, do you agree to wed Doña Abigail of your own free will?"

"I do."

"And do you, Doña Abigail agree to marry Don Isaac of your own free will?"

"I do."

Menasseh and Judah inspected and approved the ring to be used in the ceremony. After the rabbi recited another blessing, Rocamora placed the gold band on Abigail's right index finger and recited, "Be thou betrothed unto me by this ring in accordance with the Law of Moses."

Menasseh raised his hands over Rocamora and Abigail. "May you establish a loyal and fruitful house amongst the people of Israel." He recited more blessings and handed Abigail the *ketubah*.

The *Hazzan*, who was responsible for leading prayers and readings from the Torah, initiated the wedding ceremony by reciting the Seven Benedictions, and Menasseh again offered both bride and groom wine. After they drank, he placed a glass tumbler on the ground for Rocamora to shatter with his boot in memory of the destruction of the Holy Temple in Jerusalem. He lifted his right leg, hesitated, and smashed the tumbler into many pieces. The crowd shouted congratulations and good wishes.

He did not wait for permission to kiss Abigail. "My wife."

"My beloved husband."

Relations and friends surrounded Rocamora and Abigail, and they suffered through hugs and kisses. It would be a long while before they could retire to their wedding bed. Judah and Daniel had prepared a grand wedding feast for them.

34.
His First Virgin

Rocamora closed the door to their home and led Abigail upstairs to the great hall on the second floor that held their bed. For the first time, they were alone with no chaperone to watch them, no fear of intrusion. He kissed his bride. Abigail's lips were soft and warm, her body fit perfectly against his, as if both halves of a whole had become one. A virgin, she would be inexperienced. Had Abigail's aunts and married cousins prepared her for this night with wisdom or stories to frighten her?

"Did your aunts give you any advice?"

"Yes, and much of it made me blush."

"Regardless of what you may have been told, be assured of this, *mi querida*. I love you with all my heart, with all my might, with all my being. I shall be your devoted husband."

"And I shall make a home for you filled with love, comfort, and many children. Now, please wait while I attend to my person? I will call you when I am ready and in our marriage bed."

Rocamora removed his cape and doublet in the parlor. Off came his boots and the rest of his clothes. The sun began to set, the weather still warm and humid. He lit a candelabrum and closed the shutters. Wearing a thin robe of silk from China, a gift from Santcroos, Rocamora lit his clay pipe. He had imbibed small amounts of blessed wine at the wedding ceremony and subsequent banquet, and he considered then rejected drinking port or even brandy.

Rocamora had thought they might undress together. Perhaps Abigail needed time alone to gather her courage. How frightening it must be for a virgin to anticipate the impending events on her wedding night. He was perhaps no less apprehensive. Abigail would be his first virgin. How would she react to his lovemaking? Would she see it as an unpleasant requirement of marriage, solely a wifely duty, or would she be a wench in bed, a woman who naturally enjoyed pleasures of the flesh?

Based on his experiences, few women reacted the same to caresses, kisses, and probing. Where one was aroused, another was ticklish, or she reacted not at all. Where and how on her body would he give Abigail pleasure? Would she lie in bed inert as a weighty stone or engage in the action as a passionate partner? Would her scent be enticing, or would it repel him.

Women and their scents. Moraíma's orange blossoms. María's almonds and cinnamon. Catalina's heady musk, and Mina's marzipan.

He heard Abigail call him. Not Isaac or Rocamora, she used her favorite name, *Capitán.*

Rocamora snuffed his pipe, stood, and carried the candelabrum into the great hall. Abigail lay in bed clutching the sheet to her neck. "I welcome you, my husband."

"My beautiful bride. Shall I leave the candles lit, or shall I snuff them?"

"Whatever you decide."

Rocamora set the candelabrum on a table and removed his robe. He climbed into bed beside Abigail and became aroused when flesh touched flesh. She wore no bedclothes, and her scent was that of rose attar. He need not have worried how she would react to his words of love, kisses and caresses. Abigail was no inert stone.

Don Nobody wants to be Don Somebody, and
Don Somebody aspires to become Don Somebody Important.
—Spanish saying

He (Rocamora) fled the Catholic coercive system and embraced Judaism not to adhere to a new ecclesiastical system, but to find a refuge for free thought.
—Jac Zwarts, *De Uriel Da Costa, Tragedie van een monnik-biechtvader te Amsterdam, 1650.*

Part III
Physician, Husband, and Father
1647-1660

Like Uriel da Costa, Tragedy of a monk father-confessor in Amsterdam, 1650
—*Centraal Blad voor Israelieten,* May 24, 1934

35.
Doctor Isaac

Abigail surprised Rocamora daily with her purchases, and within a month after their wedding, she had furnished his study. A colorful Turkish rug lay atop his mahogany desk, another on the aqua and sand tiled floor. A bookcase covered one wall, a comfortable Moorish divan adorned with pillows had been placed against another. Abigail must have bargained well for bolts of cloth. Maroon velvet drapes hung on the sides of the large window facing the street. Attached by copper nails, the same fabric covered his armchair and the two chairs facing his desk. Abigail did not forget to add a brazier as he had requested even though the room had a fireplace.

This day, Rocamora sat at his desk in the study and listened to the complaint of two patients, Jan van der Waag, merchant son of an Amsterdam magistrate, and his wife Julia, daughter of a Groningen landowner. Married four years, they had no children. Although van der Waag's family blamed the woman and suggested they divorce, Rocamora was not yet convinced of the wife's barrenness. Her husband might be sterile, or other factors may have prevented conception.

He appreciated Julia's boldness. She declined an invitation to sit with Abigail in the parlor and insisted upon participating in the consultation, which no Spanish woman of an equivalent caste would have done.

"Mynheer, Mevrouw, may I assume you have consulted with others?"

Van der Waag hesitated and looked at his wife who nodded permission for him to continue. "My father's physician suggested my wife might have a physical anomaly that could be repaired through surgery. That is why we visited one of the best surgeons here in Amsterdam. He discovered nothing wrong with her, and he recommended that we see you."

"Jacobus Velde?"

"Yes."

Rocamora's reputation as a wise and caring physician had spread throughout the Christian community no less than within the Sephardic community. His soothing manner had been perfected by decades as a confessor. No one had a more thorough knowledge of healing herbs.

Julia nudged her husband. "Tell him about the others."

Van der Waag gestured apologetically. "My wife has sought cures on her own."

"From quacks and *curanderas*?"

"*Curanderas*?"

"Self-proclaimed healers."

"Oh, no, Doctor, I would never go to a witch."

Rocamora needed all his tact and charm to counter popular wisdom believed by many of his patients. He had never before seen so many books printed that fed upon the weakness of human vanity, all of them recommending remedies that were mostly harmless placebos, some dangerous.

"Mevrouw, may I ask what cures they offered?" His well-practiced comforting tone calmed the woman and earned her trust.

"I was to collect slime from the mouth of a hare after it fed on mallows and drink it in wine. If I were to lay with my husband two hours later, I would conceive."

"If that did not work, I was to secretly feed my wife the womb of a hare mixed into a hutspot without her knowledge, or burn it to a fine powder mixed with wine."

"Did you?"

"No, desperate as my wife and I are to conceive, they all seemed too absurd to try."

The van der Waags recounted more treatments recommended by the quacks:

Mix three handfuls of mouse-ear, and half ounces each of elecampane, liquorice, and currants. Boil them in two quarts of old wine, and drink a small amount upon awakening.

Half ounce each of old cloves and bayberries, two drams of pimpernel, one handful of mouse-ear, beat together, and place in a stone bottle. Add one pint-and-a-half of the best sherry, boil the bottle half-an-hour in a pot of water, and drink one or two spoonfuls.

"My wife tried two cures that did seem to make sense at first. For twenty-eight days, she ate each morning one new-laid egg from hens that had no cock near them for that time."

"And the other?"

"Several whom we consulted advised her to find a firstborn male child's navel-string that had not touched the ground, beat it to a powder, and mix it with wine. Nothing has worked. Can you help us?"

Rocamora agreed with Descartes' comparison of a healthy body to a well-made clock, with parts that could break down and be fixed or replaced. He doubted if that applied to the van der Waags.

"May I speak freely about the human body in front of your wife?"

"If she agrees."

"I do."

"I will ask you some questions and make suggestions that may cause you to feel uncomfortable or violate your religious tenets. May I proceed?"

Van der Waag again turned to Julia who nodded her assent. "Yes, please do."

"My first question to you is this. At what time of day or night do you make love?"

The young woman blushed and looked at her lap. Her husband answered for both, "After dark, in the darkness."

"And are you naked or do you wear bed clothes?"

Van der Waag gasped horrified. "Bed clothes of course."

"Was your marriage arranged, or was it one of choice?"

Van der Waag squeezed his wife's hand. "We have been acquainted since childhood and wed because we love each other."

"But we would not have married without our parents' blessings," Julia added.

"Ah, yes, your parents. And do you live alone or with one of your families?"

"We reside with my parents," Van derWaag said.

"That will make following my treatment more difficult."

"Why?"

"I shall explain in a moment. Mevrouw Julia, do you find your husband to be handsome and desirable?"

Her face took on a deeper hue of red. "Yes."

"And you, Mynheer, your wife?"

"From the first day I saw her."

Rocamora believed them. "I am delighted you say so, for that will make my suggested treatment more efficacious. I shall be recommending no medicines, absurd potions, or operations at this time. Because you do not have your own home, I worry it may be impossible for you to follow my instructions."

"I do not understand."

"Mynheer, to say it in a Scriptural manner, how often do you know each other during the week?"

Van der Waag hesitated embarrassed. "Several times."

"Day, night, or both?"

"I told you. At night. In the dark."

"I appreciate your honesty. Now, here is what I prescribe. You must be intimate every day or night, several times each day if you can, not as a duty, but with pleasure and love for each other. And wear no bedclothes." Rocamora paused to let the couple recover from the shock of his suggestions. "You must please each other's needs and satisfy your curiosities. If you do as I recommend for the time between your wife's menses, you should see positive results."

Deep furrows appeared on van der Waag's brow. "It will be difficult to do that in my father's house. There is so little privacy."

Rocamora made an educated guess based on van der Waag's caste. "Your family has a summer estate?"

"Yes, outside The Hague."

"Then find an excuse to go there with your wife for a month without other family members present."

For a moment, Rocamora worried the van der Waags might continue to be stifled by Calvinist attitudes toward the marriage bed and reject his advice until he saw how they looked at each other. He did not doubt they would soon be on their way to The Hague.

36.
Domesticity

"*Tía* Rebecca, I repeat. There is absolutely nothing wrong with you."

"But my cough."

"Merely an irritation of the throat." *From gossiping too much.* "I suggest drinking some peppermint tea, and the tickling will go away."

"I always have faith in your cures. I will speak with Abigail before I must return home to prepare our midday meal. Will you join us? You and Abigail are always most welcome."

"Thank you, *Tía*, not today."

After she left, Rocamora closed the door to his study. Abigail's aunts and cousins appeared uninvited daily and at odd times to gossip and to snoop. Often they used the excuse of a non-existent ailment for him to treat. It was enough that he and Abigail dined several times a week at her uncles' homes and always on Fridays for the Sabbath Eve meal. There had to be a way to break the cycle without giving offense.

An hour later, Rocamora felt the first pang of midday hunger when the aroma of Abigail's cooking wafted through the basement. He washed his hands and face and reviewed his new life as a married man. Abigail was as punctual and thorough a housekeeper as any Dutch vrouw from awakening to bedtime. She never failed to have their meals ready on time and bedding fresh and clean. Abigail had purchased a tub, which she placed in a corner of the kitchen. He now had the freedom to bathe as often as he wished, and his wife was no less sanitary.

Abigail served a midday meal of fresh fish with prunes, vegetables, and rice, and he shared with her the absurd cures quacks had advised his patients. During the three months since their wedding, she had learned much about his medicines and helped mix the ingredients. Abigail no longer polished diamonds to the disappointment of her uncles, and he had stored her mills in the attic. She never reminded him to put on his phylacteries for morning prayers at home, which he found to be a nuisance, nor did she prod him to go to the synagogue more often.

Abigail had placed one of her favorite possessions on the center of the table, part of her dowry that had belonged to the Touros for many generations. On the surface, it was a vase of coarse pewter. When twisted in a certain way, the vase opened to reveal a perfectly scaled miniature treasury of Jewish ritual all in silver: Torah scrolls, goblet, menorah, and spice box for the ceremony at end of the Sabbath, which the family had used in secret ceremonies during their sojourns in lands hostile to their religion.

"*Querida*, I like nothing more than to sup and be alone with you. I look forward to the day when we will have our own Sabbath meals."

"I am well aware you are displeased whenever my aunts and cousins come to see me."

"They mean well, but their unannounced visits are intrusions upon our privacy and my professional time."

A wry smile dimpled Abigail's cheeks. "And I have seen that when you are not available to treat them, their symptoms mysteriously disappear. You will be pleased to know that *Tía* Rebecca stopped coughing the moment she left you."

"I thought as much. What did she really want?"

"She repeated gossip that would not interest you and wanted answers to her usual questions. Am I happy in marriage? When will we have children? Why do you not go to the synagogue more often?"

"And you replied yes to the first, shrugged at the second, and suggested she ask me the third?"

"The same as I always do."

After their meal, Rocamora lit his pipe and sat beside Abigail in front of the hearth with Hombrecillo at his feet before retiring for their afternoon siesta. She hummed a cheerful simple tune he did not recognize and her sewing puzzled him.

"It seems to be an unusually small garment. For one of your nieces or nephews?"

"My physician husband has been unaware that I have not been in a state of *nidah* this month?"

Busy establishing his practice and enjoying his time alone with Abigail, Rocamora had paid no attention to her monthly cycle and the required twelve days of physical separation required by Jewish Law, which they ignored. The light in Abigail's eyes and the glow in her cheeks were not caused by the fire. He left the chair, dropped to his knees before his wife, and held her hands.

"You are with child."

"I am."

"You are certain?"

"Absolutely."

Rocamora kissed her hands, cheeks and mouth. "How far along?"

"Three months."

"Our wedding night."

"It seems so, or immediately thereafter."

Throughout the day and into the night, they made plans for their first child's future. Ever practical, Abigail had made a list of foreseeable expenses for a bowl and chair for the infant to relieve itself, large nursing basket, high chair, and child's blanket: "I believe I can purchase them for less than three florins total."

"We will need to decide on a name for our firstborn."

"After we know if it is a boy or a girl."

Rocamora understood the custom was to name males after Scriptural patriarchs, prophets, and heroes – Abraham, Isaac, David, Ezekiel, Samuel, and Solomon – and females after the patriarchs' wives and heroines – Sara, Rebecca, Rachael, Lea, Esther, Deborah, and Judith. A firstborn son would be named after his paternal grandfather. Each child, male and female carried the given name of the father.

"My father, Don Luís, had no patriarchal name of course. He was born and died a Catholic, and his Jewish blood would have been diluted over many centuries."

"Then if I should give birth to a boy, our first son shall be named according to custom after my father Moses, may he rest in peace."

Moses Isaac de Rocamora. Rocamora preferred Luís, Ramón for the first Spanish de Rocamora, or Willem, as the Dutch called Guillherme, for another of his forebears he admired most, the second Nasi, Davidic Jewish prince, of Septimania. "Moses it shall be."

"Moses Isaac."

"And I will teach him to be a fine physician."

"And an observant Jew."

But will he be so inclined? "Yes, of course. And if we have a daughter?"

"The first girl should be named after your mother."

"Her name was Gabriela, and like my father, she had no Hebrew name."

"Then it shall be Sara Isaac, after my mother. I look forward to the day when I hear our children call you *Abba* for father and me *Eemah* for mother."

"May that be so. Now, there is something I want you to see." Rocamora left the room and returned with a scrolled parchment. "No one else must see or know of this. One day, when he is old enough to understand, I will show it to our eldest son."

He untied the scroll, spread it on Abigail's lap, and told her of his encounter with Pierre Taurelle at the Abbaye de St. Roch in Roquemaure.

Abigail studied the genealogy chart. "Taurus the Jew … Taurelle … and my family was Toro in Spain, Touro in Portugal and here in Amsterdam. El Toro, the bull. Am I also truly descended from the houses of David and Arnulf?"

"It would seem so."

"Even if we are kin, it is so remote as to say we both are descended from Adam and Eve."

"Well said."

"But who is this Bodo? So strange a name."

Rocamora told Abigail the story of the apostate German noble who had been educated for the clergy. Raised to Deacon and then Bishop Palatine, Bodo was a favorite of Emperor Louis the Pious and Empress Judith. He asked to go on a pilgrimage to Rome, instead went to Spain, converted to Judaism, married, and became a polemicist warrior Jew.

"And from him through your mother you inherited your unusual beautiful green eyes. I pray our children also will have them."

Rocamora rolled and tied the chart. "No one else must know of this."

He returned to the attic and placed the scroll in the chest that contained his plays and poems that even Abigail had not seen, nor would she ever read them. He had not destroyed his poems to María and Moraíma. Odd that Catalina never inspired him to compose even one couplet to her other than the superficial extempore attempts during poetical jousts at her salon gatherings.

Rocamora found Abigail in bed, naked, awaiting him. They had made love many times by day and candle light despite the prohibitions.

"My beloved *Capitán*, the genealogy chart, your past life … and now I am with child. Do you feel confined in a world so small? There are moments when I sense you are on a shelf, not here, but idealizing your former life in Spain."

Uncanny how Abigail has guessed my thoughts.

"I confess I do find the Vlooienburg community to be confining and at times stifling, and the weather here in Amsterdam often too cold, misty, and gloomy in contrast to Madrid and most of all my lost fragrant coast of Valencia. But know this, *querida*, you …." Rocamora paused and placed a hand on her belly. "… you are my entire world now and all the world I need."

37.
Ashkenazim

Rocamora arrived home late in the afternoon after visiting his patients, and Abigail welcomed him with a kiss. He looked at her extended belly. "The birth of our first child is two months away. We have postponed long enough the hiring of a servant to help you with the daily chores of cleaning, marketing, and preparing meals."

"I prefer a young girl to train instead of a woman set in her ways."

"I agree, *querida*, but I do not want in our home any widow or spinster from the community who will gossip about our every move and repeat each spoken word. I prefer a robust country girl, the same as I have seen in Christian households, but decrees of the *Ma'amad* forbid the employing of gentiles."

"Then where can we find a servant?"

"I will select one from the Ashkenazim, as other families in Vlooienburg have done, with your approval of course."

Ashkenaz was the Hebrew word for the German, and Ashkenazim became the name for all European Jews not from Iberia. Some had attended prayer at Talmud Torah. Many more begged for coins or food on Jodenbreestraat and a few at the front door of their home.

The Sephardim regarded the Ashkenazim as inferior, lacking *hidalguía* and refinement, with no appreciation for art, literature, and music. They understood no Spanish or Portuguese and spoke a language harsh sounding to Iberian ears similar to German, which they called Yiddish.

In an effort to keep their community separate from these alien Jews, the *Ma'amad* decreed that no one from the congregation should purchase kosher food from Ashkenazi butchers or attend their prayer services. They forbade Sephardic *mohels* from circumcising their newborn males. No member of the community was to have social intercourse with the Ashkenazim, with specific exceptions. The community gave money and food to the needy to reduce their begging. They could be hired as servants; and Sephardic rabbis consulted Ashkenazi sages on interpretation of Jewish law because the latter had never lost continuity with their religion.

The Ashkenazim lived in overcrowded wooden tenements in the poorest section of Vlooienburg. They numbered a few hundred, but it was their market day, and the street teemed with a noisy throng inspecting, selecting, and haggling over produce, chickens, meat, and goods displayed in stalls and on carts. Ragged musicians, singers, and beggars added to the din. Their physiognomy fascinated Rocamora. Some were fair with blond or red hair, snub noses, and porcine blue eyes. Others had features and coloring similar to the Iberians without the dignified bearing.

Gestures, language, and garb of the Ashkenazim made their overall appearance different from the Dutch styles of the Sephardim to the extreme. Their men refused to dress as proper burghers and wore instead long dark caftans, peculiar conical hats or battered caps, and they left their beards untrimmed.

These strange looking people, dare I bring one of them into my home as a servant?

Rocamora encountered a crowd gathering around a half dozen haggard and shivering individuals barely covered in rags, four men, a woman, and a girl he guessed to be no older than twelve with hair the color of a blazing fire. As best he could understand, they were refugees from different villages in Poland and had escaped one of the worst massacres of Jews since the days of San Vicente de Ferrer at the end of the fourteenth century. Cossacks and Ukrainians had rebelled against their Polish masters and killed every Jewish man, woman, and child they encountered. Mere murder was not enough for them. Rocamora listened horrified to their tales of Jews being flayed and buried alive, trampled to death by horses, and suffering the worst tortures, which reminded him of the monstrous acts he had witnessed committed by Catholic and Protestant mercenaries against defenseless populations during his journey through the Germanys more than ten years earlier.

According to the refugees, more than three hundred communities of Jews no longer existed in Poland and Ukraine. Tens of thousands had been slaughtered. Rocamora wondered why they had not converted to save their lives as so many had done in Spain and Portugal. The redheaded girl had not spoken, and he suspected from her angry expression that she would have taken a sword and killed a Cossack had she been able.

When the adult refugees saw Rocamora, they gathered around him wailing, lamenting, and begging. He would have given them some florins so they could buy food and purchase proper garments to withstand the cold of an Amsterdam winter, but that might have the caused beggars and layabouts to riot.

He recognized two members from the Iberian community haggling with one of the male refugees. Abraham Nieto and Jacob Salvador owned a bordello near the docks. Nieto gave the man several coins, and Salvador seized the girl who screamed and struggled.

Rocamora confronted the refugee who received the coins. He spoke German so the man might understand him. "Are you this child's father or her brother?"

The refugee dropped to one knee and kissed his gloved hand. "No, my lord, but I need the money so I can eat."

Rocamora recoiled at his touch "I am not anyone's lord, nor are you. You have no right to sell her." He struck the refugee a hard blow on the wrist with his stick causing him to drop the florins. Several men and women pounced on the coins.

Rocamora ignored the scuffle. "You, Nieto and Salvador, release that girl."

Nieto drew his dagger. "We paid fairly for her. It is none of your business."

"I repeat. Release the child now."

Nieto lunged. Rocamora sidestepped and tripped him. He drew his sword from the walking stick, placed it at the prone man's throat, and kicked the dagger from his hand. He turned to face Salvador who continued to grasp the little redhead. "I will count to three, and if you do not let her go, I will end this dog's life and you will be next. One ...."

The girl broke free, hurried to Rocamora's side, and retrieved Nieto's dagger.

Rocamora placed his sword in the stick and allowed Nieto to rise. "Leave now, and I advise both of you not to cross my path again."

After Nieto and Salvador disappeared from sight, Rocamora confronted the crowd. His stentorian voice commanded silence. "Cowards all. So many of you and only two of those swine. You could have prevented this girl from being taken away to a life of slavery and shame. Do not wait for Yom Kippur to ask God to forgive you."

Rocamora turned his back to them and appraised the girl. Malnourished but not starving. Intelligent blue eyes. Fearless too. She might do well as a servant.

"What is your name, my child?"

The softness of his voice calmed her. "I am Miriam, daughter of Yankel, the Leaseholder. I thank you for saving me from those men."

"What happened to your family?"

"The Cossacks killed them all. I was away on an errand and returned after the murderers left. Who are you?"

She had responded in better German than his and not Yiddish, which convinced him Miriam came from an educated family. "I am the physician, Don Isaac de Rocamora. Can you read and write?"

"Hebrew, Yiddish, German, and Polish. My father taught me numbers too."

Rocamora believed he could never have found so rare a gem amongst the Sephardim. "Are you willing to come live with me and my wife as a servant? She will be giving birth to our first child in two months."

She studied his face and clothes. "Are you a Jew?"

"Yes, a Jew from Spain. I assure you, Señorita Miriam, you will be fed, clothed properly, and treated well."

"But will your wife want me?"

"Of that I am certain."

"What is her name?"

"Abigail."

Miriam's jaw quivered, and she struggled not to cry. "My sister's name, may she rest in peace." She handed Rocamora the dagger. "Yes, I will go with you."

"First, we must find you some new clothes and give you a decent meal … and a bath."

"You did well, *Capitán*. She is a lovely child and intelligent."

Rocamora smoked his pipe in a chair beside Abigail, who spun yarn to make a linen garment for their baby to come, and he stroked Hombrecillo curled in his lap. "Daughter, son, it matters not if you and the infant both survive in good health."

Miriam entered clean from her bath and wearing a new plain dress, white apron, and cap. "Herr Doktor, I thank you again for rescuing me, and your wife for accepting me into your home."

Rocamora translated for Abigail before he replied to the girl. "Miriam, you can show your gratitude best not by words but by attending to my wife and soon to be child."

"Si, Señor."

"She has a good ear for languages, *mi querida*."

"Then I shall teach her Spanish and Portuguese."

"Doctor Isaac, does your wife keep a kosher kitchen?"

"Yes, she does."

Unfortunately.

38.
Greatest Accomplishments

Arce and his minions have been busy.

Rocamora counted increasing numbers of refugees from Spain and Portugal appearing in Vlooienburg. They claimed to be caballeros, soldiers, former nuns, priests or monks. Most said they were related to the great families, which Rocamora disbelieved. Many settled in the community. Others left to join kin in cities throughout the United Provinces and in Hamburg. Some returned to Iberia.

After one of his rare Saturday morning appearances at Talmud Torah synagogue, Rocamora walked with Judah Touro along Jodenbreestraat. "In answer to your question, Abigail should give birth the first or second week in April."

"May God grant you a healthy child."

Rocamora preferred to rely on his knowledge and skills. "There should be no complications."

"Don Isaac, I hope you will not misunderstand what I am about to say and take no offence. Some in our community continue to voice concerns regarding your activities. You have been seen associating more with gentiles than Jews. You have been observed going to taverns and baths, dens of thieves and whores."

"Am I accused of thieving and whoring?"

"No, of course not, but appearances …."

"Are deceiving. And when I defecate, will they know if I wipe my ass with my left or right hand?"

"Is there no talking to you?"

"Of course there is, when one makes sense."

Judah and no one else need know his reasons for going to the baths. Velde had arranged for him to become physician to the city's regulated prostitutes there and at the taverns where he enjoyed the camaraderie of the surgeon and van Noordwijk when the latter was in Amsterdam.

"Who are these spies, Judah? Man or woman, kin to wife or not, point them out and I will knock some sense in their heads."

Judah recoiled at his vehemence. "I mean well. I am thinking of Abigail. The women gossip so."

The men no less.

They parted at St. Anthony's Lock. Rocamora did not go home. He walked throughout the city and dwelled on the spying and absurd rules of the Sephardic community and the pretentiousness of too many of its inhabitants with their concept of *hombres de nação*. They had taken as their own, the *cinco excelencias*, the five characteristics of Spaniards, which presumably distinguished them from other people.

One, superiority of physiognomy.

Two, military valor.

Three, great wealth.

Four, authentic literary taste.

Five, a combination of knowledge, devout piety, genuine nobility, and purity of blood.

The same as Spain, too many Don Nobodies pretending to be Don Somebody Important resided in Vlooienburg.

When he first arrived in Amsterdam, Rocamora sympathized with the Law of Moses, but he now realized it had been in abstract terms, not with its practice. He had not fled Spain to trade one coercive ecclesiastic system for another.

This was not the first time Rocamora considered converting to Velde's liberal Protestant sect. The Collegiants would allow him to live as he chose, eat whatever he wanted, and not bother him with annoying religious rituals and prohibitions. Although Abigail was devoted to her family and religion, he believed his wife would follow him even though they faced certain ostracism and excommunication by the Sephardic community. Could he force so terrible a choice upon the woman he loved?

Miriam met Rocamora at the front door speaking a mix of German, Yiddish, and Spanish. "Doctor, thank God you are home. The Señora has gone into labor."

"Three weeks early?" One thought dominated: this birth must not be a repeat of what happened to Brianda and little Vicente. No one but he would deliver his child.

Rocamora hurried to Abigail. Miriam followed. "Doctor, I have begun to boil water like you told me if you were not here when it happened. I served the Señora a pot of red raspberry leaf tea and set clean towels, linens, and everything else on your list on a table at her bedside"

"Very good. Now bring a slab of butter to the great room. After that, I will instruct you further."

Rocamora dropped his bag on the floor in the great hall. Abigail sat in bed wearing a shift. Her calmness surprised him. So did Hombrecillo. The cat lay beside his wife meowing softly and licking her hand as if to comfort her. He kissed his wife, felt her stomach, and timed the contractions.

"*Calma, mi Capitán.* I am fine. Soon I will give you our first child. He is so impatient to be born."

"He?"

"It will be a boy."

"Hush, save your strength."

Miriam ran into the room with a pound of butter. "Is it enough, Doctor?"

"Yes, put it on the table. Place the towels on a chair, move it close to the fire, and bring me a basin of hot water and soap."

Rocamora set a candle on the table by the butter, opened his bag, and laid his instruments beside it and the items Miriam had prepared earlier: scissors, needle, and thread to cut and tie the umbilical cord; dried lavender and perfumed oils for the newborn's skin. For the first time he noticed the girl had prepared a *rolkoets* on the side of the bed with linens and a blanket.

He poured another cup of red raspberry leaf tea for Abigail. "*Querida*, drink all you can. It will help ease the delivery of our baby."

Miriam laid a basin of hot water on the table, and Rocamora scrubbed his hands with soap. He dried them and sat beside Abigail.

Miriam refilled the cup of tea. "What else can I do, Doctor."

"Take Hombrecillo from the bed and bring more hot water and towels when I say so."

Contractions came at shorter intervals. Rocamora's heart beat faster. Again, the specter of what happened to Brianda intruded, and he caught himself praying for both his wife and the baby.

"Now, *mi Capitán*, now."

Rocamora stood and applied butter to Abigail's womb to smooth her delivery. He reached inside for the baby. No need to turn it. Abigail's shrill scream was more of triumph than pain when the newborn emerged smiling. Completely out of her womb and definitely a boy, he bellowed to the world he had arrived.

Rocamora held his breath and examined the newborn so tiny and helpless. Ten fingers and toes, bright eyes, strong heart, powerful lungs, about seven and a half pounds. Well proportioned.

"*Mi Capitán*, you are weeping. Is there something wrong? Or are they tears of joy?"

Rocamora lifted the newborn so Abigail could see him. "We have a healthy son, *mi querida*." Abigail never looked so beautiful, not even on their wedding day. "You have kept your promise. Know that I love you beyond words, beyond the height of the sky and oceans' depths, beyond the value of gold."

Abigail reached to touch a tear on his cheek. "I do, *mi Capitán*. Our son shall be named Moses Isaac de Rocamora at his *berit milah*."

"Moses Isaac de Rocamora, my son, our son, flesh of our flesh, blood of our blood. I already think of him as Moses"

"I will give you more sons and daughters too. Look how handsome our firstborn is, so very much like you."

Rocamora placed Moses on linen cloth at the bottom of the bed. He cut, tied, and sewed the umbilical cord. "I will bring Moses to you shortly." He laid their newborn on a soft warm towel atop the table beside the bed. He washed his son with lukewarm water from a bowl, dried him with heated linens, and applied scented oils.

Abigail opened her arms. "Our son is hungry."

No restrictive swaddling for his son, Rocamora dressed Moses in a warmed white flannel smock and placed him in the crook of Abigail's arm. She bared a breast for their hungry firstborn to suckle.

Rocamora was certain of one fact. No mother would be more loving and nurturing than Abigail. He kissed her moist brow, eyes, cheeks, mouth and their son's forehead. After she finished nursing, he lifted Moses to his shoulder, patted his son's back, and started at a baby sound.

"A most manly belch."

Overwhelmed with love for their firstborn, Rocamora spoke to him. "My beautiful boy, always be proud you are a de Rocamora. Your lineage is no less than kings and emperors and greater than most rulers. Who else can trace descent from the Houses of David and Arnulf, Roman consuls, princes of Alamannia, renowned soldiers, and grand Señores de Benetorrente? I shall teach you arms and all I know about medicine if you are so inclined. If you prefer to take a different road, I will encourage you to live a life of your own choosing, which I was denied."

Doubts intruded.

Will you become the man I envision? Can I be a good father to you?

Rocamora returned Moses to Abigail and sat on the bed beside them until they fell asleep. He beckoned Miriam. "You did well today."

"Doctor, I will be pleased to help the Señora and take care of your baby."

"His name will be Moses. They are sleeping now. Rest here beside them. Call me if I am needed."

Rocamora went to his study, poured a glass of brandy and lit his pipe. Until now, he had not realized how much his hands shook. The moment he settled in a chair by a brazier, Hombrecillo leaped onto his lap and purred. Calmer now, thoughts of past and present came to mind.

In Spain, he never could have married and sired children. Yet, at age forty-six to his amazement, he wed Abigail, and a few weeks before his forty-seventh birthday she gave him an heir. Better to have her love and now a son than transient offices and titles of royal confessor and Inquisitor General.

Despite its sun, palms and cypress, fields of melons, and groves of orange, Spain and all connected to it became in memory a land of darkness. He remembered his father's assassination and death of his mother when he was a boy. He grieved over the loss of those he loved, too many taken before their time: Don Lope, Moraíma, Yusef and Koitalel, Ramon, court *bufónes* Hombrecillo and Inéz, Catalina, María, and Brianda.

Amsterdam, so bleak and dark during winter now became a city of light and life. Here, he found Abigail, the great love of his life, and wed her. Here, she gave him a son. From Dominican royal confessor in Spain to married physician and father of Moses in Amsterdam, the course of his life had changed one hundred and eighty degrees.

Rocamora laughed aloud at another thought. Arce and all the celibate inquisitors of the Holy Office would die without issue, whereas his seed through Moses would multiply over subsequent generations. He credited Abigail for taking him to a paradise greater than the fragrant coast of Valencia.

Abigail has made me the happiest of men. Marrying and having a son with her are the greatest accomplishments of my life.

Rocamora's euphoria continued throughout the eight days to his son's *berit milah*. The great hall filled with guests for the circumcision. Abigail sat in bed attended by Miriam and her female relations. The men gathered around two chairs and blocked the women's view of the ritual, Rocamora in one holding his crying firstborn on a soft white satin pillow. The infant had been bound to prevent him from squirming during his circumcision.

According to tradition, *Tío* Judah, the oldest male relation and godfather to Moses, should have held him. Rocamora would let no one except the *mohel* touch his precious son. Were it not for Halakah, he would have performed the *berit milah* on his firstborn.

The empty second chair was reserved for the prophet Elijah, symbolic witness to the enduring loyalty and commitment of Jews to keep Israel alive.

Rocamora scanned the great hall pleased to see his friends Santcroos, Gaspar Hendrijks, Velde, and van Noordwijk in attendance.

The *mohel* washed his hands in a basin on a nearby table, dipped each tool in an engraved silver flagon of wine, and held them over a candle flame. Dropping to one knee, the *Mohel* adjusted the baby's position on the pillow in Rocamora's lap and exposed his penis. With thumb and forefinger, he stretched the foreskin to its limit and pulled it through a small loop extending from one of the instruments. Rocamora winced when the *mohel* cut his son's foreskin.

Menasseh intoned over the baby's screaming, "Blessed art Thou, Lord our God, King of the Universe, Who has sanctified us by Thy commandments, and commanded us regarding *milah* ... Who has sanctified Thy beloved from birth."

All responded with "Amen."

After the *mohel* poured wine on the infant's raw penis and dressed it with clean linen, Rocamora unbound his son and recited, "Blessed art Thou Lord our God, King of the Universe, Who has sanctified us by Thy commandments and commanded us to bring our son into the covenant of Abraham our father."

The men responded, "As he entered the covenant, so may he attain a life of Torah, mitzvah, and go to the wedding canopy."

Menasseh recited a blessing over Moses to invoke God's special protection, and Rocamora stood holding his son on the pillow. "Welcome my firstborn, Moses bar Isaac de Rocamora y Touro y Cornel."

Rocamora carried Moses around the room on his pillow for all to see and brought him to Abigail. "Here, *mi querida,* here is Moses, our son."

He kissed his wife and left the women who fussed over Moses. At a table laden with food and drink, he poured a much-needed glass of wine. After Menasseh, the Touro relations, and other guests toasted Moses' birth, Santcroos took Rocamora aside. "My son David is entering manhood. God willing, he will wed soon and sire many children. Perhaps he may have a daughter for your Moses to wed and link our two houses."

"That would be a *mitzvoth*, Don Samuel."

"Yes, a true blessing."

Van Noordwijk raised his glass to Rocamora. "You are a braver man than I."

"I can assure you that my knees turned to water during the ceremony."

"I have good news of my own. Our families have given their consent for Arabella and me to marry. Our wedding will take place the last Saturday in June at The Hague. I am inviting you and Doña Abigail."

"Congratulations, my friend, we will be delighted to accept."

Velde also raised his glass to Rocamora. "May you have many more sons. I thank you for inviting me. It was a most interesting and moving ceremony. Don Samuel translated the prayers and explained the rituals. I cannot help but wonder how much money I could be making if circumcision were allowed in the Protestant faiths."

"A fortune unless the clergy took it upon themselves."

"And they would too."

Rocamora turned toward Abigail, impatient for all guests to leave and he could be alone with his wife and son in their private world.

39
The Peace of Exhaustion

Shortly after Moses' birth, the European wars that had continued for thirty years ended. Amsterdam and other cities throughout the Dutch Republic held stirring parades, elaborate pageants, thanksgiving services, open-air theatrical performances, bonfires and fireworks, and sumptuous banquets for the militia and governing bodies. The celebrations lasted through April and May, and on an early day in June, Rocamora stood with Velde in the middle of a cheering mostly drunk mob in the square outside the Town Hall. The festivities rivaled any fair. Strangers embraced. Backs and hands ached from many hearty slaps. Women kissed freely.

The Dutch had every reason to celebrate. Treaties signed months earlier at Münster ended the war against Spain, and the magistrates chose to announce the particulars in the Supreme Court of Justice at precisely ten in the morning on the fifth day of June 1648 for a specific reason, which Velde explained to Rocamora.

"This is the same day and hour the Duke of Alba executed the Counts of Egmont and Hoorn in 1568, and began our eighty year War of Independence from Spain. Ah, here are the terms."

They read the broadsides distributed by officials throughout the crowd. Rocamora shut out the shouting and cheering and read that Spain renounced its claim on the seven northern provinces of the Netherlands and recognized the Dutch Republic as free and sovereign. Of equal importance for trade, the Spanish could not sail in the waters of territories controlled by the Dutch East India Company.

Rocamora recalled the glorious now futile military exploits of his kinsmen Jerónimo, Ramón, and Francisco de Rocamora, and that of the Cardinal-Infante. So ended thirty years of relentless warfare that left countless dead and lands devastated.

"Let us go to an inn," Velde shouted above the noise. "I swear, peace has already given me a great thirst."

"Peace, war, day and night, you need no excuse to satiate your thirst, Jacobus."

Jan van der Waag waved and approached them. "Dr. Isaacus, Mynheer Jacobus, I thank the Lord I found you in this crowd."

"Is there something wrong?"

"Far from it, Doctor. My wife has gone into labor, and you promised to be there for her and my child, my firstborn."

"And so I shall."

Rocamora and Velde followed van der Waag to the home of his father not far from the Town Hall. Both families were excited and apprehensive about the impending birth of a grandchild. Rocamora reassured them that the midwife was competent and both Julia and the baby would survive.

After an hour, they heard a scream and the crying of a newborn. The midwife parted the curtains. "You have a boy."

Rocamora inspected the infant nestled in the crook of her arm. "All fingers and toes are there, no deformities, and his crying tells me he has a healthy pair of lungs and strong heart."

They heard Julia scream again, and her husband gripped Rocamora's arm. "My wife. Go to her."

He went behind the curtain with the midwife and took the baby from her so she could deliver a second child. A few minutes later, they stood before Jan and Julia's families, each holding a newborn.

Rocamora held the second infant high for all to see. "Mynheer Jan, your wife has delivered a second perfectly formed male child. You have twin boys."

His manhood proclaimed and Julia's fertility assured, van der Waag embraced Rocamora in tears. "We are so grateful."

"May you have many more."

Magistrate van der Waag raised his *flapkan* filled with beer. "An auspicious day for our city and nation, a significant day for our families. Come, one and all, let us celebrate the birth of my grandsons and full independence of our United Provinces with food and drink. May they live a life of peace and prosperity."

Prosperity perhaps, but little peace. Although the wars of religion had ended, Rocamora did not forget that the French still had an insatiable appetite for conquest, and the English coveted the Dutch trade and colonies.

New wars did not come immediately. By October 1648, other treaties ended the European wars that had lasted thirty years. Some referred to it as the Peace of Exhaustion.

The clauses that interested Rocamora most when he read them on the walls of the Town Hall were the formal recognition of the Dutch Republic by all European powers and abolition of trade barriers erected during the long war. He saw irony in many other clauses. Protestants could now vote to elect the Catholic Holy Roman Emperor. Spain had failed to establish Habsburg hegemony in Europe. Instead, France emerged as the greatest victor and expanded its territory.

Peace eluded England, which suffered through another year of civil war. In January 1649, Rocamora was distressed to learn the English Parliament beheaded King Charles. Although both Jews and Dutch celebrated the triumph of the Protestants over the Catholic-leaning monarch, they ignored one obvious fact: England would continue to be their most dangerous mercantile rival.

Rocamora sent condolences to the unfortunate monarch's daughter, Princess Royal Mary Stuart, with flattering descriptions of her father during his courtship of the Infanta.

As if Rocamora had merely blinked, more than a year sped by. During those months, his practice grew, and so did his love for Abigail. She amazed him with her cool efficiency running their household and making it their private sanctuary from the outside world.

At the end of each day, Rocamora enjoyed most their sitting together in the parlor where he relaxed with pipe and glass of Port and they described the events of each other's day. He even looked ahead to the coming winter, for no pleasure was greater than sharing a bed with his wife on the coldest of nights and embracing to feel her warmth and passion.

Moses thrived at nineteen months, walking, talking, and large for his age, and soon to have a brother or sister. Each night when Abigail put their son to bed, she sang him the Hebrew alphabet.

Rocamora enjoyed a small circle of good friends principally Velde, Santcroos, Hendrijks, Menasseh, and van Noordwijk when the diplomat was in Amsterdam. He comforted himself that however strict the *Ma'amad* might be at times, it could not compare with the dungeons, torture, *autos*, and *quemaderos* of the Holy Office.

At misty dusk in mid-January 1650, Rocamora walked home from the center of town where he had seen a patient. He sensed someone following but saw and heard no one suspicious. On separate occasions earlier in the day, Velde, Santcroos, and Menasseh had alerted him that a stranger was inquiring about the Dominican Vicente de Rocamora. Each described him as slight of build with spade beard and mustachio, a well-dressed, typical Spaniard to all appearances. Rocamora wanted to believe the Holy Office would have forgotten him by now, but Arce was no less vengeful than any Valencian.

Abigail awaited him with Moses clinging to her dress. He kissed his wife and son and washed his hands and face. Before supping, Rocamora sat at his desk and made notes regarding the progress of his patients. Hombrecillo, now a muscular fifteen pounds, bounded into his lap. "Ay, my friend, I may have misnamed you, for you are no longer a little man but a giant amongst cats."

Rocamora and Abigail shared a light evening supper of spicy vegetable soup, bread and cheese, tea for his wife and wine for himself served by Miriam. He studied Moses, secure in his child's chair. The lively boy was likely to surpass him in height. Would he be a physician or succumb to the de Rocamora martial spirit of his forebears? For a moment, Rocamora also speculated about the imminent birth of their next child. Boy or girl, what type of person would it become?

After the meal, Rocamora played his guitar and serenaded Abigail and Moses until he heard persistent knocking at the front door. The hour was late but not unusual for patients to call or their kin to summon him. The clock did not regulate ailments and injuries. Or he might be the stranger who had inquired about him.

"Miriam, I will see who it is."

Alert to potential; danger, Rocamora opened the front door where he faced a slight man covered in a cloak with plumed hat, boots and spurs, and a scarf across most of his face. The stranger held no weapon but might have a hidden brace of pistols and dagger.

"Are you ill, Mynheer?"

Off came the scarf. "At last. Vicente, *mi amigo*."

40.
From the Past

Rocamora embraced his old friend. "Pablo, come inside out of the wind and warm yourself. I believed we would never meet again."

"As I also feared. I have been told you are now a physician and married."

"Yes, I am a padre of the proper kind. One son and another child due at any time." He brought Pablo to the table. "*Querida*, this is Pablo de Royaya, my loyal friend from Valencia, of whom I have spoken so many times. My wife, Abigail."

Pablo doffed his hat, executed a bow worthy of any grandee, and kissed her hand. "I am honored, Doña Abigail."

"Don Pablo, I am so pleased to meet you. Please sit and share our meal." She raised her voice so it could be heard in the kitchen. "Miriam, we have company."

"A handsome boy you have there, and a beautiful wife. A fine home too. I am pleased to see you living well."

Rocamora could not take his eyes from Pablo. "And judging by the quality of your clothes so are you."

"A façade to impress, as we Spaniards are wont to do." Pablo opened his eyes wider when Miriam appeared. "I have never seen hair so red."

"Miriam, this is Don Pablo, Doctor. Isaac's friend. Bring him a bowl of hot soup, for he is still shivering from the cold, and bread and cheese. Prepare a bed in the unused room on the fourth floor. He will be our guest for as long as he wishes."

"Si, Señora." The girl curtsied and left.

"She cannot be Spanish or Portuguese with such hair."

"She is from Poland, Pablo. A long story."

"So here you are in Amsterdam at last, physician, husband, and father."

"And what brings you here? The Holy Office?"

"Arce is relentless. He has expunged every document where your name is mentioned. Your defection to the Jews has been a great embarrassment to the Church and *la Corte*. They have tried to erase all memory of your existence in Spain."

"That explains why they never excommunicated me or paraded my effigy at any of their *autos de fé* and burned it at the *quemadero*."

"They prefer to create the lie you never existed."

"You may be right. To include me in one of their shows would embarrass Crown, Church, and all presumed *limpio* de Rocamoras."

"I regret to tell you that your and my blood enemies have triumphed in Valencia. Your family's *señorio* no longer exists. It has been given to an Angesola kin of Violante."

"But that violates all law. Benetorrente is entailed, and I made Juan de Rocamora my heir."

"Forgeries now exist to prove otherwise. Your kin the Dominican Tomás and Gaspar de Rocamora, who is now the Second Marqués de Rafal and a Familiar of the Inquisition, have joined the Holy Office in purging Valencia of your existence. I had no choice but to flee. There are rewards for denouncing and capturing all your associates and partisans. Also, you are being shown no less respect than Olivares himself. Did you ever see Velázquez' painting The Riding Academy?"

"Yes, Olivares was portrayed as one of the spectators watching Infante Baltazar Carlos on a horse."

"No longer. Velázquez painted over him as if he never existed."

"Olivares was too great a man to disappear from history. Is there any good news?"

"Juan has been made *maestro de campo de infanteria*."

"A field commander like his father. Has he married?"

"Very well. A daughter of the powerful Cascante family."

Rocamora explained for Abigail the family connections in Orihuela, careful to omit the crimes of Rafal's depraved eldest son Jacinto.

"Juan is likely to be the third Marqués de Rafal. Orihuela was decimated by fever, which took the lives of Gaspar's children. I have other interesting news from Spain. King Philip will wed the late Empress María's daughter, his niece, María Anna."

Rocamora calculated. Philip was forty-three and the princess but fourteen. "The unfortunate child."

"Have you heard how the king reacted when he discovered his future bride has no legs?"

Abigail gasped. "Is that true?"

"*Querida*, I suspect it may be another instance of Habsburg *punctilio*, their court etiquette taken to the extreme."

"What Vicente says is true, Doña Abigail. During her journey from Austria last year, María Anna arrived at a town near Barcelona renowned for its rare and near priceless silk gloves and stockings. The magistrates gifted their future queen with pairs of gloves. The leader of the royal entourage accepted them on María Anna's behalf, but when they presented her with several pair of silk stockings, he flung them away because they had made an error of *lèse majesté*. When he said, 'Know, that a Queen of Spain has no legs,' María Anna burst into tears and pleaded to be taken back to Austria. Because she had no understanding of Spanish Habsburg punctilio, she believed they would amputate her legs. It is said King Philip never laughed so heartily when he heard the story."

Rocamora doubted the latter part of story was true. During his twenty-two years at the Alcazar, he had never seen Philip laugh, and the King's smiles came as seldom as a cool breeze during a Madrid summer.

After Miriam served Pablo soup, bread and cheeses, Abigail gave Moses to the girl and stood. The men also rose.

"I shall leave the two of you alone to talk. Moses is asleep now, and I wish to put him to bed. Don Pablo, I am pleased to have met you, and I welcome you to our home."

"You are very kind, Doña Abigail, and I thank you for your warm reception."

Rocamora kissed his wife and son. "Sleep well, *querida*, and you my strong, handsome Moses."

41.
Old Times, New Decisions

Rocamora took Pablo to his study. They sat by the fire with a bottle of brandy and two glasses on a small mahogany table between them.

Pablo flinched when Hombrecillo leaped onto Rocamora's lap, curled into a comfortable position, and purred. "What is this creature?"

Rocamora lit his pipe and stroked the cat. "He adopted me when he was a kitten. I named him Hombrecillo."

"For your good friend at the Alcazar."

"Yes." Rocamora touched glasses with Pablo. "I cannot begin to express my surprise and delight to be with you again, old friend."

"I worried I might not find you even though I heard rumors that you had gone to Amsterdam and became a Jew. I never imagined I would find you a settled married man wearing *quevedos* and dressed as any burgher. I remembered you always in Dominican robes and your disguises. You must tell me everything that happened to you these past seven years."

"A few days after you and I parted in Madrid, Queen Isabel warned me to leave Spain. If I did not, my rivals in the Holy Office would either have taken my life or tossed me into some dungeon to rot."

Rocamora described his escape from Spain, the time he spent in Roquemaure where he discovered the Jewish origins of his family, and his arrival in Amsterdam.

Pablo interrupted horrified. "You circumcised yourself?"

Rocamora explained the reasons why and related all that transpired afterward until Pablo's arrival. By the time he finished, they had drunk half the bottle of brandy.

"You have married well, Vicente. Abigail is a fine woman."

"The last and greatest of my three loves, as predicted by your sister."

"I still mourn Moraíma and my niece, Philippa."

"As do I, and so many others. Now, it is your turn. You must tell me about your adventures these past seven years."

"After we saw each other last, I returned to Valencia and organized the last survivors of Don Lope's band."

Pablo entertained Rocamora with his life of banditry, debasing of coinage, cheating at games, and raiding local *señorios* for food and valuables. At the same time, Gaspar de Rocamora became obsessed to avenge what Pablo and Rocamora had done to his brother Jacinto. He organized a posse and chased Pablo from Valencia to Alicante, the forests and mountains around Elx, and beyond Orihuela to Murcia. A Familiar of the Inquisition, Gaspar had the added support of the Holy Office.

"He vowed to send you my head. I heard too many rumors you had gone to Amsterdam to disbelieve them. Tired of running, I decided to do the deed myself and bring my head to you, attached to my body of course."

"A surgeon could not have done a better job sewing."

Laughing and weeping, they spent the rest of the night reminiscing about their past, from their childhood to the night they arranged a fitting end for Jacinto.

"Tell me, Vicente, how is it to live a life without fear of the Inquisition?"

"Freedom from fear of denunciation and imprisonment is a most exhilarating experience, but Judaism has its annoying restrictions."

Pablo listened amused to Rocamora's description of the congregation's rituals and customs. "And have the Jews truly converted you, Vicente?"

"No more than the Catholics did." Rocamora was well aware that Pablo refused to call him Isaac and decided not to correct his friend. Vicente was still and always would be how he called himself, thought of himself. "And now, *amigo*, tell me. What are you plans?"

"Nothing specific."

"You are a resourceful rogue. You can make a life with a new family in the Dutch Republic as I have done."

"I would prefer to find a way to make my wealth first. I have heard that they pay well here in Amsterdam for jewels and spices."

"That is true, and I am acquainted with several merchants and many ship's captains."

"Still a dock rat like the boys we were?"

"El Grau, Barcelona, and Amsterdam, they are all the same."

"Vicente, tell me the truth, Are you truly happy and content here in Amsterdam?"

"I often yearn for melons and the sight of palm and cypress. But yes, I am happy and content. I have found the love of my life in Abigail and my true calling as a physician. And as I told you, I live without fear of denunciation and arrest by the Holy Office and far away from the blood feuds of Valencia. That is worth more than all the melons, cypress, and palms in the world."

"I think some of our best times were at *el Paraíso* in Madrid."

"Yes, it was a paradise. Pablo I mean it. I want you to settle here in Amsterdam."

Pablo listened to Rocamora's suggestion for a business. "That would take many more escudos than I have or whatever they call your money for me to succeed, and I fear I may never learn the harsh infernal language of the Dutch."

"You are as good at tongues as I. How much wealth did you bring with you?"

"Outside the city, I buried about five hundred escudos."

"You must retrieve them immediately. The entire land is prone to flooding."

"Then where can I hide my coins?"

Rocamora explained the workings of the Wisselbank "There they will be safe from theft, or you can risk them all at the Bourse, the one place where you can become wealthy in a short moment or penurious."

"Gambling?"

"Remember, you and I never gambled. We either cheated at cards or wagered on sure outcomes. Pablo, the Bourse is more like pirating. A friend of mine, whom you will meet, says it is better to let your money work for you than to work for it. You may purchase shares in a voyage for as low as one sixty-fourth of an enterprise's value. Some speculators will buy and sell paper obligations before the ship leaves and do the same when they receive news in advance of any ship's arrival. Trading in the wind, they call it. It is a skill, a diabolical gift, to know when to buy low and sell high."

"Do you play that game, *amigo*?"

"Small amounts only when I have inside information."

Pablo laughed again. "It is good to know you have not changed completely."

Abigail entered and smiled at the empty bottle of brandy. "Good morning, *mi Capitán*, Don Pablo. Did you know it is already past six?"

Both men rose, and Rocamora kissed Abigail. "Good morning, mi querida. Forgive me. The hours passed as minutes."

"I understand." Abigail touched the skin below Rocamora's eyes. "When will you sleep?"

"There is much to do this morning. We can siesta after we return home for our midday meal."

"I charge you with the responsibility to see that he does, Don Pablo. Now, come with me. I have prepared your breakfast." Abigail took their hands and brought them into the eating kitchen. Moses sat in his baby's chair. Miriam stood at the table ready to serve a hearty meal of bread, cheese, and savory eggs scrambled with onions and spices

Rocamora encouraged Pablo to sit. "We have an array of teas for you to choose, but no beer."

"Beer? Who drinks beer in the morning?"

"You shall soon see, my friend."

42.
A Business Plan for Pablo

"It is but nine in the morning. Do the Dutch drink beer all day and night?"

At the table he shared with Pablo in *The Three Crows*, Rocamora lit his pipe and touched *flapkans* with him. "Yes, even their women and children."

"Astonishing, and you say this is the best tavern in Amsterdam?"

"Without question."

"It cannot begin to compare with *el Paraíso*."

"That is why I brought you here first. Ah, here he is now." Rocamora waved Velde to their table. "Jacobus, meet my childhood friend who arrived from Spain yesterday, Don Pablo de Royaya. Pablo, Jacobus Velde is one of the finest surgeons in the United Provinces."

"A pleasure to meet any friend of Isaacus, Don Pablo." Velde ordered a single beer, sausages, and waffles. "Are you going to reside here in Amsterdam?"

Rocamora answered for Pablo. "My friend does not understand Dutch, but he knows what I have to discuss with you. Pablo, show Jacobus the drawing you made this morning."

Velde took the paper. "It is a floor plan of a house, a very large house. Has he brought a shipload of escudos from Spain to build it?"

"Jacobus, This is no mere house. Remember when you wanted to invest in the expansion of this tavern?"

"And you advised me not to, for which I am eternally grateful."

"I have a better investment for you now if you are so inclined."

Velde listened wide-eyed and speechless to Rocamora's description of *el Paraíso*, the grand casino and theater Pablo and Yusef owned in Madrid. "So fabulous an establishment would be costly to replicate here in Amsterdam, but if it can be done, I would willingly purchase shares if you so advised and if the major investors were trustworthy."

"I know of at least one we shall be approaching whose word is as unimpeachable as that of the Wisselbank."

Velde returned the drawing to Pablo. "Then keep me informed of the progress, Isaacus. Now, please, tell me in more detail about the gambling and women of *el Paraíso*."

Later that morning, Santcroos sat with Rocamora and Pablo in his office at the warehouse, studied the drawing, and spoke Spanish. "*El Paraíso*. I visited there in my youth when I went to Madrid on business. I never forgot a woman who sang and danced there. She was deservedly celebrated as *la Hermosura*."

"Moraíma. She was my sister, may she rest in peace."

"My condolences."

"I followed Vicente's suggestion, and in this sketch, I replaced the theater with a bath house."

Santcroos returned his attention to the drawing. "Amsterdam has nothing like it. This would be a costly enterprise to build or if we were to remodel an existing structure expensive to maintain as well. Also, the Amsterdam statutes require that the owners be citizens, preferably a magistrate amongst them."

"I can accept partners if they are trustworthy. Vicente has praised your honesty, Don Samuel. How many guilders would we need?"

"Tens of thousands. How many do you have to invest?"

"Five hundred escudos."

"Not nearly enough to become an equal partner in your own enterprise."

"We thought Pablo might sail on one of your ships, find wealth and booty overseas, and return here to sell whatever he can for a considerable profit."

"Your experience?"

"I have many skills to which Vicente can attest."

"Don Samuel, I can assure you that Pablo is one of the most resourceful of men you will ever meet. I am confident he will come back with riches."

"Or I shall not return." Pablo pointed at a map of the world that covered one wall of Santcroos' office. "What do those pins represent?"

"Each red-topped pin is at a port where we trade. Each blue-topped pin represents a ship of the East and West India Companies. To which port would you sail?"

"Wherever I can find or steal precious gems, gold, coral, and rare spices."

Santcroos swept his hand across a line of islands to Malaya, Siam, and Burma. "The East Indies."

"A long journey to places unfamiliar. I may be away for several years."

"Yes, Don Pablo, but that will give me time to arrange the partnership, find the best property, and begin construction. I believe an establishment similar to *el Paraíso* with a bathhouse can be a profitable business. Because you are my good friend's friend and he vouches for you, I shall offer two propositions even if you lack sufficient funds to invest. I can guarantee that at the very least you will manage the establishment and be a minor partner. If you return with riches, I will sell you enough shares to be a full financial partner. Do you agree?"

"That seems fair enough."

"Good. When can you leave?"

"I will be delighted to escape your Amsterdam winter as soon as possible."

"One of my ships sails for the Indies in two weeks." Santcroos thought for a moment. "You said if you did not bring back wealth, you would not return."

"I did."

"That is an investment with the greatest risk of all. Your five hundred gold pieces are nothing compared to your life."

"Then what shall I do with them?"

"Since you are risking your life on a voyage to the Indies, why should you not also wager all your escudos on its success?"

"Of course. If I do not return, the financial loss will not affect the condition of my corpse. Will you also invest, Vicente?"

"Because it is you, my indestructible friend, I shall."

Santcroos shook Pablo's hand. "Upon your return, you shall be a partner and manage the establishment. Is that agreeable to you?"

"It is."

"And, our mutual friend Don Isaac is our witness. Now, have you any ideas about furnishing the interior?"

"I have. I thought …."

Miriam appeared at the door breathing heavily, her face red as her hair. "Doctor, Doña Abigail has gone into labor."

"You left my wife alone?"

"Her aunts are visiting, and they sent for a midwife."

By the time Rocamora and Pablo returned home, Abigail had given birth to a healthy boy with no complications. Eight days later on the twenty-seventh of January 1650, Vicente sat at her bedside after their last guest left. He touched the tiny fingers of their second son secure and sleeping in the crook of her arm after the ordeal of his *berit milah*.

He kissed Abigail. "*Mi querida,* I thank you for giving us two healthy boys."

"May God grant us a daughter next time."

"Yes, I would like that, a lovely girl exactly like her mother, whom I love with all my heart. No Madonna has ever been painted or sculpted to equal your beauty."

"Can you not make a comparison with a woman of our *nação*, *Capitán*?"

Rocamora adored Abigail's wry wit. "Miriam, whom the Christians worship as Mary, was a Jew to the day she died. Were they of Israel, I would praise your loveliness as being beyond that of Aphrodite, Helen of Troy, and Delilah. Still, it may be best to compare you with Judith who slew Holofernes, for in truth like the Assyrian general I have lost my head over you. Your wisdom and courage are greater than Judge Deborah's. Had you been married to another, I would have been David to your Bathsheba and rid you of your husband. Were I King Solomon, I would have no other wife and no concubines."

"You are *mi Capitán*. That is enough for me. Look our Moses is restless. Please bring him to me."

Rocamora kissed Abigail and went to the far end of the great Hall where Moses cried despite the attention Miriam and Pablo gave him. The moment he saw his father, he stopped bawling. "*Abba.*"

Pleased his firstborn had learned the Hebrew name for father, Rocamora lifted his son and carried him to the bed. "Moses, your brother has been named Solomon."

"Sowmon ...."

"Sol-o-mon. You shall be Solomon's protector and best friend, and he will be loyal to you. Kiss your brother and love him."

Moses kissed Solomon's forehead, and Abigail stroked their eldest's cheek. "My handsome Moses, my precious firstborn, I love you, and we shall love Solomon."

Rocamora led Moses from the bed. "You did well, my son. Miriam, give Moses sweets to celebrate the *berit milah* of his brother."

Pablo took Rocamora aside. "Do babies always scream like cats mating when they are circumcised?"

"Yes, but their crying stops when they are unbound and returned to their mother's arms."

"Then tell me if you can, *amigo*, how you endured the pain when you operated on yourself."

"With much difficulty and too little wine, but I did not cry out. And you, my Morisco friend, will you honor your forebears and do the same in the East Indies, for Islam is the dominant religion there."

"If it is better when making love I might consider it."

Rocamora glanced toward Abigail. "It is always the woman who makes it better or worse."

43.
Discontent

Early in February 1650, Rocamora waited on the docks with Pablo before he boarded a caravel bound for the East Indies. "I wish you were not leaving so soon."

"I have a restless spirit and these northern cities and climes are too cold and gloomy for this Valencian."

"That, I understand all too well. You have the list of herbs, spices, and opiates I require?"

"On paper." Pablo touched his temple. "And here. Will the inn and bath house be completed upon my return?"

"That depends upon how long you will be away. The design you and Santcroos agreed upon is unique. It will be the talk of the entire United Provinces and beyond."

"Something has puzzled me for years, and now that you are a physician, can you tell me why I recovered from the fever when my sister and her child did not?"

"I have given much thought to that and why I never succumbed as well. From my experience, observation, and the collective wisdom of medical science, no answer explains why anyone survives fevers and plagues. It may be the gift of a strong constitution, personal cleanliness, or the use of tobacco. It could be the same blind luck I have seen on the battlefield when men are killed or maimed and others beside them survive. Perhaps one day science will have the answer."

"Good fortune is preferable to brains in any endeavor, it seems."

"I cannot argue against that. May the Lady Fortune favor you."

They embraced, and Pablo gathered his belongings. "*Amigo,* I expect to see more children when I return. It seems Catholics become celibate priests, and Jews breed children."

"You Moriscos spread your seed no less. May your Allah provide you with your seventy-two virgins in the Indies while you live."

"That could be the death of me."

Santcroos joined them. "Again, let me wish you a safe and prosperous voyage, Don Pablo."

"I shall not disappoint you."

After Pablo's ship sailed, Santcroos walked with Rocamora to his warehouse. "This morning I received reports from Spain that will interest you. One is in regards to Royal Physician Fernando Cardoso. Did you not tell me he strongly supported your candidacy to become Inquisitor General?"

"Until he anticipated the fall of Olivares and joined the reactionaries."

"Apparently that did him no good. Cardoso has fled Spain and reappeared in the Venice ghetto where he submitted to circumcision and took the name Isaac."

"Cardoso came from a Portuguese new-Christian family. I always suspected he was a Judaizer."

Santcroos stopped in front of his warehouse. "There is more. Familiars of the Portuguese Inquisition in Lisbon arrested and jailed another of your former allies, the gifted man of letters Fernández de Villareal."

"He returned to Portugal? Why could he not have stayed in Paris as the Portuguese Counsel where he was a respected member of the literati and praised for his biography of Richelieu?"

"Perhaps it was an irresistible yearning for his native land that caused Villareal to return. It happens to many who come to Amsterdam."

"Did your report say how and why he was denounced?

"Spies of the Holy Office intercepted a letter Menasseh sent him. No other details were given to me. I am sorry, Isaac."

Menasseh, what have you done?

Rocamora decided to speak to the rabbi about the letter that most certainly would cost Fernández de Villareal his life but changed his mind by the time he reached the synagogue. Nothing he could say to Menasseh would undo the damage done to Villareal, and he did not want to increase the rabbi's burden of guilt for his gaffe.

He found Menasseh on the steps of Talmud Torah arguing with three men who glowered when they saw him. Bent elderly Abraham da Mexia had wanted to marry Abigail. Mexia's punctilious cousin, Dr. Ephraim da Bueno, continued to be suspicious of him because he had been a Dominican. Their kinsman, recent arrival Benjamin da Ferrar, a poor and prideful boaster, affected a *hidalguía* he most certainly never had in Spain and toadied to the other two because of their wealth and prominence in the community.

Menasseh greeted Rocamora. "Doctor Isaac, perhaps you can offer your wisdom on a subject we have been discussing."

Rocamora ignored the trio. "If I can, Rabbi."

"Today, the Council will be taking under advisement decrees against giving alms to Ashkenazi beggars and that Sephardim who marry outside our community shall no longer be buried in Ouderkerk. As you probably know, they have already forced David de Almeida to apologize to the congregation because he bought a chicken from one of their *schochets,* ritual chicken slaughterers."

"How petty. Do their butchers observe the Laws of *Kashrut* any less than ours?"

"Then you would not vote the same were you a member of the *Ma'amad*?"

"No, Rabbi, but I am not likely to serve on the Council."

Mexia forced a scornful snort. "You have never spoken truer words. I say we cut off the Ashkenazim completely from our congregation and community. All of us have seen their outlandish costumes. Tall hats, greasy cloaks, tunics of old sacks tied with ropes, faces covered with moth eaten mufflers up to eyes, feet encased in rags, women in tattered shawls with ugly wigs like witches, pale children of skin and bones."

"Which is why we must help them." Rocamora had treated several Ashkenazim gratis as required by the Hippocratic Oath he had sworn to uphold and his conscience demanded.

"Well, there is a positive side to their infestation," Mexia said. "The refugees are willing to work cheaply as our servants provided one can tolerate their smell."

More congregants joined them, and Ferrar strutted before them. "The Ashkenazim are not like us. We have superior manners."

Other men spoke:

"We blend with our Dutch hosts except for religion, whereas they are peasants, fanatics, ignorant, dirty, and destitute."

"And more thousands are coming."

"God forbid our daughters and sons should marry one of theirs."

"Mine would be dead to me."

Rocamora heard enough, and his powerful voice silenced all. "Sephardim are Jews. Ashkenazim are Jews. Inferior in wealth, education, and status they may be, repugnant to many, their rabbis and congregants never left their faith, unlike the Sephardim in Spain and Portugal. And our rabbis go to theirs for interpretations of scripture and ritual."

Ferrar faced him. "You are fortunate you have been accepted by our congregation considering your suspect ancestry."

"Suspect?" Rocamora removed a glove and slapped Ferrar's cheek with such force the young man fell onto the steps. "Pretentious dog, I will fight you here and now, any time and place. Choose your weapon."

Ferrar rubbed his cheek "He is mad."

"Stop whining. Stand and face me like a man. If you fail to fight, I shall publicly horsewhip you up and down the Breestraat and brand you the cowardly cur you are. Honor must be satisfied."

Mexia and Bueno helped Ferrar to his feet, and Menasseh stepped between them and Rocamora. "Don Benjamin, you must apologize to the esteemed Doctor Isaac." When Mexia and Bueno protested, the rabbi raised his voice. "If he does not apologize here and now to one of our most illustrious congregants, I shall bring him before the *Ma'amad*. We cannot allow dueling. We do not want the Dutch authorities involved."

Ferrar stiffened. "I spoke in haste without thinking, Doctor Isaac. Please accept my apology."

"I do so only to spare our community trouble from the magistrates." Rocamora fixed his eyes upon Mexia first and next Bueno. "Listen to me carefully. Each one of you. The next man who insults me or my family will have spoken those words with his last breath."

Menasseh took Rocamora aside. "Don Isaac, you know I wish you the best and have done everything possible to sponsor you. I married you and Doña Abigail. I led prayers at the *berit milah* of your sons. Please listen to what I have to say. Everybody knows you seldom come to pray here."

"Enough, Rabbi. I will not accept any lecture regarding my behavior, even from you whom I hold in the highest regard. Before I say more, I bid you good day."

Still furious when he reached the bridge, his mood became night dark. Their false *hidalguía*, their spying, their messianism, and the annoying external demands of ritual were becoming more impossible each day.

Early in February, Rocamora met with Reverend Wachtendorpius, a member of the Amsterdam Church Council, in the minister's austere rectory in the Nieuwe Kerk adjacent to the construction of the new Town Hall begun in 1648.

"To answer your question, Reverend, I have come to you because I am unable to accept Talmudic Judaism and its millennial fantasies. My inclination is to join your Reformist religion. Of course, I cannot allow my situation to be discovered by anyone, especially my wife, until I come to a final decision."

"I understand your dilemma, Doctor Isaacus, but you must consider my position. Your inner conflict may be sincere, but you should know that many of your Spanish brothers and sisters come to us for the generous charities we offer because they are impecunious and not because they see the true light. Such men and women have betrayed the Amsterdam Church Council in its missionary spirit many times. That is why, regarding your case, I cannot accept you so easily."

"Why not if I give you my word?"

"You have been a Dominican royal confessor, preacher at *autos de fé* and at the burning stakes. You persecuted Protestants. Then you accepted the Jewish faith. Now you wish to convert to ours. I do not understand how one can change his faith so easily, as if merely donning a change of clothes."

"What can I do to convince you of my sincerity?"

"First, you must repent wholeheartedly of your horrible apostasies by showing this in fact. Before we can accept you, you must leave Judaism openly and declare your belief in Jesus Christ as Savior and Son of God."

Which I did so often in Spain.

"Reverend, I am not prepared to do so this day. I need to learn more about the requirements of your faith and prepare my family."

"We can meet as often as you like until you decide."

During the next several months, Rocamora vacillated between converting to the Protestant faith and staying with the Iberian community and congregation. Each time he looked at Abigail, he doubted he could follow through with his intention to join the Dutch Reformed Church. If he did, it would destroy her. Abigail was devout in her Judaism. She attended synagogue regularly and observed all holidays and Holy Days. She recited the *Shemah* each night before retiring. Each day, she sang the Hebrew alphabet to Moses and Solomon.

In May 1650 after many meetings with Wachtendorpius and discussions with Velde, both of whom kept their promises to be discreet, Rocamora came to an irrevocable decision. To avoid offending Wachtendorpius, he shaded the truth.

"Reverend, as you know, my family and I would be ostracized by the Jewish community should I convert. My patients would abandon me. I must know if your church will support us if I make a clean break from the congregation."

"As I have explained, you must make that break and repent publicly before our Council agrees to your request. If you do so with convincing sincerity, you can be assured that God, the Lord, shall not leave you and your family uncared for."

"You cannot guarantee financial support for me and my family this day?"

"I cannot. I shall await your decision and so write to the Assembly."

That was what Rocamora expected to hear. He thanked Wachtendorpius and left the rectory with his mind no longer cluttered with vacillation. His love for Abigail and his sons was too strong. For them, he must conform more to the external rituals required by the congregation.

44.
A Surprise in the Attic

Stadhouder Willem II and his army approached Amsterdam, and Rocamora stood with Velde in Dam Square amidst a crowd of armed citizens outside the Town Hall. He carried a satchel filled with medicines and salves. Velde's bag contained his surgical tools and bandages. The city prepared for a siege, and they had volunteered to aid the wounded.

Inside the Town Hall, Willem's emissaries conferred with the City Council in a final effort to prevent battle, and Rocamora thought about the roots of the conflict that began the previous year after Parliament beheaded Charles I, the *Stadhouder's* father in law. Bellicose Willem II failed to obtain a declaration of war against England and permission to continue the struggle against Spain despite the Treaty of Münster. Preferring peace and prosperity to war, the provincial governments further enraged the *Stadhouder* by reducing military spending, disbanding part of the army, and refusing to pay the full amount of wages they had promised the soldiers.

Loyal to his troops, Willem sent a delegation to the principal cities of each province to negotiate for the payments. After they refused to meet with his representatives, the *Stadhouder* decided to attack Amsterdam and make it an example.

Rocamora saw Santcroos and several major shareholders of the Dutch East India Company emerge from the Town Hall and linger in front. "Look, Jacobus, they are smiling."

"But not those Members of the City Council who followed. See how grim their expressions are. What is going on? Is it peace or a siege?"

Rocamora recognized two men who joined the others on the steps. "It will be peace, Jacobus. There is my friend, Dirck van Noordwijk, one of the *Stadhouder's* delegates, and he is with a patient of mine."

"I recognize him too, Jan van der Waag, whose father is a magistrate."

"And like Santcroos, they too are smiling."

Moments later, town clerks posted bulletins confirming there would be no siege. The crowd in Dam Square cheered and dispersed to celebrate the peace. Bells rang from the Town Hall, Nieuwe Kerk, the Waag, and from churches throughout the city. Concerned the clanging would alarm Abigail, Rocamora declined Velde's offer to celebrate in a tavern and hurried home.

He searched for his wife and children in the kitchen, great hall, and the parlor, Miriam too, but the girl was not in her room. Rocamora heard voices coming from the attic above and hesitated at the top of the stairs astonished when he saw Abigail, her back to him, teaching two year old Moses numbers in Portuguese and Miriam holding nine-month-old Solomon.

The attic had been transformed from a dark empty space to a cheerful classroom, one wall a bright yellow, another a pale blue. Sheets of paper had been attached to them, each with hand drawn numbers, the Hebrew, Spanish and Portuguese alphabets, and maps of Europe and the world. Maps were expensive, and Rocamora could well imagine Abigail's relentless bargaining with the mapmaker until he met his wife's price.

Moses sat in one of four small chairs at a child's table. Rocamora applauded when Abigail pointed at a number and his firstborn responded correctly. He noted how nine-month-old Solomon also seemed to be paying attention to the lesson.

Moses saw Rocamora, left his chair, and ran to him. "*Abba*."

Abigail turned to Rocamora. "You are home at last, *mi Capitán*, but those bells and the commotion outside ... is Prince Willem's army so near?"

"Do not be alarmed. The bells are not a call to battle. They are celebratory." Rocamora tousled Moses' curls when the boy clung to his leg. "There will be no siege. The City Council resigned en masse, and the new government has agreed to the *Stadhouder's* terms. His soldiers will be paid. My patient, Jan van der Waag, replaced his father as a magistrate, so I doubt if there will be any significant change in the city's government."

"Then all is normal again."

"Not all. You have done all this without my knowing."

"The furniture arrived this morning, and I wanted to surprise you."

"You left me speechless, mi querida. You created these charts?"

"I did, and Miriam helped me paint the walls."

"You have a fine artistic hand. I can imagine how well you bargained for the maps and furniture."

"*Mi Capitán*, shopkeepers tremble whenever I enter their stores. I am pleased to say our Moses is a quick learner. So is Miriam. I found Dutch and English grammars for her. She says those languages are similar to German."

"Indeed they are." Rocamora tickled Solomon. "I believe he too is learning. When they are older, we will need to purchase books for them."

Abigail led Rocamora to an open trunk filled with books in the recess of the attic. "I could not resist several bargains."

Rocamora embraced her. "You are the most amazing woman I have known, the best mother, and my great love. I cannot imagine life without you."

45.
"The Worst of all Harpies"

An enemy more powerful than Willem II attacked Amsterdam, small pox, which the Dutch called, *de vreselijkste aller harpije*, the worst of all harpies. Rocamora appreciated the metaphor of the vicious beasts of Greek mythology that came with the west wind and brought unbearable suffering and death. The disease infected Willem and his army while they were still in the field and spread rapidly throughout the provinces.

To prevent further smallpox contagion within his patients' families, Rocamora offered remedies proven efficacious by the Indians and Chinese: rubbing pus from a smallpox victim into the healthy family members' skin lesions, or blowing powdered smallpox scabs into their noses. If the treatment brought on a mild case of the disease, the patient might become immune to its worst effects. Most families Rocamora treated gave their consent so great was their trust in his skills and knowledge.

"Are you ill, Dirck?"

Van Noordwijk arrived at Rocamora's home disheveled and in a state of distress. "Better I were dead. I buried my wife and son. They fell to smallpox."

Abigail invited van Noordwijk to sit at the dining table. "We grieve with you."

"It happened while I was away." Van Noordwijk regained his composure. "Please forgive my lack of manners, Doña Abigail. I have come for your husband. Our *Stadhouder* has not left his bed since August, and we fear he is close to death."

"I am sorry to hear he is so ill, but surely Prince Willem is attended by the best physicians. What can I possibly do that they have not?"

"Another opinion is always welcome, and it is well reported that more of your patients so afflicted have a better chance of survival." Van Noordwijk emptied his glass of wine in one swallow. "There is another reason why you are needed at the palace. Princess Mary is with child. If she loses the baby due to shock and stress, we would have no heir to the *Stadhouderate*. I trust you above all other physicians to attend her."

"My Abigail is also with child."

"I congratulate you."

Rocamora refilled van Noordwijk's glass. "When is Princess Mary's baby due?"

"Mid-November. Isaacus, I would not have come to you had she not remembered your kind comments about her father, King Charles when you appeared before Frederick Hendrick and his family. She also appreciated the condolences you sent after Parliament executed the Martyr King."

"You mentioned my name to her?"

"Yes. She is looking forward to seeing you and hearing more anecdotes about her father."

"November, you said. That means I shall be away from my family for several weeks at best. I would prefer not to leave them alone for so long a period."

Abigail waited until Miriam served van Noordwijk a warm plate of fresh fish and vegetables on a bed of seasoned rice. "*Mi Capitán*, you must go to Princess Mary. I am not due for another five months, and she needs you now."

During their ride to The Hague, Rocamora listened to van Noordwijk's laments over his great loss. "But you are still young, Dirck. Time is a great healer of grief. Surely you will wed again and have more children."

"That is what my family says, but I know I can never again feel the love, the strong love I had and still have for my beloved Arabella and my son, may they rest in peace."

"Dirck, let me assure you that I too have loved and lost others and believed I would never find happiness again. Yet, fortune smiled upon me and brought Abigail into my life. I have loved no one more than my wife and sons."

"You give me hope, my friend, but I do not foresee myself so fortunate as you."

Rocamora thought it best to change the conversation away from death to a subject more light and trivial. "Is a clean shaven face the latest fashion at court?"

Van Noordwijk touched his cheek. "Another fad we have borrowed from the French."

Rocamora thought of Velde. "A good business for barber-surgeons." *Because of the Law of Moses, that fashion will never be received in Vlooienburg.*

The following day, Rocamora and van Noordwijk arrived at the *Stadhouder's* palace in The Hague. They went directly to the bedside of Prince

Willem who slept. Pox pustules covered his face and body. The *Stadhouder* would not survive the week.

Van Noordwijk next escorted Rocamora to Princess Mary's chambers. "So young a life, so short a reign, a mere three years. I pray the child will be a boy. Regardless, difficult times lie ahead. Should Prince Willem die, there will be a struggle to become regent between widow and mother-in-law, and the Republicans will plot to abolish the office of *Stadhouderate* for all time."

Dressed in black, Princess Amalia approached them with a stern expression the moment they entered Princess Mary's apartments. "What is this intrusion?"

"Madame, you remember Dr. Isaacus de Rocamora. He was acquainted with King Charles, and I thought Princess Mary might be distracted by his ability to calm her during these terrible days with stories of her father, the King-Martyr."

"Yes, I remember. Doctor, will you talk some sense into that stubborn woman?"

Rocamora listened patiently to Amalia's complaining. Princess Mary wanted to name her child, if a boy, Charles after her father and brother. Amalia insisted on the name Willem, which, she believed, would help lay the foundation for her grandson to become the next *Stadhouder*.

"Colonel Van Noordwijk, we are all too aware that in a moment of weakness, the *Stadhouder* appointed his wife to be his son's guardian. Fortunately, he has not yet signed the document. We must prevent him from doing so when he is conscious, lucid or not. Doctor, have you seen my son, Prince Willem?"

"I have, Madame."

"And your diagnosis?"

"It is not what you wish to hear. He is close to death. Nothing more can be done for him."

"As I feared. All right, you may now see the woman."

Rocamora's audience with Princess Mary was brief in her new brightly painted and furnished chambers of French influence. Arguments with her mother-in-law and worry over her husband's condition exhausted the Princess Royal, and their meeting lasted less than five minutes.

Van Noordwijk was waiting for him. "Our *Stadhouder*, Willem II, has succumbed."

Rocamora remembered not to cross himself. "May he rest in peace."

Rocamora attended Mary for longer periods when Amalia permitted and cheered the grieving princess with anecdotes about her father and Aunt Isabel, the late Queen of Spain. Evenings, he commiserated with van Noordwijk.

House of Rocamora

Eight days after her husband's death, on the fourteenth day of November 1650, the Princess Royal delivered a healthy male baby. Amalia had her way. Christened Willem, the infant was proclaimed Sovereign Prince of Orange-Nassau. As if she were Queen of the United Provinces, Amalia peremptorily dismissed Rocamora. He said farewell to Dirck and returned home.

46.
Reawakened Grief

With Miriam assisting at his side, Rocamora blocked Abigail's view of the stillborn lying on a table away from their bed, washed and covered with a linen cloth, its placenta and umbilical cord in a bucket. He modulated his voice to a soothing tone and spoke as physician to a patient. "Drink this *calmante*. It will help you sleep"

"Where are Solomon and Moses?"

"In the attic schoolroom. You know what must be done, *mi querida*."

Abigail nodded she did. In Vlooienburg, several of her relations and Rocamora's patients had given birth to dead fetuses or babies who had not lived past the thirtieth day. Under *Halakha*, collective Jewish Law, they were called *nefels*, and the *Hebra Kaddisha*, Last Rites Committee, a volunteer group of righteous men and women of the congregation, immediately buried them in unmarked graves without ritual at the farthest edge of Ouderkerk. Abigail had served as a committee member, which was why she had not asked to hold or see it.

"Miriam, save your weeping for later but never in front of the boys. You did well. Now hurry to the synagogue and tell the *Shamash*, our sexton, to notify the Last Rites Committee. If you encounter any of the Touros, tell them they may visit tomorrow."

Rocamora sat beside Abigail. Exhausted from giving birth and feeling the effects of the *calmante,* she fell asleep.

"Doctor Isaac, the Last Rights Committee is here."

He closed the curtains around their bed and greeted the committee members who brought with them a tiny plain wood coffin. They worked swiftly and left within a few minutes of their arrival.

Rocamora went to the attic. The boys ran to him. He embraced confused and anxious four year old Moses and lifted two year old Solomon in his arms. "My sons, I am proud of you for being obedient."

"Is *Eemah* hurt?"

"No, Moses, she is well and sleeping now. You and Solomon must wait until morning to see her. Then you will learn what happened."

Night fell. Silence prevailed throughout the house. Rocamora drank brandy in his study illuminated by a full moon. He relaxed for the first time since Abigail went into labor. She had survived the ordeal in good health, but now the loss of a child brought forth unwanted painful memories.

The agonized screams of his beautiful daughter.

The horrors of those long hours watching helplessly while Brianda lost too much blood and suffered excruciating pain.

Brianda calling for him after giving birth to a fetus, blue and strangled by its umbilical cord.

Brianda dying in his arms having lived but a brief seventeen years.

Rocamora recalled each year he and Brianda had shared with the bright promise of so many more, now never to be fulfilled.

47.
Bento's Confession

Rocamora left a patient he treated for insomnia and walked toward Dam Square to read the latest bulletins posted at the Town Hall before going home for his midday meal. He moved slowly on crowded streets along canals filled with commercial sailing boats and smaller craft rowed by farmers and tradesmen. When Rocamora stopped at a stall to purchase a bouquet of roses for Abigail, a slight pale and handsome young man he recognized approached from the opposite direction.

"Doctor Isaac."

"Bento, what are you doing in this part of Amsterdam?"

"I have come from the home of Franciscus van den Enden who has been teaching me Latin. He has freed my mind as no one before. I would like to introduce you to him some day."

Rocamora had heard much about van den Enden from Menasseh and the rabbi's Christian friends. They spoke of the scholar, not always kindly, as one of the leading freethinkers in Amsterdam. After failing as a dealer in art, van den Enden opened a Latin school, which Bento attended regularly to the displeasure of his family and many in the Sephardic community.

"Doctor, may I walk and speak with you?"

"Of course, Bento, if you do not mind accompanying me to Dam Square."

"I believe you are the one man in Vlooienburg to whom I can reveal my thoughts and intentions."

Am I to don my Dominican's robe and play the role of confessor yet again?

"I am confiding in you, Doctor, because I have long suspected we share the same beliefs, beliefs that are not those of the congregation."

Rocamora withheld comment and listened to Bento's rant against the inflexible orthodoxy and messianism of the rabbis and his praise for the Mennonites and Collegiants, the latter the most anti-clerical sect of the Remonstrantors. The enthusiastic nineteen year old described how van den Enden taught more than Latin and introduced him to science and philosophy, including the writings of René Descartes.

"Doctor, I would not be surprised if you agree with Descartes' mind-body dualism, that the human body is a self-contained, entirely material machine composed of parts, and those parts are composed of smaller parts."

"One need not be a physician or surgeon to know that, for it is obvious to the eye."

"Not prayer, not Torah and Talmud, science alone can lead us to know what causes our body to malfunction and what can be done to repair it."

"We physicians do our best, Bento, but my observations lead me to believe the condition of the mind also can affect one's health."

"But no God or Supreme Being plays any role in that. All can be learned through science."

Rocamora believed young d'Espinoza would be happiest if he became a secular professor of philosophy at a respected university. "Bento, I have suggested before it is best you keep such thoughts to yourself."

"And you, Doctor, is that what you have been doing?" He did not wait for Rocamora to reply. "No rabbis, Franciscus van den Enden is my teacher now. Doctor, I trust you not to repeat what I have said and will say."

"You have my word."

"Although I am not yet ready to break from the community and congregation, I confess to you that I am a freethinker, and yes, one day I shall leave Talmud Torah and Vlooienburg, most likely after my father's death."

"Whatever you decide, Bento, consider most carefully the consequences."

"Excommunication? That superstitious ritual cannot hurt me if I choose to reject the congregation and community. Do not tell anyone yet, but van den Enden and other freethinkers call me by a name I now prefer, the Christian equivalent of my given name Baruch. Outside of Vlooienburg, I am Benedict Spinoza."

"Most of our Iberian brethren have several names, even I."

They arrived at Dam Square and joined a crowd standing before a bulletin freshly attached to a wall. It announced the Dutch *Hoge Raad*, Supreme Council, ruled that the guardianship of Willem III born the previous November would be shared by a triumvirate consisting of his mother Princess Royal Mary, his paternal grandmother Princess Amalia, and an uncle by marriage, Frederick William, Elector of Brandenburg. To counter the royals' influence over the future *Stadhouder*, the Estates General elected Jan de Witt to head the Republic with the title and powers of Grand Pensionary and to supervise Willem's education.

"This is a wonderful decision, Doctor. Now that de Witt and the republicans lead the United Provinces, they will initiate a period of true freedom of thought and religious tolerance. We will have a government without control by any religion, a state that offers education to all children and rejects slavery. Doctor Isaac, I thank you for listening to me and for your advice."

"Feel free to speak with me any time, Bento."

I listened, but he already decided which road to take before we spoke.

48.
Yèying

Pablo embraced Rocamora the moment he disembarked. "By the Prophet's beard, you are as grey as I."

"And you, my friend, you are fit and brown as a Turk."

Late summer of 1654, Pablo returned from his four and a half year voyage wearing aqua and gold silks with sash, turban, and jewel-encrusted scabbard for his scimitar, more flamboyant than even the pirate Gaspar Hendrijks. "Vicente, I was tempted to stay in a paradise worthy of a sultan. Instead, I have brought that paradise with me."

Santcroos, Velde, Magistrate Jan van der Waag also greeted Pablo. Other investors great and small ogled and commented on the goods Don Samuel's men unloaded and transported to his dockside warehouse supervised by his son David.

Rocamora imagined the excitement and chaos at the Bourse now that it had confirmation of the successful voyage. He heard more shouting from the expanding crowd when a dozen young Asian women in colorful native costumes disembarked.

Santcroos appraised them. "How lovely they are. So delicate."

"Pablo, I thought your Koran allowed for no more than four wives, you randy rogue."

"Not wives for me, Vicente. They will be serving our customers."

Rocamora frowned. "As prostitute slaves?"

"They are free to sell their favors or not. They have come here in search of husbands and a better life. Don Samuel, how is our enterprise progressing?"

"The gaming tables are ready for the adventurous, the bathhouse too, and the requisite magistrates bribed. Now that you have returned, I will have our men stock it with food and drink. After we add the furniture and decorations you have brought, we can open the doors. Before that, however, we must give it a fitting name."

Pablo gestured towards the women and goods still being unloaded. "I have an appropriate name, *The Fragrant Peony*."

Santcroos conferred with van der Waag, and the other major investors. "We agree. *The Fragrant Peony* it shall be. But who is that?"

A woman disembarked followed by men from the Indies carrying her trunks. A pretty female servant shaded her with a parasol. The woman wore silks of crimson and yellow decorated with colorful birds and flora, her expressionless features a mix of European and Asian, her manner authoritative, and her age indeterminate. Two muscular men wearing short sleeveless vests carried on their shoulders long poles bearing a palanquin, a sedan chair encased in a rosewood structure, its silk curtains decorated with images of Asian women.

Rocamora turned to Velde who stared wide-eyed at the woman. "Jacobus, I suggest you close your mouth before your chin drops to the dock. Who is she, Pablo, a princess you have claimed for yourself?"

"Her name is Yèyīng. Observe how she gestures with her fan and the servants obey."

"I have been told that Chinese names often have poetic meaning."

"Yes, *amigo*, and Yèyīng translates as Night Hawk. She will oversee the women, manage the gaming rooms, and deal cards at the tables where our prey wager the most."

"We agreed that you would manage *The Fragrant Peony*."

"And so I shall, Don Samuel, but I also intend to make more voyages to the East Indies. For there, the sun shines as it did in Valencia."

Yèyīng gestured again with her fan, and Vicente watched fascinated while the woman's servants helped her into the palanquin. The exotic woman was more imperious than any Habsburg, even María.

The following day Pablo arrived at Rocamora's home with two servants from the Indies carrying a rosewood trunk carved with exotic birds and flowers. Abigail was giving lessons in numbers to Moses and Solomon in the attic classroom, and Rocamora sent Miriam to summon them. In the great hall, he took Pablo to the bed and showed him an infant sleeping in a *rolkoets*.

"My third son, Joseph, born this past twenty-sixth of April." Rocamora did not tell Pablo about the stillborn boy and death of a daughter the previous year who lived four days.

Abigail, Miriam, and the boys came into the room, and the commotion awakened Joseph, who began to cry. Abigail swept him into her arms and cooed to calm him.

Pablo opened the trunk. "I brought these for you, Doña Abigail, and for my *amigo*." He gave Rocamora a padded robe of the finest silk from Shantung embroidered with fire breathing dragons and placed another on the bed.

Rocamora felt its weight. "They are exquisite and will keep us warm in the winter."

Abigail handed Joseph to Miriam. "Thank you, Pablo. It is a most thoughtful, elegant yet practical gift."

"I have more."

Abigail opened an ivory fan so all could admire the vivid flowers and birds in the silk. "This is so beautiful. Thank you again, Pablo."

"And Señorita Miriam, here is an ivory and silk fan for you and a coral necklace." Pablo laughed when Hombrecillo leaped into the trunk. "Your cat has chosen his own gift."

Abigail restrained their eldest son who was fascinated by Pablo's scimitar. "No, Moses, it is rude to touch other people's possessions."

"I do have something for the boys." He gave Moses a lacquered cup with a ball attached to its handle by a string. "The Portuguese sailors call this a *bilboquê,* the Spanish a *boliquê.* And for you, Solomon, this yo-yo is from the Philippines."

The boys laughed because the Spanish translation was I-I, and Rocamora prodded his sons. "Thank your *Tío* Pablo."

"Gracias," they said together.

Abigail told Moses and Solomon they could play with their gifts if they did well with their lessons, and she took them to the attic. Miriam returned Joseph to the *rolkoets* and left for the kitchen. Rocamora moved Hombrecillo from one side of the trunk to the other and inspected the herbs, spices, teas, and oils inside. "You have brought me a fortune in medicines."

"I wish I could have given you the entire cargo."

"Not the women though. One loving wife is all I need."

"Ay, *amigo,* marriage has tamed you."

"A wife whom I love above all else, three sons, and a thriving profession … not tamed, my friend, but a contentment I could never have achieved in Spain even though I do have moments when I yearn for our lost Fragrant Coast of Valencia."

"Speaking of which, Vicente, have you any significant news from Spain?"

"Fernández de Villareal died at the *quemadero* in Lisbon, and after the death of another erstwhile partisan, Cortizos de Villasante, Knight of Calatrava and royal financier, Familiars arrested his family and delivered them to the Inquisition. Cortizos' kin here in Amsterdam. revealed he had sent 600,000 escudos to the Wisselbank to live on if he ever fled Spain, which he should have. At least, Arce and the Holy Office failed to seize all his wealth. One more thing, my cousin Tomás de Rocamora, Viceroy and Bishop of Mallorca, died last year."

"May you outlive all your enemies."

"At least I am outbreeding them."

49.
The Fragrant Peony

Rocamora toured *The Fragrant Peony* with Pablo and Velde the day before it opened for business. It was not a replica of *el Paraíso*, no plays to be performed, no *la Hermosura*. Instead, the rooms and bathhouse provided an Asian fantasy of silks, satin, velvet, lush pillows, incense, and exotic women. Other houses of pleasure in Amsterdam required their women to stand outside and attract or seize the arms of potential customers, but *The Fragrant Peony* had something unique, a window where Madame Yèyīng's girls took turns lounging on divans in their native costumes. Two large and threatening men stood on either side to protect the glass.

Pablo brought Rocamora and Velde into a room containing several gaming tables and ornate Chinese screens along the walls. Yèyīng sat at one instructing two of her girls in dealing cards, throwing knucklebones, and manipulating individual beads for a game unfamiliar to the men.

Pablo introduced them to Madame Yèyīng, who did not respond. Rocamora thought her face resembled a porcelain mask, eyebrows shaved and marked with fine lines above almond shaped eyes, and lips painted a vivid crimson. The expression in her eyes when she looked at Rocamora puzzled him. Definitely not indifference, was it instead hostility, desire, or perhaps even pain?

"Pablo, how did you find her?"

"Yèyīng led a pirate band and attacked our ship off the coast of Sumatra. She fought like an Amazon queen. We were fortunate to win the battle. No, *amigo*, I did not bed her. My life would have ended had I tried. Her father was a Portuguese sailor and her mother the daughter of a Chinese merchant. Because Yèyīng speaks Portuguese, I was able to convince her to join my enterprise and come here to work at *The Fragrant Peony*. Why she agreed, I cannot say. In truth, there is much about her life I do not know, and it is impossible to read her thoughts. Perhaps you will learn her secrets one day by using the same skills you had as confessor."

"Perhaps, and why are you frowning, Jacobus?"

"This may be too elegant an establishment given its proximity to the docks and the coarseness of the general population."

"What we will charge for food, drink, use of the baths, and minimum amounts to gamble will exclude the worst of them."

"Pablo makes sense," Rocamora reassured Velde. "And do not forget that Amsterdam is a city that attracts aristocrats, scientists, and scholars from all over Europe. They will soon be extolling *The Fragrant Peony* as a wonder that must be seen and experienced."

Pablo took them to the bathhouse. It had three pools, one heated, one cold, and a third filled with seawater. "Vicente, will you show the girls how to avoid *mal frances*?"

"And to recognize the French sickness. I shall inspect them weekly to ensure they are free of Cupid's mischief."

Velde kneeled to test the temperature of the heated pool and stared at one of the Asian girls lighting incense. "I may never be farther away than the dining table and these baths."

"And of course, *amigo*, you will sample the delights these beauties have to offer."

Rocamora conceded only to himself the temptations he resisted. "I look forward to enjoying the waters of these baths, but as I told you, Pablo, I am loyal to Abigail and must save my aging seed so we can have more children."

"How many more do you plan to have?"

"Pablo, I would like one for every accursed priest and friar as revenge against the Church. Realistically, a daughter will suffice, and I must think first of Abigail's health. But you, my friend, why do you not wed?"

"I have. I took several wives in the Indies after I converted to Islam to please their families and honor my ancestors. And yes, my surprised *amigo*, I submitted to circumcision but drugged myself first with opium. As you have done here in Amsterdam, I successfully spread my seed in the Indies, and my children will be raised as Muslims, my own revenge against the Spanish Church and Crown."

"I congratulate you. Will you bring them here to Amsterdam?"

"No, it is best they grow up with their own, and I shall visit them during my subsequent voyages."

"I prefer that you live here permanently."

"I do not know if I can. I asked you this before. How does one endure life here without palm trees, melons, and days of clear sunshine?"

"It was difficult at first, and in truth, I shall always think of myself as a Spaniard. I also know this, and I told you so before you left on your journey to the Indies. No other place in the entire world allows me to live so free without fear of any Church and Crown, with no capricious government or monarch to tyrannize the population. Here I have married the great love of my life, and she has given me three healthy sons. Is that not the best paradise of all?"

50.
Infantiña

Rocamora delivered the baby from Abigail's womb, severed the umbilical cord, and kissed his beautiful perfect daughter. She stopped crying and smiled. He believed her gurgling sounds also indicated pleasure at being in his arms. "*Mi infantiña,* my little princess."

Rocamora wept unashamed. He would see his *infantiña* grow and develop each day of her life, hold and kiss her whenever he liked, proclaim her to the world as his daughter unlike Brianda, whom he did not see for the first time until her eleventh year and could never acknowledge as his child. Rocamora smiled back at his daughter and described his plans for her until he heard Abigail calling.

"*Capitán*, have you forgotten me? I would like to know if we have a girl or a boy."

"Forgive me, querida." Rocamora carried their newborn to Abigail. "Here is our daughter."

"I have given you a daughter at last."

"And none has ever been born so beautiful."

"Yes, she is lovely and sweet of temperament. Look at her dimple here. Oh, and another there. Are you truly pleased?"

"You have kept your promise and given me, given us the best daughter ever born."

"We must establish a dowry for her."

"In time, querida, in time." Rocamora parted the curtains. "Miriam, again I thank you for your help. Moses, Solomon, come behold your beautiful little sister. You must be her protectors for all your lives."

Moses thrust his chest forward and placed an arm around his smaller brother. "Like I protect Solomon?"

"Yes, and the way Solomon looks out for you."

"Will she be pretty like eemah?"

"Yes, Moses, I believe she will."

Precocious five year old Solomon moved closer and stared at his sister. "She looks healthy, *Abba*. She will live."

"An excellent diagnosis, my son, Yes, she shall live and thrive."

"*Abba*, when can I watch a childbirth?"

"When you are older, Solomon, you may follow me on my rounds. One day, you shall learn all I know about the practice of medicine and be well prepared when you go to medical school."

"I am going to be a soldier like Colonel Dirck."

Rocamora struggled not to smile. In spirit, his eldest son resembled himself at the same age. "Moses, you will change your mind many times before you become a man."

The physical and mental development of his children fascinated Rocamora. His two oldest boys were different physically, in temperament, and interests. One would not know they came from the same parents. Year old Joseph had yet to reveal his mind and personality. Would his newborn daughter resemble most his beloved Abigail, his dearest mother, Brianda, or one of the many Touro cousins and aunts?

Rocamora kissed Abigail. "Thank you, mi querida, for giving us three strong sons and a beautiful daughter."

"Her name shall be Sara for my mother.

"Sara, Hebrew for princess, our *infantiña*."

After Abigail regained her strength, they invited relations and friends for the naming of their daughter at a traditional ceremony called *fadas*. According to custom, a young female cousin dressed as a bride held the baby on a linen pillow of floral design, and all sang verses from the Song of Solomon.

Rocamora shocked everyone except Abigail when he snatched his *infantiña* from the girl. No one but he should hold his daughter. He paid little attention to the guests and doted on the exquisite cheerful little girl on his lap.

Because Menasseh had gone to England in the hope of obtaining Cromwell's consent for the resettlement of Jews, Rocamora invited his neighbor Rabbi Saul Morteira to recite the traditional blessings. He did not hear them. He saw his *infantiña* in the best clothes and educated in languages, history, literature, art, and music. He expected her voice to surpass those of angels and nightingales.

Rocamora heard Morteira's final benediction, "We welcome to our community, Sara bat Isaac de Rocamora."

He stood and carried his *infantiña* around the room on the pillow for all to admire. During the feast that followed, guests speculated which of their young sons, nephews, and cousins scattered from Bordeaux to the Dutch Republic, Hamburg, the Venice ghetto, and beyond to Morocco and Salonika, Sara might marry. Prodded by his father, David de Santcroos described the virtues of his two boys Samuel and Benjamin. Rocamora doubted if anyone would be worthy of his daughter.

After the last guest left, Rocamora placed Sara in the *rolkoets* beside that of Joseph. He watched over her while Abigail sang a children's song to their sons.

Life could not be sweeter.

51.
Confinement

Mournful bells tolled throughout Amsterdam. Town criers alerted the citizenry. Rocamora hurried home mid-morning concerned for his family. After he scrubbed his hands and face with soap and hot water, he went to Abigail in the great hall where she looked out the window. Joseph sat on the floor clinging to her skirt. Sara slept in her *rolkoets*.

"*Capitán*, those bells."

"Plague. Velde brought me to a corpse covered with bulboes. It is not the only one in the city." Rocamora's deep voice resonated throughout the house. "Moses, Solomon, Miriam, come here immediately." The boys ran from the attic into the great hall followed by Miriam. "Quiet, all of you."

With the same theatricality he used to sermonize and harangue in Spain, Rocamora spoke in an ominous authoritative tone they had not heard before. "Listen to me and do not interrupt. Plague has come to Amsterdam. You must do all I say. Wash often with soap and hot water. No one, not one of you may leave our home. No one may enter. No exceptions. I will arrange for food to be delivered."

Rocamora saw Hombrecillo watching them from atop a cabinet. "Do not let the cat out. If he escapes, do not let him back in. Moses, Solomon, be obedient. Do everything your mother and Miriam say. I do not know when I will return."

Rocamora went to his laboratory, filled his satchel to bursting with medicines and opiates, and left.

Fear ruled Amsterdam. Panic increased with each death. Many remembered the plague of 1623 that lasted three years and took more than sixteen thousand lives, one of every six Amsterdammers. It returned in 1636, and now yet again. The least change of mood or appearance of something new on the skin frightened the healthy into believing they had the plague.

Congregants and former disbelievers filled churches and synagogues beyond normal capacity to hear sermons and pray to God for forgiveness. Calvinist ministers terrified their congregations with threats of hellfire and damnation. They called the plague the Justified Anger of God, a warning for sinners to repent, which added to the hysteria.

Magistrates closed brothels, alehouses, and banned wedding feasts. They forbade imports of anything suspected of causing the plague including cucumbers, spinach, and especially plums, because they resembled bulboes.

Rocamora advised Pablo to stay inside *The Fragrant Peony* with Yèyīng, the girls, their servants and employees. Santcroos and others of great wealth fled with their families to country homes. He assumed van Noordwijk had gone to his estate. Gaspar was at sea.

The night sky lit when the city burned two hundred barrels of pitch and set wood fires everywhere to prevent further spreading of the plague. Rocamora found the odor preferable to the foul stink of death that became unbearable when the churches filled with more bodies than they could hold for burial. He could not douse his handkerchiefs with enough perfume, and he smoked heavily to rid his nostrils of the stench. Many believed tobacco prevented the spread of plague.

Families left infected members alone to recover or die from neglect. Officials marked houses of the dead and dying P for plague and boarded doors and windows. Everyone who lived with the plague-ridden had to carry a white stick.

Quacks and charlatans posted notices on shuttered homes and shops promising false immunity and cures. Their powdered concoctions labeled Unicorn's Horn or Toad reminded Rocamora of incompetent court physicians at the Alcazar who recommended powdered crocodile dung for tertian and quartan fevers. The gullible purchased amulets filled with quicksilver or arsenic and walnut shells containing mercury.

Rocamora never encountered so vile a sickness. Unbearable headaches came with the first symptoms and drove many to madness. Severe chills, shaking and trembling, nausea and vomiting followed. At work or in the middle of a conversation, one might fall asleep and die if not wakened. Spots spread over the entire body without warning of infection and caused death within a few hours. Blisters developed into excruciatingly painful purple tumors in armpits, groins, and behind the ear, each of varying size and sickening stench, each seeming to be on fire. If the bulboes did not break naturally, surgeons incised and cleansed them, a treatment so painful patients often collapsed.

Rocamora worked with Velde and his son Peter to treat victims of the plague. They also had to deal with patients afflicted with familiar summer diseases and other ailments: ague, typhoid, tuberculosis, rheumatism, gout, insomnia, diabetes, depression, appendicitis, and broken limbs. He seldom arrived home before midnight. He rose before dawn.

Throughout the summer of plague, Abigail created a sanctuary of love and comfort for Rocamora. She and Miriam provided hot water for him to wash, tea to refresh, and warm meals for nourishment no matter how late he came home.

Most nights he arrived exhausted, barely able to move. Abigail brought him soup, hot tea, and lit his pipe in the study. She sat beside Rocamora catering to his every need, waiting for him to speak, never complaining if he did not.

Following his morning ablutions, Rocamora ate breakfast, refilled his satchel, and left.

Rocamora sat facing Vrouw Cornelia in her parlor, his first patient of the day. He visited his former landlady every week to reassure her that she had not caught the plague.

"Mevrouw, that little spot on your cheek has always been there. It is but a mole."

"You are absolutely sure?"

'I am."

She touched the amulet hanging from her neck with a quotation from the Gospels inside. "Praise the Lord, and you too Doctor."

Rocamora felt her forehead. "No fever. You are healthy."

Vrouw Cornelia gripped Rocamora's hand. "You were my best lodger, and now you are my physician, better than any I have had. Is your lovely wife all right? How are your children?"

"Thank you for asking. They are well."

"But you are so gaunt. Your clothes hang loosely. You must make time to eat. Before you leave, stop in my kitchen. I have baked your favorites."

Vrouw Cornelia wanted company, and Rocamora lingered to chat with her. She still bred Chartreaux cats, selling some to the wealthy for pets and pelts of those she fattened to furriers.

Hombrecillo, you do not know how fortunate you were to adopt me.

One night in late September, Rocamora came home, washed, and went to his study. Abigail brought him his usual bowl of soup, cup of tea, and fresh tobacco for his pipe surprised to see him standing.

He kissed her good evening. "*Querida*, it has been several days since Velde and I have seen a new patient afflicted with the plague."

"Has it ended?"

"Not officially, but we believe the worst is over. Everyone agrees the plague is most virulent during the summer months. The weather has been cooler. I believe I can end your confinement. Tomorrow, you and Miriam will be free to shop for food, and the boys can play in the park. *Mi querida*, I cannot praise you enough for how well you ran the house and took care of the children and me during these trying times."

Rocamora took a small narrow black case from his doublet, removed its contents, and clasped a necklace of matched pearls around Abigail's neck. "Perfect as pearls go, but far less than your own perfection and beauty."

52.
Shabat

From the day he committed to marrying Abigail, Rocamora thought many of the Sephardic rites intrusive and annoying. Before the plague, they had gone to the homes of Abigail's uncles for Sabbath Eve meals, Passover Seders, and breaking the Yom Kippur fast. During the months of confinement, Rocamora's views changed regarding certain religious observances in his home, especially the Sabbath meal, which Abigail insisted they observe. To his surprise, he came to accept it as necessary mucilage to bind and strengthen the family.

The first Monday after the confinement, Abigail selected and ordered food for the Sabbath Eve meal. Thursday and Friday, she and Miriam scrubbed and polished every room, floor, and piece of furniture. On Friday, Abigail made time to bathe the children and herself in water scented with aromatic herbs.

All wore their finest and freshly laundered clothes, their sons resembling miniature *caballeros* in their doublets, breeches, and hats, his *infantiña* in white linens more beautiful than any French fashion doll. Abigail, Miriam, and the older boys lit candles throughout the house and kindled fires to last through sundown Saturday.

Each Friday, Rocamora came home to a house filled with pleasing aromas of food cooking with spices and herbs and each body washed and scented. Abigail had hot water waiting for him so he could bathe and dress in time for the meal.

At the dining table, Moses sat to Rocamora's right, Solomon to the left, Miriam between his *infantiña* and Joseph in high chairs, and Abigail at the opposite end. Rocamora filled the etched silver cup Abigail inherited from her father with wine beyond the rim to symbolize the overflowing joy welcoming the Sabbath as a bride coming into the home of her betrothed.

More than anything, he looked forward to Abigail's lighting of the table candles. A diaphanous ivory-white tatted linen veil covered her hair and ears while she made a circle with her hands three times over the flames, as if washing the light toward her face, and recited a blessing over the Sabbath lights. Abigail's beatific expression reminded Rocamora of icons, sculptures, and paintings of the Virgin.

They sang in Hebrew melodic Sabbath prayers and blessings. Before Miriam served the first course, Moses brought Joseph to Rocamora and Abigail, kissed his parents' hands, and placed his crying younger brother in his mother's lap to quiet him. Solomon followed, and Rocamora held his Sara while he and Abigail blessed their children.

Rocamora wallowed in contentment. He had a beautiful loving wife who created a sanctuary from the outside world filled with joy and laughter. Life had again become sweet.

"Isaac, I cannot thank you enough. I did not lose a single employee. They followed your commands. Word has spread throughout Amsterdam that all your patients who did so survived the plague."

Never given to false modesty regarding his profession, Rocamora did not argue with Santcroos who returned with his family from the country estate a few days before Rosh Hashanah, the Jewish New Year. "Unfortunately, Don Samuel, Velde and I could not save everyone who became afflicted."

"Still, it is well known throughout the city that you healed more patients than any other physician. So far, somewhere between ten to fifteen thousand have died in Amsterdam alone. Every city in our Dutch Republic has suffered the same, if not more. Entire families have died."

Rocamora smoked, accepted a refill of coffee, and did not speak. He did not know where Santcroos was leading him.

"Men have been left destitute, women widowed, children orphaned. Many are so weakened they will never be able to work again. All will be desperate for food and will need to sell their possessions on their own or at auctions to survive. Think of the silver objects, precious gems, Turkish rugs, and fine furniture you can purchase for as low as a florin on the guilder."

Rocamora did not tell Santcroos, nor would he ever reveal to Abigail that it was how he acquired her pearl necklace.

53.
Memories of el Paraiso

The wealthy returned from their country estates. Magistrates allowed brothels, alehouses, and theaters to open again. The last death from the plague occurred in November. By then, close to seventeen thousand Amsterdammers had died, ten percent of the population.

The Fragrant Peony thrived, and by the early months of 1656, Pablo learned to speak a passable Dutch. This day, customers filled the grand dining salon. The aroma of spiced food from China and the Indies competed with tobacco smoke for olfactory dominance. Rocamora went to Velde and his son Peter who were eating at one of the tables.

"I compliment you on your dexterity."

Velde held a pair of chopsticks. "I would be a poor surgeon if I lacked the coordination to master these infernal twigs. As you can see, Peter is more skilled than I, for he can pick up a single pea."

"He is already a fine surgeon and barber. I may visit you tomorrow for a trim of my mustache and beard."

"Doctor."

Rocamora exchanged greetings with Magistrate and principal investor Jan van der Waag who sat at a nearby table with several city officials. "How are your lovely wife and children?"

"All in good health thanks to your advice and our escape to the countryside. Julia is expecting our fifth child due in about three months. You will attend the birth as usual?"

"Of course."

Pablo came to their table, and Van der Waag smacked his lips. "Mynheer, your cook from the Indies is a genius."

"I would have abducted him if he had been unwilling to come. Are you not gambling?"

"I risk with investments in property and trade, never at cards and such."

Rocamora went with Pablo into a separate room with tables for cards, bones, and Fan Tan, a game unfamiliar to him and the Amsterdammers, excepting those who had traveled to the Indies and China.

A large square outlined in gold lay on green felt at the center of the table. Its sides numbered in gold from one to four. One of the delicate girls from the Indies Pablo identified as the banker removed at random a double handful of beads from a large jade bowl, laid them on the table, and covered them with a smaller metal bowl. The gamblers placed coins at the side of the square bearing their numbers of choice. Some wagered on the corners between numbers.

After the banker stopped all betting, she lifted the bowl. With a small wooden stick she removed beads from the pile four at a time until from one to four were left. That number determined the winner, who collected three times his wager minus the house fee of ten percent. Those who bet on the corners won a return of one and a half times their wager.

"They believe it to be a game of pure chance, *amigo*."

"She has exceptional dexterity."

"Good enough to create a winner of choice to pay our bribes to certain city officials."

Rocamora followed Pablo into another smaller and more intricately appointed salon. Painted Chinese screens lined the walls. Well-dressed gamblers sat on silk cushioned chairs and wagered high stakes at elaborately carved tables, two for Fan Tan and another at which Madame Yèyīng dealt Bone Ace and other card games.

"A most formidable woman, Pablo."

"As skilled a dealer of cards as you and I, *amigo*, and always impenetrable of mind and body. All who work here fear and respect Yèyīng. Santcroos and the other investors are pleased with her dedication to making *The Fragrant Peony* the success it has become."

"I have never seen anyone cheat so cleverly."

"The Night Hawk devours her chickens completely, beak, feet, feathers and bone. If she allows a player to win a hand, he will always wager more and lose the next."

Rocamora remembered the evening at *el Paraíso* when he took Ramón's place at the table in a game of pharaoh, recouped his losses and more. He yearned to be in his older kinsman's genial company again. No greater wit existed in all Spain or now in the Dutch Republic.

"You are lost in thought."

"Memories of *el Paraíso*. Another world. I thought Yèyīng would be managing more than dealing."

"She does, but we make exceptions for wealthy men who are enamored. Some have given her expensive gifts of gems and gold. They sit at Yèyīng's table and are willing to lose simply to be in her presence."

"A Moraíma who does not sing and dance."

"Nor sell herself to men."

Rocamora recalled the effect his presumed celibacy had on the women at the Alcazar and others he confessed. "Unattainability may be the greatest aphrodisiac of all."

"Well said, Vicente. You will stay a while for a meal and a bath?"

"I have more patients to see. Many fear each new mark on their bodies is a sign that the plague has returned."

"I pray we shall not see it again in our lifetimes."

"Or those of my children."

"I want to see mine. Next week I sail for the East Indies. If not for the plague, I would have left sooner."

"You are unhappy here in Amsterdam?"

"It is the weather, the climate. I need more sunshine. There are other reasons. Most of the girls I brought from the Indies have found husbands. I will have to collect many more for *The Fragrant Peony*. I promise you. I shall return. Ay, *amigo*, I believe we are indestructible and ageless."

"But slower of movement. Do not stay away for too long this time."

54.
Excommunication

Saddened and brooding, Rocamora left his neighbor Rabbi Morteira and hesitated before entering his home to digest what he had heard. After saying *adios* to Pablo earlier at the docks, he made the rounds of his patients, visiting Morteira last to see how his affliction of hemorrhoids was healing. The Rabbi had company, Santcroos and Rabbi Isaac Aboab da Fonseca, whom Rocamora met for the first time since the esteemed sage's return from Recife the previous week.

They were discussing the imminent excommunication of Bento d'Espinoza. The rabbis did not care what Bento believed if he would be silent and outwardly conform. They even gave approval for Santcroos to offer Bento a thousand guilders income annually if he returned to the congregation and appeared at Talmud Torah once or twice a year.

Because Bento refused the offer, Santcroos and other oligarchs of the congregation demanded his immediate excommunication. The young man's politics and associations with secularists worried the *poderosos* more than his theology. So far, the government had left it to the congregation to deal with Bento. No one in Vlooienburg wanted the magistrates to accuse any Jew of subverting the foundations of their Protestant religion and system of government. That would give the more intolerant Calvinists an excuse to take away privileges granted to the Jews.

Rocamora agreed Bento had gone too far taking positions contrary to that of the Amsterdam government and the Orangists. The young philosopher and his secular friends opposed the Calvinist Church's dominance in political affairs, and they wanted to dissolve the Dutch East India and Dutch West India Companies, the sources of Holland's wealth.

Rocamora well understood that Holland tolerated Jews because the *Bet Din* and *Ma'amad* enforced orthodoxy and discouraged freethinking. The Amsterdam government granted citizenship equal to Dutch Christians to the most successful Jews such as Santcroos. The Dutch were not bigots when it came to making money.

Rocamora's bleak mood dissipated when he held his *infantiña*, gave attention to the boys, and sat with Abigail in their parlor at night to share the events of their day and plan the next. Each evening after the children fell asleep and he made sure his Sara was secure in her *rolkoets*, Abigail provided an upholstered stool for his feet and lit his pipe. She served him tea, wine, brandy, or an occasional cup of hot chocolate and his new favorite, coffee, the most expensive of all drinks.

Never idle, Abigail tatted a lace tablecloth and described how well their children learned and behaved. She never gossiped or dwelled on trivial matters. Abigail waited for Rocamora to speak. When he did not, she touched his arm.

"You are troubled, *mi Capitán*?"

Rocamora sipped his coffee, "Nothing that concerns us and the children."

"Are you worried Pablo may not return?"

"Not that. I saw Rabbi Morteira and met Rabbi Aboab. Santcroos was there too. It has been decided. Bento will be excommunicated."

"How terrible. Bento admires you. Can you not influence him?"

"No one can. Even if I were so inclined, it is too late."

"I suppose you are right. I remember that after Bento won a suit against his half-sister Rebecca over their father's inheritance, he renounced his claim and left Vlooienburg."

"He has formally Christianized his name to Benedict."

Abigail gasped. "He converted?"

"No, Bento is too committed a freethinker to accept any religion. He now lives with van den Enden teaching in his mentor's school and associating with secular Christian thinkers."

"Do you believe Rabbi Menasseh might have counseled Bento otherwise if he had not gone to England?"

"Morteira also was Bento's teacher and loved him as a surrogate son. If he no longer has influence over his former pupil, the same holds true for Menasseh."

"How awful for Bento. At least our community has no dungeons, *autos de fé*, or stakes for burning."

"It would not matter if we had. Bento will forever be banned and dead to our community and all Jewish communities throughout the world. *Mi querida*, Bento may be the one of the most courageous men I have ever encountered."

"But no one is braver than you. And now, *mi Capitán*, I have saved the best news to cheer you. My time of the month has passed. I am with child."

On the sixth day of *Ab*, 5416 years from the day of the Creation, the tenth day of July 1656 according to the Christian calendar, Rocamora sat inside crowded stifling Talmud Torah for the excommunication of Spinoza who was not present.

Selected members of the congregation began the ceremony by lighting the synagogue candles and extinguishing them to symbolize the death of the person to be excommunicated. The hazzan blew the *shofar*, the ram's horn, and Rabbi Aboab dressed all in white as on The Day of Atonement walked to the platform in the center of the synagogue. Aboab was an imposing figure with a full white beard, hair that exploded from the sides of his head, fiery eyes, and a majestic promontory of a nose.

Rocamora's thoughts moved back and forth from the present to his past in Spain as he recalled both witnessing and participating in the similar awesome Anathema of the Catholic Church. He became aware of the present when Aboab intoned:

> "... with the anathema wherewith Joshua cursed Jericho, and with all the curses which are written in the Law. Cursed be he by day and cursed be he by night. Cursed be he in sleeping and cursed be he in waking. Cursed be he in going out and cursed be he in coming in. The Lord shall not pardon him. The Lord shall destroy his name under the sun and shall damn him with all the curses of the firmament, written in the Law"

Rocamora heard much similarity between the Hebrew and Spanish condemnations except Spinoza was not here in *sambenito* and *coraza* to be scourged, humiliated, and condemned to the stake. He saw Aboab's face becoming as one with those of Inquisitor Generals Zapata, Sotomayor, and Arce Reynoso when the rabbi continued:

> "The Lords of the *Ma'amad*, having long known of the evil opinions and acts of Baruch de Espinoza, they have endeavored by various means and promises to turn him from his evil ways. But having failed to make him mend his wicked ways, and, on the contrary, daily receiving more and more serious information about the abominable heresies, which he practiced and taught, and about his monstrous deeds, and having numerous trustworthy witnesses who have deposed and born witness to this effect in the presence of the said Espinoza, they became convinced of the truth of this matter."

Aboab's doom shrouded pronouncements caused many in the synagogue to cringe because they remembered their years in Spain and Portugal fearing denunciation.

> "And after all of this has been investigated in the presence of the honorable sages, they have decided, with their consent, that the said Espinoza should be excommunicated and expelled from the people of Israel.
>
> "By decree of the angels and by the command of the holy men, we excommunicate, expel, curse and damn Baruch de Espinoza, with the consent of God, Blessed be He, and with the consent of the entire holy congregation, and in front of these holy scrolls with the 613 precepts, which are written therein.
>
> The Lord will not spare him, and all the curses that are written in this book shall lie upon him, and the Lord shall blot out his name. And the Lord shall separate him unto evil out of all the tribes of Israel, according to all the curses of the covenant that are written in this book of the law. But you, that cleave unto the Lord your God, are alive, every one of you this day."

Aboab paused yet again, taking on the mien of a righteous prophet as if he had emerged from the pages of Scripture.

> "No one should communicate with him neither in writing, nor accord him any favor, nor stay with him under the same roof, nor within four cubits in his vicinity of nor shall read any treatise composed or written by him."

Rocamora remembered Bento as the precocious skeptical boy of eleven the day they first met in 1643. Even then, Vlooienburg had been too small to contain him. Would Amsterdam allow him to thrive?

55.
The Father

Rocamora had looked forward to Menasseh ben Israel's return to Amsterdam, but it was not to be. In September of 1657, the rabbi's son Samuel died in England and two months later, the rabbi passed away in Middleburg. Rocamora never had an opportunity to discuss Bento's excommunication with Menasseh or Oliver Cromwell's thoughts about the likelihood of any formal readmission of Jews to England. He mourned the man, who, in his opinion, was the greatest ornament of the Sephardic community.

Other concerns took precedence. Abigail had given birth to a boy they named Daniel, whose bones were developing malformed, and a year later David, their fifth son. A month after the infant's *Berit Milah*, Rocamora listened to his heartbeat and difficult breathing.

"*Querida,* it will be a miracle if David survives the grippe he is so weak and small."

"But another precious gift from God."

Rocamora did not voice his thoughts that any God who bestowed such gifts had a malicious nature. He believed his seed had weakened with age and brought forth four consecutive damaged sons, one premature and stillborn, another who survived less than a week, deformed Daniel the previous year, and now sickly David. Then there was a daughter, who lived a mere four days.

He took Abigail's hand. "*Querida,* we have more than fulfilled the commandment to be fruitful. We should no longer burden your body with more birthing."

"You wish to abandon our bed?"

"Never. I would be lost without the comfort of your nearness, but we must be careful. I do not want to risk losing you. As we both know, so many women die giving birth. It is a miracle you have survived nine."

"I so want to give you another daughter."

"Our *infantiña* is the center jewel in your crown of motherhood."

"Yes, Sara is a dutiful and respectful child. I do not worry about Solomon, who is obedient, brilliant at his studies and will join you as physician. Nor have I concerns for Joseph, who is respectful no less than Solomon. However, our Moses, named for my beloved father, may he rest in peace, is not doing well at the *Yesibót*. I fear he will not be ready for his bar mitzvah next year."

"Our eldest has no head for study. He prefers manly pursuits, sport and arms."

"Which you encourage. They are not for observant Jews. What shall become of him?"

"Moses is resourceful and courageous, protective of his sister and brothers, a chivalrous *caballero*."

Abigail smiled. "A *caballero*? But you forget, we are not in Spain."

Rocamora sat across from Rabbi Aboab's desk at the *Yesibôt* and waited for him to explain the purpose of their meeting. He had never warmed to the director of the school. Aboab was both a messianist and a Kabbalist, and Rocamora remembered the rabbi unfavorably in the context of Bento's excommunication. He wished Menasseh still lived.

"Doctor Isaac, Your son Moses did not come to school yesterday afternoon. Solomon refused to tell me where his brother was. This morning, when their teacher attempted to punish them, Moses took the strap and threatened to beat him if he laid a hand on Solomon or himself. We cannot permit such outrageous behavior, nor can we tolerate such blatant disrespect. Your sons must be punished."

Rocamora held Aboab's gaze and spoke in a menacing tone that caused the rabbi to recoil. "First, know that if anyone ever strikes my sons, regardless of any infraction, rabbi or not, I will give that person a thrashing he will never forget. Have I made myself clear?"

"Yes, yes, you have, but will you discipline your sons?"

"Solomon protected Moses, as Moses has always protected Solomon. I shall never punish them for being loyal to each other, nor shall you or anyone else in the *Yesibôt*. As for Moses, I will learn why he absented himself and deal with him myself."

"Moses should be doing better with his studies."

"He will be well prepared for his *bar mitzvah*."

That evening Rocamora summoned Moses and Solomon to his study. He did not smile or give them permission to sit. He stared at each for a long time and worried if he had been a proper father. At home, they were obedient sons. Rocamora left it to Abigail to do the day to day disciplining, breaking up their arguments and settling grievances.

"Solomon, your brother placed you in a difficult situation, and I applaud you for your loyalty to him. Tomorrow, you must apologize to your teacher and Rabbi Aboab for your defiance but not for anything else."

"Yes, *Abba*."

"You may leave, Solomon, and close the door behind you." Rocamora waited until he left. "Moses, were you playing *Groote Kolven* instead of attending the *Yesibót*?"

"Yes, *Abba*."

"You left Solomon with the impossible choices of lying, betraying you, or not speaking at all."

"I did not think …."

"Exactly. Our actions always impact others. Now I must decide your punishment for disobedience."

Rocamora never struck his sons and seldom needed to reprimand them. Abigail had given them no more than light slaps when they were toddlers to get their attention when they were too rowdy or recalcitrant. His own father never gave him beatings, and he would never forget the severe lashing from Fray Bernardo, which scarred his back for life. It made no sense to take cane, stick, or strap to a good chi---ld who made a mistake.

Aware that Moses admired and respected him above all others, Rocamora did not need to raise his voice. A proper rebuke stung more than any lashing. "You have disappointed your mother and me."

Tears came to Moses' eyes. "I am sorry, *Abba*. I promise. I will not absent myself from school again."

"I believe you."

Moses fidgeted. "*Abba*, what punishment will you give me?"

"What do you suggest?"

"I … I do not know. Extra hours of studying? More chores? A beating?"

Rocamora struggled to sustain a stern expression. Moses, so much like himself, would never know how many times he had missed school to frolic in the sea and learn survival on the docks of El Grau. "My son, if the knowledge you have disappointed your father and mother is not enough to shame you, all other punishments are meaningless. Do you know which of the Ten Commandments you have broken?"

"The Fifth."

"For which you will atone later this year on Yom Kippur."

"Yes, *Abba*."

Now, tell me, did you score any goals? Did your side win?"

56.
Miriam's Surprise

"*Abba*, can I dissect it?"

Rocamora stood over Hombrecillo with his two eldest sons. His little friend had lived a long life. He remembered that day sixteen years earlier in the room he rented from Vrouw Cornelia when the Chartreaux kitten took command of his lap and adopted him. He did not want to discourage Solomon's interest in anatomy but preferred that his longtime companion should rest in deserved peace.

"We will bury Hombrecillo here in the back of our house."

"*Abba*, is there a *Kaddish* for cats?"

"No, Moses, but we can improvise whatever prayer for the dead we wish."

After the boys buried Hombrecillo, they left for the *Yesibót*, and Rocamora went to the great hall where Abigail sang lullabies to Daniel and David. He worried about the health of his two youngest. Daniel's spine and chest were malformed. The irony that his fourth son would be hunchbacked was not lost on Rocamora. That had been his disguise the day he took revenge upon Anglesola and another when he escaped from Madrid. Frail and sickly David would require much observation and attention.

Rocamora looked with amusement at his *infantiña* playing in another part of the great hall. She was dressing one of her dolls and lecturing it to behave as any mother would. Each day she resembled Abigail more in both appearance and mannerisms. So did Joseph who could pass as Sara's twin.

"Where is Joseph?"

"In the attic."

"Studying?"

"Joseph sits on the floor with my diamond mills. He prefers them to his lessons and pesters me to teach him bruting."

David coughed, and Rocamora listened to his breathing. "*Querida*, this bed will always be our Eden, but you will soon be thirty-eight and I fifty-nine. You have given us four healthy children, and we must do all we can for Daniel and David so they may survive and thrive. We have been fruitful according to Scripture, and I know of methods to prevent childbirth."

"Yes, *Capitán*, I understand."

Daniel and David had fallen asleep, and Rocamora helped Abigail make them comfortable in the *rolkoetsen*. "Joseph seems to have chosen his path at a young age the same as our Solomon, who will be a physician."

"But what shall become of Moses?"

Before Rocamora replied, Miriam came into the great hall. "Doctor, may I speak to you and Doña Abigail?"

"Of course, Miriam."

"I wish to wed."

Abigail stared at Miriam speechless, and Rocamora appraised her before answering. Now twenty-three years of age, she had matured into a plump, healthy young woman with flaming red hair, vivid blue eyes and features suggesting Slavic rather than Jewish forebears. He appreciated why men might find Miriam desirable.

"Whom do you wish to wed?"

"His name is Lyzor ben Nachum, Doctor."

"An Ashkenazi."

"Yes."

"What does he do?"

"Lyzor is a *schneiderl*."

"*Schneiderl?*" Abigail repeated. "What is that?"

"A lowly tailor, *querida*. Surely you can do better than that, Miriam."

"*Calma, mi Capitán.*" Abigail reached for Miriam's hand. "You always have been free to do as you wish."

Rocamora caught himself reacting the same as any father. "Miriam, as you know, we love you as our own daughter, and we shall miss you after you leave."

Tears came to her eyes. "Are you casting me out?"

Abigail squeezed her hand. "Of course not, but when the time comes for you to wed, you will have to establish your own household."

"Oh, that will not be for a long while. Lyzor cannot yet afford to marry. He arrived here penniless six months ago. I met him at our Ashkenazi synagogue. In Podolia, Lyzor was a respected furrier, but the one job he could find in Vlooienburg was with a tailor. Everybody likes him. I hope you will give us your blessing."

While Miriam extolled Lyzor's virtues, Rocamora decided to see for himself if the young man was worthy of her.

Abigail brought Rocamora tea in his study after he arrived home in the evening. "Did you meet the young man Miriam wishes to marry?"

"I have. Lyzor is a typical Yiddish corruption of the Scriptural name, Eliezer. He is an observant Jew and knowledgeable about furs and pelts. His employer, a vile creature, exploits Lyzor and deserves a thrashing."

"Miriam cannot marry if Lyzor continues to slave for an exploiter. Can you find him work elsewhere?"

"You have read my mind, *querida*. I spoke with Pablo, and he promised to find something for Lyzor to do at a proper wage."

"You are a good man, *Capitán*, the best of all men."

Rocamora did not mistake her expression. He rose, closed the shutters, and locked the door so they would not be disturbed.

Rocamora and Abigail invited Lyzor to share an evening supper, and the young man bore their children's scrutiny with good humor. Lyzor had gained weight, shed his outlandish Ashkenazi garments for doublet and breeches. Rocamora thought he still needed to trim his beard and mustache. Pablo had told him Lyzor was doing well at *The Fragrant Peony* because of his quick mind and good ear. He had learned enough Portuguese, Spanish, and Dutch to converse adequately in those languages.

After the meal, Abigail and Miriam put the younger children to bed. Moses and Solomon went to the attic to study their lessons from the *Yesibót*. Rocamora offered Lyzor tobacco, which he declined, and encouraged the young man to talk about his life in Podolia.

When the women returned, Rocamora smiled at the young couple to put them more at ease. "Miriam, Lyzor, before you came here tonight, my wife and I discussed at length the practicalities of your marrying, specifically the amount of money necessary to begin a life together."

"If I may speak, Doctor, Señora, my lodging is adequate, and Don Pablo pays me a fair wage. Miriam and I can live on that."

"And my savings," Miriam added.

"That is subsisting, not living, not good enough for our Miriam. The Señora and I love you, love you as a daughter. You have lived in our home for twelve years. You have been a sister to our children. We cannot allow you to dwell in that squalid section of Vlooienburg. That is why we offer you a dowry, which your parents, may they rest in peace, would have provided for you. We want to give you and Lyzor the opportunity to make a new life for yourselves."

"A new life?"

"Yes, Miriam. Lyzor should work at what he does best. If he returns to the fur trade, so be it. Or, after you marry, he may wish to do something else here in Amsterdam."

"May I speak, Doctor?"

"Of course, Miriam."

She touched Lyzor's hand to silence him. "*Liebschen*, I will speak for both of us, for I am more fluent in their languages. Lyzor and I are of like mind. Excepting you and Doña Abigail, the Sephardim treat the Ashkenazim as inferior. Lyzor knows furs. He can hunt, kill, and skin animals. He can sew their pelts and make them become coats, hats, and gloves. That is why we will save our money until we can afford passage to New Amsterdam, or we may go to one of the English colonies where we can worship as we please. All who have been there say the lands are vast with unlimited opportunities to prosper for those who work hard."

"So far away from us?"

"Do not cry, *querida*. Miriam, I would be as distressed as my wife to lose you to the New World. Yet, if you are serious about going to North America, we will give you enough florins to pay for passage to New Amsterdam and more for you to purchase some land or a house and to begin a business."

Lyzor sat speechless. Miriam wept and kissed Rocamora's and Abigail's hands. "God bless you both. I promise I will find you the best possible cook and housekeeper to replace me."

Rocamora rose, went to a sideboard, and poured wine into four goblets. He raised his in a toast. "Miriam, Lyzor. *Salud*. May you prosper and have many healthy children."

57.
Don Somebody Important

Miriam convinced Geitl, an energetic Ashkenazi widow in her late forties, to leave her Sephardic employer and work for the de Rocamoras. Geitl had lost her husband and children to the plague, and her motherly instincts won over the children. Although she had learned to cook in the Sephardic style, Rocamora acquired a taste for several Eastern European dishes the woman prepared well, specifically *gefülte* fish, cabbage borscht, and blintzes.

In May, Rocamora gave Miriam away at the Ashkenazi synagogue despite possible fines or sanctions from the *Ma'amad*, and the children did not stop weeping the following day when she and Lyzor sailed for New Amsterdam. Rocamora and Abigail felt both sadness they would never see Miriam again and pride. They had given her a good life in Amsterdam and a bright future with Lyzor.

That same day, Santcroos died. Rocamora grieved over the loss of a great friend and man he admired and sat Shiva with the family. After the intense period of mourning, they invited Rocamora to the reading of Don Samuel's will. He tried not to listen to the details and recalled the years of friendship they shared until the notary mentioned his name.

"To Don Isaac Israel de Rocamora, my esteemed friend and brilliant physician who saved the life of my precious son, David, I bequeath the house in which he and his family reside at St. Anthony's Lock, and all its attendant property."

Rocamora sat stunned by his friend's generosity. Afterwards, David Samuel de Santcroos took him aside. "Doctor, I want to reassure you that my entire family is in accord with our father's bequest to you. He admired you more than any other, and I owe my life to you."

"I am truly speechless."

"Here is the document that legally transfers the house to you."

Rocamora embraced David. "Don Samuel, may he rest in peace, was a great man and a true friend. He is irreplaceable."

The following night, Abigail wearing a light linen chemise greeted Rocamora the moment he arrived home. Her face etched with concern, she held a candelabrum to his face. "*Capitán*, it is so late. Did you see that many patients today? Has the plague returned? No, I should not have asked. You have been with your gentile friends. I smell alcohol in your breath."

"I confess, *querida*, I have imbibed prodigiously, and I will explain why. But first, awaken our children, except for Daniel and David, and let Geitl sleep. I have much news of importance for all of you to hear."

Rocamora awaited them at the eating kitchen table. Abigail returned wearing a lightweight dressing gown, and each child wore bedclothes. The heat from a summer day lingered in the house.

After all sat at the table, Rocamora stood. "I have important news. Tomorrow, the magistrates will post a bulletin announcing that Amsterdam's population has exceeded 200,000."

"That means more patients."

"Yes, Solomon, and also more physicians to compete for them. That is why you must strive to be better than the others."

"*Capitán*, surely that is not the reason why you summoned our children."

"You understand me all too well, *mi querida*. As we know, this day of Ab is when Jews mourn the destruction of the Temple in Jerusalem and our expulsion from Spain if we did not convert to the false faith, but I shall always remember this ninth day of September as my moment of personal triumph that also brings great honor to my family. Today, I was summoned to the Town Hall on the pretext my services were needed by one of the magistrates."

"Pretext?"

"My good friends Jacobus Velde, Dirck van Noordwijk, and Jan van der Waag awaited me with other magistrates and notables I have treated over the years. The municipal clerk sat a table with an open register. Dirck told me to give him my name, profession, place of birth, and religion. Van der Waag then announced I had been enrolled as a full citizen of Amsterdam equal in privileges and duties to Dutch Christians." Rocamora raised a hand to silence Abigail and the children. "There is more. They next took me to the *Collegium Medicum* where their clerk also registered me as a full member equal to Christians. I am only the third Jewish physician in Amsterdam to be granted citizenship and membership in the *Collegium*."

Abigail left her chair and kissed him. "I am so proud of you, *Capitán*."

"Are we citizens too, *Abba*?"

"No, Moses, Jews cannot inherit citizenship. Each of you will have to earn it on your own."

"I can marry a citizen, *Abba*."

Rocamora had begun to address his daughter differently. "Tiña, many years will pass before we find you a suitable husband."

"I want him to be as handsome as Moses."

Rocamora smiled at his eldest. "That may be an impossibility."

Solomon tugged his sleeve. "Who are the other two physicians that became citizens?"

"Joseph Bueno, who was physician to *Stadhouder* Frederick Hendrick, and his son, the esteemed Ephraim da Bueno, who also served the House of Orange. I would have come home sooner, *querida*, but after we left the clerk who registered me for *Collegium Medicum*, my friends and I went to *The Fragrant Peony* to celebrate. That is why I have come home so late. Now that I am a citizen, with that honor comes the obligation to pay taxes to the city, which of course we can afford. It is called the two-hundredth tax, one florin for every two hundred of income. There is a household tax too, which we must pay because I earn more than two thousand guilders a year."

"Why are you laughing, *Capitán*?"

"To be a common citizen is a great honor in Amsterdam. Thus, I have become a *pechero*, a taxpayer, who would have been looked upon with contempt in Spain."

"As I continue to remind you, you are no longer in Spain."

"I know, *querida*, and I am thankful for that."

Rocamora explained the Amsterdam taxation system further to answer his children's questions. Beer is taxed at sixty percent, wine twice that of beer when sold to an individual and half as much again by tavern owners. All articles of consumption may have been taxed many times by the time we purchase any one of them. Now, Solomon, no more questions. The hour is late. We can talk more tomorrow. All of you, off to bed now."

Rocamora believed not even Abigail could possibly know the elation he was experiencing. He had found his place in this world at last, not as a *caballero, conquistador*, soldier, royal confessor, or inquisitor general, not even as a Jew in his mind. Now an honored physician with a loving wife and children, he had become a free citizen and Don Somebody Important in the city of Amsterdam, but still forever a Spaniard in the essence of his being.

A week after Rocamora received citizenship, he stood with Abigail and his children on the street outside their home and watched an artisan remove a cloth from what he had secured above the front door lentil.

"*Abba*, it is a shield."

"Yes, Moses, the de Rocamora coat-of-arms. The blue and white waves on the bottom represent the waters of the Rhône River in France. The tower atop a rock above those waves represent castle Roquemaure, Rock of the Moors. The mulberry branches and flowers are from the lands we owned in Spain, *mora* also being the Latin root word for mulberry. The *fleur de lys* on either side of the tower on a sky blue field identify our French origins, for Don Pedro Ramón, the first Spanish de Rocamora was a grandnephew of King Louis VIII. Your mother has seen it, and one day I shall allow you to read the chart that traces our bloodlines to even greater monarchs."

At their midday meal, Rocamora explained to Abigail and his children why the Sephardic community celebrated Charles' restoration with such joy and optimism.

"After Oliver Cromwell's death in 1658, bigots tried to suppress the nascent Jewish community, but now the new king has intervened in their favor. He has given them de facto recognition and opposes all religious oppression against the Jews."

"Why, *Abba*?"

"Solomon, it is because of their mercantile value. Charles received aid from several Jewish financiers during his exile. One of them, Augustino Coronel, also known as Nuñes da Costa, has secured a significant loan on his behalf from Alfonso VI of Portugal and is financing the dowry of Portuguese Princess Catherine de Braganza should they wed."

The freedom to return and worship as Jews in England for the first time since the reign of Edward I had other ramifications that concerned Rocamora, which he did not discuss with his family. The messianists believed the Anointed One would soon appear and fulfill Scriptural prophecies.

Given human nature, any charismatic charlatan might convince the gullible he could be the Messiah.

The one who lives out of delusions, dies of reality.
—Spanish Proverb

The opinions of many Christians and mine do concur, that we both believe that the restoring time of our Nation into their native country is very near at hand.
—Menasseh ben Israel, from a letter to Oliver Cromwell, 1654

Part IV
Difficult Years
1660-1667

58.
A Different Calendar

Although Rocamora continued to count in Spanish and mark months and years according to the Christian Gregorian calendar, he also measured time according to Jewish fasts, feasts, festivals, and holy days based on a thirteen-month calendar that followed the cycle of the moon. T

Rosh Hashanah, the Jewish New Year, came in late September or early October. It began the ten days of repentance culminating with Yom Kippur, the Day of Atonement for all sins and transgressions committed during the past year when all fasted from sundown to sundown

Sukkoth, Feast of the Tabernacle, based on harvest festivals, came next. At home, the children decorated a booth and trellis with palms, myrtle twigs, willows, citron, festoons of cranberries, and fruits shipped from the Holy Land.

For Rocamora, the three celebrations of Jewish survival were the most important days on the lunar calendar. Hanukkah, the Festival of Lights, came first in late November or early December and lasted for eight days. It commemorated the victory of Jewish rebels led by Judah HaMakabi, the Hammer, and his brothers known as Maccabees over their Greco-Syrian oppressors who banned circumcision, outlawed Judaism, looted the Temple in Jerusalem, and erected an altar to Zeus where they sacrificed pigs.

After the Maccabees saved Judaism from extinction, the Temple's Eternal Light had enough oil to burn for only one day. During the time needed to press more oil, a miracle occurred. The Eternal Light continued to burn for eight days. Judah Maccabeus then decreed an annual festival symbolized by the lighting of a menorah, a nine-branched candelabrum with four candles on each side of an extra light in the middle raised above the others. One candle was lit the first night, two the next, and so on to the eighth.

The festival and feast of Purim came on the full moon in February when Jews celebrated with costumes and processions the story of Esther, the crypto-Jewish queen of Persia who saved all Jews in the empire from a planned massacre by the King's chief advisor Haman. In Spain and Portugal, crypto-Jews revered the Persian queen as St. Esther and a martyr because she was willing to sacrifice herself for her religion and her people. Many secretly observed a three day fast as written in the Book of Esther to emulate the Jewish Queen. After her fast, Esther proclaimed to King Ahasuerus that she was a Jew and revealed Haman's plot to massacre her people. The King's love for Esther was so great he executed Haman and gave permission for the Jews to defend themselves.

Another eight day celebration and most significant of the three, Passover, arrived a lunar month after Purim in late March or early April. Each night at the family dinner known as Haggadah by the Sephardim of Vlooienburg, Rocamora read from a book of the same name. It told the story of Israelite slavery in Egypt, the heroics of Moses the Lawgiver, the Ten Plagues during which God slew all Egyptian first born but passed over and spared Jewish children, the Exodus from Egypt, the Ten Commandments, and promise of a land of milk and honey.

A joyous time for his children, Purim became Rocamora's favorite of all. He wrote a short play in which Queen Esther, played by Tiña in a robe and crown made by Abigail revealed herself as a Jew to her husband, King Ahasuerus, a role Moses acted regally and well. Solomon created a mask for little Daniel to wear for the character of Haman, the king's advisor who planned to massacre all the Jew within the Persian Empire. It resembled the Christian images of Satan. Solomon also took on the role of Esther's Uncle Mordechai, a court official who advised her. Joseph helped his mother replicate gemstones for Sara's crown and robe. By now, all her brothers addressed her as 'Tiña.

Before the feast began, Rocamora asked his children, "What does the word Purim mean?"

Solomon responded first, as he usually did to any question posed from Scripture. "Lots, *Abba*, which wicked Haman cast to select a date for the massacre."

The children booed and stamped their feet at Solomon's mention of Haman's name, as if to erase it. Rocamora stood and held his goblet of wine.

"The Talmud says that during the feast of Purim we are required to drink until we cannot distinguish between cursed Haman ..." He paused while the children again made noise to blot out the villain's name. ... "and blessed Mordecai, Esther's courageous uncle. That is why I have given each of you a small portion of wine to honor that command symbolically."

After they drank, Abigail and Sara helped Geitl serve the holiday delicacies they all loved, which came from differing Jewish cultures: Iberia, North Africa and the Ottoman Empire, and the Ashkenazim. The dishes included chicken soup with saffron infused matzoh balls, peppers and eggplant stuffed with vegetables and spices, onions fried in garlic and oil, and an assortment of pastries filled with nuts, raisins, honey, meats, and spices.

Throughout the meal, Rocamora reflected on the different personalities, diverse interests, and abilities of his children. Moses, who would be fifteen in March, had his features and physique. Often, Rocamora saw his own father's face when he looked at his eldest, other times that of Brianda. Intelligent but not studious, Moses would never be a physician, and he had no interest in trade. For the time being, he worked in the Santcroos dockside warehouse. The most Spanish of his children, Moses preferred a life of adventure, preferably as a soldier, a phase Rocamora hoped would pass.

By way of contrast, swarthy thirteen year old Solomon, the one son likely to join his practice as a physician, resembled several of Abigail's uncles. From the time he began to walk and speak, Solomon decided to be a physician, and he was the most observant of the children.

Physically soft with his mother's face, shy Joseph was already learning the craft of diamond polishing from Abigail.

Rocamora adored Tiña. His daughter also resembled Abigail feature for feature and inherited her mother's serene temperament. They had begun to save guilders and purchase necessary items for her dowry.

He worried most about his two youngest. Daniel was hunchbacked and frail of body with a twisted foot that caused him to limp. Like Solomon, he resembled the Touros. It was too early to know if the boy had a head for study or numbers, but his cheerful smile and sweetness of temperament charmed everyone who met him. Perhaps that would be all Daniel needed to survive in this world.

David was sickly, quiet, and passive. Rocamora told the older brothers and sister to give him much attention. That he was a physician ensured a longer life for David than the boy might otherwise have in another household.

"*Abba*?"

"Yes, Moses."

"If Esther could marry a gentile and be revered as a prophet, can a Jewish male marry a gentile?"

Rocamora noted Abigail's expression of alarm at their eldest's interest in marriage between Jew and gentile. He suspected Moses had a specific Christian girl in mind and intended to learn her identity.

"To answer your question, my son, it is against the law in Amsterdam for any Jew, male or female, to wed a Christian. Even if it were possible, children born of a gentile woman who converted, cannot be a Jew according to the rabbis. Yet, there is an irony to that because in Spain and elsewhere those same children are persecuted as Jews by the Christian populations."

"A Jew must marry someone born of a Jewish woman."

"Yes, Solomon, if he wants to be part of the community even though Boaz married Ruth the Moabite, and their great-grandson was King David."

"Then there can be exceptions."

"No, Moses, not since the rabbis codified Jewish Law a thousand years ago."

"Why did they do that?"

Solomon answered Moses. "At the *Yesibót*, the rabbis teach us that Italians, Frenchmen, Spaniards, Germans, and Greeks are mixtures of each other and also of Phoenicians, Chaldeans, Egyptians, Goths, Huns, Alemanni, Vandals, and Carthaginians. Israel, by contrast, although scattered throughout the world, has remained a separate and distinct people with our Law and a lineage we can trace to the patriarchs."

"Be careful, Solomon, when you repeat much of what you do not yet understand. You have described our own mixed though noble lineage through my parents and antecedents."

Solomon blushed. "I am sorry, *Abba*. I did not mean to offend."

"Better than taking pride in one's lineage, which is a mere accident of birth, you should be most proud of what you accomplish in life. I can assure you of this. Nothing is more rewarding than to triumph over obstacles and adversity and achieve worthwhile goals." Rocamora raised his glass. "Except to be blessed with a loving wife and children of whom to be proud."

59.
Kermis

Rocamora's calendar also included Dutch holidays and festivals he sometimes celebrated with his Christian friends. Now that all his children were old enough to enjoy it, he looked forward to the local Kermis each year when the celebrations did not conflict with Rosh Hashanah, the Jewish New Year. In September of 1663, Rocamora and Abigail decided to take them to the annual Amsterdam fair except for David who stayed home in bed watched over by Geitl.

He lifted undersized Daniel onto his shoulders so his son could see rows of temporary shops, stalls, and booths lining the streets where craftsmen exhibited examples of their art and wares and charlatan healers and fortunetellers gulled the credulous. Tradesmen, farmers, and entertainers filled city squares and fields beyond. Bakers sold flat oval griddlecakes with lettered pink sugar iced phrases surrounded by preserved fruit such as For your Kermis, With my Love, and With all my Heart for swains to offer girls they fancied. Rocamora purchased a cake for Sara, which read For my beautiful Tiña and another for Abigail with the dedication, *Por mi Querida*.

Rocamora led his family to a field where the populace sat on long benches, barrels, or on the ground eating and drinking beer in large quantities. All about them adults danced and children frolicked. Some walked on stilts. Others beat drums and tambourines and blew whistles. Minstrels carried placards displaying words for the populace to join them in songs. Fiddlers played amidst strollers inspecting wares at the stalls. Mischievous youths poured beer inside the shirts of the unwary or smeared their faces with flour and wax reminding Rocamora of pranksters in Valencia on Shrove Tuesday, the day of carousing before Lent began.

Abigail told her children not to stray. "So much to see it makes one dizzy."

"Yes, *querida*, it is difficult to focus on one entertainment."

They paused to watch acrobats, tightrope walkers, troupes of gymnasts performing Egyptian pyramids, talking dogs, and horses counting with their hooves. Cages held elephants, lions, and other exotic beasts from Africa and India.

At a merry-go-round, Rocamora showed Sara how to sit side-saddle on a wooden horse and secured Daniel in his seat. Their cries of delight mingled with those of other children and the creaking and groaning of the merry-go-round.

Moses left them to watch the militia parade in uniforms and display skills in archery, musket, carbine, and pistol. Solomon lingered to study how a beekeeper commanded the insects to return to their hive and a limbless man who could sew and weave using his mouth alone. Joseph was most interested in the mechanical theaters where clockwork puppets played drum and bugle.

Solomon asked Rocamora how cows, pigs, and dogs on display could have been born with two heads or with three to six feet and other anomalies.

"It is either the result of disease or injuries that occurred before or during birth."

"*Capitán*, where is our Moses?"

Solomon pointed. "Over there watching a game of *Groote Kolven* on the grass."

"Our eldest son is too fond of meaningless games … and gentile girls."

Rocamora followed Abigail's glance and saw Moses talking to a comely ash blonde. Not a hand's width of space separated them. Was she the girl who prompted Moses' question at the Purim feast about a Jewish male marrying a gentile woman? He could not blame the boy. She was pretty and obviously adored him.

"Did you hear me, *Capitán*?"

"Yes, *querida*, but do not worry. It appears to be a harmless flirtation."

"But if he becomes enamored of a Christian, Dutch law forbids."

"Solomon, watch your brother. If Moses strays too far from the festivities with that girl … wait, bring him here. We must leave now."

Abigail breathed with difficulty. Perspiration drenched her face. Rocamora held his wife to prevent her from falling. The peak summer heat affected others. Rocamora saw ladies fainting and men suffering shortness of breath when he led his family home.

In bed that night, Abigail clung to Rocamora. "I worry about our Moses. He is so reckless. I know he will not be a physician, and he has no head for learning scripture or any trade. What shall become of our eldest? He cannot, he must not work in a warehouse for the rest of his life."

"Moses should become whatever he wants, which I was not allowed to do at his age. Had my father and mother lived, I would have soldiered for the

Crown or sought adventure and riches in the New World."

"I shall never consent to Moses being a soldier, living amongst gentiles, or marrying one, God forbid."

Rocamora did not misread his wife's tone of voice. When Abigail held an opinion, she could be as immoveable as the stone walls of Toledo. "Would you say *Kaddish* for him?" Tears came to her eyes, and Rocamora realized he had gone too far "Perhaps it might be best for him to go to New Amsterdam where there is a thriving Jewish community."

"Never. Moses is our firstborn. He will stay at home with us here in Amsterdam. All our children must. Promise me you will speak with Moses and dissuade him from all that would cause us displeasure and grief."

"I promise."

"Will you promise me something else?"

Rocamora remembered his pledge to Rafal without knowing what it was until too late and sensed his wife might ask of him that to which he could not agree. "What is it?"

"Should anything happen to me, promise you will marry again so our children will have a mother to look after them."

"Is there something you have not told me?"

"I have dreamed often that you wed another."

"And you did not take a dagger to me?"

"I am serious."

"I have seen no unhealthy signs. You recovered quickly from the heat. Your eyes are clear, your complexion healthy. You have boundless energy. Now tell me. Who is it you saw me wed?"

"My cousin, Sara Eliahu."

"God spare me that. You cannot be serious."

"She loves you no less than I."

"That is her misfortune."

"But it is my wish that if anything does happen to me, you must marry her. She will look after you and the children."

"Wed Sara? The best I can promise is that I would consider it most carefully and ask the opinion of our sons and daughter." He kissed Abigail and held her. "I cannot imagine being wed to anyone else. You are my Aphrodite and my Athena."

"My pagan *Capitán*, you could not compare me to anyone from scripture?"

"You still bewitch me as Delilah did Samson."

"A gentile."

"Very well, as Esther enthralled Ahasuerus, with all the wisdom of Deborah. I cannot conceive of my life without you."

Later, while Abigail slept, Rocamora lay awake troubled. Other than her near fainting at the Kermis, which could have been caused by the intense midsummer heat, he had diagnosed no evidence of illness. He believed Abigail would outlive him given the twenty-one year difference in their ages. Yet, there was much he did not know about the failings of the human body.

Abigail showed no signs of ill health during the following months. Assisted by Geitl, she marketed, cooked, taught and mothered their children with her typical energy. Over those same months, significant events caused excitement throughout the community. Charles II of England knighted the Jew, Coronel Chacon, for negotiating his marriage to Princess Catherine de Braganza of Portugal, who brought with her a sizeable dowry. Rabbis and the congregation of Talmud Torah believed England would be as tolerant a sanctuary for Jews as the United Provinces. That further encouraged the messianists who anticipated the imminent appearance of their Anointed One.

Rocamora avoided all messianic discussion so as not to offend the credulous with his skepticism. He did not understand why any rational man would want to trade the good life in Amsterdam for a return to Zion, that pile of sand in the desert surrounded by hostile Muslims.

The latest news from Spain interested Rocamora more than the messianic speculations of the Sephardic community. His former partisan, Rodrigo Méndez de Silva, former Royal Councilor and Historiographer to Philip IV and renowned as the Spanish Livy, fled to the Venice ghetto where he submitted to circumcision, took the name Jacob, and married an eighteen year old at age sixty-eight.

May he be virile enough to please her.

Rocamora did not feel any significant burden of age himself except for weaker eyes and an occasional tooth at the back of his mouth that needed removing. Men much younger than he showed more severe symptoms of aging, further proof that one's chronology was not necessarily his destiny.

60.
Father and Son

Not until an evening at the end of December 1663 did Rocamora summon Moses for a serious talk. He gave the boy permission to sit opposite him by the fire, proud he and Abigail had created so strong and handsome a son.

"Have I done something to offend you, *Abba*?"

"No, Moses, but I am concerned, and so is your *Eemah*. That girl who commanded all your time at the Kermis and whom you have been seeing...."

"So Solomon has been spying on me again."

"I have asked him to watch over you for your own good. You are aware of the laws prohibiting Jews from becoming intimate with Christian women."

"Yes, *Abba*, I know, but we were doing nothing wrong. Solomon would have told you. Delia is so beautiful, and I ... I cannot find the words to explain it, but I am happiest when I am with her."

"Yes, I know what you mean."

"You do?"

"That is how I feel when I am with your mother." Rocamora would never tell Moses of his passion for Moraíma when he was the same age.

"*Abba*. If Delia converted ...."

"Forbidden by the civic authorities. Surely, you have noticed many young girls of good family in Vlooienburg who will be available one day for marriage."

"I care not for any of them."

"There are other communities of Sephardim here in the United Provinces, Rotterdam for instance, and your mother also has kin in Venice and Bordeaux. Perhaps in a few years, we can find a suitable girl in one of those communities who would please you as a wife. But first, you must decide what you wish to do with your life."

"You know I want to be a soldier like *Oom* Dirck."

"Perhaps I made a mistake teaching you weapons."

"I would have found a way to learn."

"Yes, I am sure you would have. You want to soldier, and so did I at your age. A martial spirit seems to flow in our blood."

"You never told me what you did in battle at Nördlingen."

"I experienced the worst horrors of war." For the first time, Rocamora described for Moses the deaths and misery he had witnessed and caused on the battlefield.

"I wish I could have been there with you, *Abba*. I know you are disappointed that I lack the desire and ability to become a physician like you and have no interest in Scripture and trade. Solomon and my brothers will fulfill those dreams for you. Give me your blessing and let me join the army."

"And live as a gentile?"

"Yes, if I must, as you did for all your life before you came to Amsterdam."

Moses' quick answers reminded Rocamora of his own responses to Ramón that day when his kinsman told him he must enter the Dominican Order. "Do you want to break your *Eemah's* heart?" Rocamora lowered his voice. "Perhaps I should not tell you this, but firstborns are always the favorites of their parents, especially their mothers, although we love all our children equally."

"I will speak the truth, *Abba*. I have considered running away."

"To the army?"

"Yes, that or to the English Colonies where Miriam and Lyzor live."

Rocamora was of two minds. If the boy left, it would devastate Abigail and create a void in his own life. She might blame him, which could create a chasm between them. Still, Rocamora wished his son the life of choice that Rafal and his own commitment to honor had denied him. "I need to think more on the matter, Moses. Promise me, you will do nothing rash in the meantime."

"I promise, *Abba*. I will not run away to join the army or sail to the New World until we discuss my future again. But please, let it be soon."

"It shall be. And about the girl …." Rocamora hesitated when Moses set his jaw in the same manner as Abigail when she became immovable in an argument. He did not want to force a promise his son might not be able to keep. "Tell me about Delia's family, their name and religion. Are they educated people of substance?"

"Her father is Martin Schiffer, a member of the Bricklayers Guild."

"A Calvinist?"

"I am not sure because her father is drunk much of the time. Delia says he is inflexible and hates Jews, Catholics, and the Remonstrantors. He knows nothing about me."

"There are other children?"

"Two older brothers and a younger sister."

"How old is your Delia?"

"She is two months younger than I."

"We shall talk about her again. Until then, continue to be discreet."

Rocamora said good night to Moses and considered how best to deal with him. His eldest still wanted to soldier, but the army did not accept Jews. All to the good, for were Moses to convert to the Dutch Reformed Church and choose that life, Abigail would suffer grief as if her firstborn had died. Perhaps Moses would thrive best in the New World. Rocamora discarded the Spanish and Portuguese colonies as too dangerous and the Caribbean too pestilential. On the morrow, he would write Miriam and Lyzor for detailed information about the Jewish communities in New Amsterdam and the English colonies. Yet, were Moses to leave for the New World, that too would cause Abigail to suffer as if he had died. The best alternative to separate Moses from Delia was to send him away from Amsterdam and the United Provinces to live with one of the Touro families in Venice or Bordeaux until his infatuation passed or she wed another.

Rocamora worried he may have been too lenient and indulgent a father to Moses, to all his children. He wanted them to be happy and free to choose their own lives.

Deep in thought about his children, Rocamora reacted as if his heart had stopped. He sprang from his chair. "No, *mi querida,* no."

61.
Irreplaceable

Rocamora dashed to their bed in the great hall. He held a candle over Abigail. Her face glowed in the flickering light never so beautiful, her expression one of saintly repose. Twice he called her name. She did not respond. He touched his beloved's cheek still warm and her soft neck. No pulse, no movement.

Rocamora the husband refused to accept what Rocamora the physician diagnosed. He pulled away Abigail's bedding, sat on the bed, and held her. No mistaking it, her heart stopped moments ago sometime after midnight on the thirtieth day of December 1663, at age forty-one.

Rocamora snuffed the candle. Throughout the night, he clutched Abigail to his chest rocking back and forth, recalling their life together. She had been his anchor, the glue that bound him to the Sephardic community, his partner, his lover, his confidante, his better self. His *querida* made their home a wider realm than the Spanish Empire he once served and his existence in the narrow confines of the Amsterdam Iberian community tolerable.

He had made a permanent place for himself as a respected physician and citizen in Amsterdam and had sons and a daughter, but without Abigail, did it have any meaning? Rocamora wished an afterlife existed where he could reunite with his *b'shert*, destined soul mate.

A voice brought him back to his surroundings. "Doctor, it is late. Breakfast is … is the Señora ill?"

Geitl had entered the great hall. Rocamora shielded Abigail' face. "Stay where you are. Do not come closer. Listen to me, Geitl. My Abigail died in her sleep."

"No."

"Geitl, please, calm yourself. There is much to be done. Return to the serving kitchen. Say nothing to the children, but tell Moses to come here. I will send for the children in turn so they may kiss their mother goodbye."

After Geitl left, Rocamora laid Abigail atop the bed and covered her to the neck. When Moses entered, he placed a hand on his son's shoulder. "My firstborn, your mother is dead. You may kiss her goodbye."

"She looks asleep, *Abba*."

"Your mother died peacefully." He watched Moses kneel and kiss his mother's cheek. "Save your tears for later. You must be strong for your brothers and sister. Now send Solomon to me. I want you and Geitl to comfort the younger children, and until I give permission, not one of you is to leave the serving kitchen."

Moments later, Solomon darted into the great hall. "*Abba,* is it true?"

"Yes, Solomon."

"But how, when?"

"We shall speak of it much later. Kiss your mother goodbye. Good. Now go to Talmud Torah and notify the Last Rites Committee and Rabbi Morteira. After you return, help Moses and Geitl console your brothers and sister."

Joseph wailed at Abigail's bedside, crying, kissing her face and hand until Rocamora pulled him away. "Joseph, that is enough. Must I shake you? Now, send your sister to me"

After Tiña, Daniel and David kissed their mother goodbye, Rocamora sat with Abigail in the great hall disengaging from reality and dreaming of their life together until he heard the Last Rites Committee approaching. He kissed Abigail for the last time.

"*Mi querida,* this must be our final moment together in body, but in spirit we shall always be united beyond the grave throughout eternity."

The Last Rites Committee entered with their ritual paraphernalia, and Rocamora went to his study, each step an ordeal, his legs heavy as if bearing iron weights. He brooded by the fire unable to watch strangers touch his beloved Abigail. Still, he heard them moving about and the chanting of their prayers. During his more than sixteen years practicing medicine, he had been present at many such rituals and could not avoid seeing in his mind's eye everything the Committee did to his Abigail.

Rabbi Morteira recited prayers from Ezekiel and Leviticus. The women removed Abigail's night shift, placed her on a freshly washed board, and covered her with a clean sheet. They poured pitchers of lukewarm water over Abigail three times, replaced the soaked sheet with a dry one and reached underneath to clean her most intimate parts.

The women next washed their hands and poured three pails of cold water over Abigail from head to foot. After they dried and covered her in a plain shroud of the finest white linen, the men of the Committee lifted Abigail into the coffin, making sure she lay in a position of tranquil sleep.

Morteira placed bits of earth from the Holy Land on Abigail's eyes and recited, "Let them not draw near to gaze when what is sacred is covered, lest they die."

The men closed and sealed the coffin, never to be opened again.

62.
Year of Mourning

Rocamora thought it undignified to grieve in front of family and strangers. He refused to tear his doublet, and Solomon brought him a black cloth to rend instead, which satisfied the rabbis. He bore the subsequent burial rituals and Shiva, the intense seven days of mourning and prayers at home, in a state of *desengaño*, disillusionment and stoic detachment.

Alone at night, he grieved unable to weep and spoke to Abigail. He gave Geitl money to purchase the finest fabrics, which he placed over his *b'shert's* chairs in the eating kitchen and dining room out of respect.

After Shiva ended, Rocamora sat with his children in the study, Sara on his lap, Moses in the other chair holding David, and Solomon on the divan with Daniel beside him.

"Where is Joseph?"

Moses looked at the ceiling. "He is in the attic. Shall I get him, *Abba*?"

Rocamora supposed Joseph was clinging to Abigail's diamond mills as if in communion with his mother, which the boy had been doing from the day she died. "No, I will speak with him. Moses, Solomon, because you have been bar mitzvahed, you are men of the congregation. We cannot shave or cut our hair during our year of mourning. There are external rituals we must observe to satisfy traditions, but I want you to know this. You have my permission and support to grieve for your mother, may she rest in peace, however you like. Now listen to me, children. Listen to me carefully. Your mother loved each of you with all her heart and being. She wanted you to be happy and live fulfilling lives. It will be painful at first, but we must resume our daily routines. I have patients to see. I shall begin my rounds tomorrow. Moses, return to the warehouse. Hard work will help you through your grieving. Solomon, you will stay at my side and assist me with my patients. I want you to learn all I know so that you shall be better prepared than any other student for medical school when the time comes."

"Thank you, Father."

"*Abba*, I will help Geitl clean and cook and take care of Daniel, and David."

Looking after her younger brothers would be enough work for Tiña. Too many girls Sara's age became little mothers and old before their time. Rocamora wanted his daughter to continue learning to read and write in several languages and play the harpsichord he had purchased for her. Although death silenced Abigail's voice, music and laughter must return to their home. How and when, it was too soon to know.

He kissed his daughter and stood her on the floor. "Tiña, I will hire a woman to help Geitl cook and clean."

"Daniel, David, come here." He hugged his two youngest. "We all miss your mother, may she rest in peace, but know this. Your older brothers, Sara, and I will take care of you and love you."

Rocamora sent the children to bed and asked Moses to stay. Staring at his eldest was the same as looking in the mirror and seeing his own reflection. "Moses, you did well to comfort your brothers and sister these past trying days. Once the year of mourning has passed, we shall speak again about the road you wish to follow. But for now, tell me the truth. Which is it you prefer? The army or the New World?"

"I prefer the New World. I want to marry Delia and take her with me. I would like us to have a *señorio* like Benetorrente in Valencia and own my own land, the same as your father and our ancestors in Spain."

"An admirable aspiration, but you are only fifteen."

"I will be sixteen in March. That is two months away, and Delia's birthday is in May."

"Her family will never consent to your marrying."

"We could leave without their knowledge."

"Well, many things can change in a year."

"Not our love for each other."

"We shall see. I will introduce you to men who have been to New Amsterdam. They can tell you what to expect. Although we are in an extended period of mourning, I think it best for you to sharpen your proficiency at arms and other skills to ensure your survival. Should you go to New Amsterdam, you must first visit Miriam and Lyzor."

"I cannot believe she has two children."

"And a third on the way. Her letter arrived today. You may read it later. Speak of our conversation to no one."

Rocamora went to the attic where Joseph clung to the diamond mills. He patted the boy's head. "It will be all right, Joseph. I will tell Geitl to bring you food and drink today, but tomorrow, you will return to the *Yesibôt*. If I must, I will take you there myself. Do you understand?"

"Yes, *Abba*."

Rocamora came home with Solomon exhausted from seeing his backlog of patients and maintaining a façade of stoicism. "Geitl, where are the children?"

"I called them twice to come and wash for supper. Shall I look for them?"

"No, I will go."

Rocamora went through each room of the silent house until he heard voices coming from the attic. Atop the last step, he hesitated surprised to see Tiña giving lessons to David and Daniel. An earlier moment in time flashed before his eyes. He saw Abigail teaching young Moses and Solomon.

Sara ran to him. "Eemah would have wanted them to continue their lessons."

"I am proud of you, Tiña, you too, Daniel and David. Joseph, leave the mills. All of your, go down for your supper."

Rocamora had no appetite and went to his study. By the time he settled in a chair by the fire, Tiña entered carrying a tea service..

"*Abba*, I tried to make you tea the way eemah did. I know you like coffee better, but I have to be shown how to do it."

"Thank you." He took the cup from Tiña and sipped the tea. "Delicious, the best I have ever tasted."

"Really, *Abba*?" She lit his pipe. "Then I will bring it to you every night."

Rocamora turned his head so his daughter would not see the first tears he shed since Abigail died.

At each meal Abigail's shrouded chair intensified Rocamora's sense of loss. Sabbaths, Purim, and Passover were no longer joyous. A return to daily routines did not lessen his and the children's grieving.

When Moses arrived home from work, he played with his younger brothers and sister always mindful to be gentle with frail Daniel and sickly David. Solomon watched Rocamora treat his patients during the day and studied medicine at night. After school and supper until bedtime, Joseph practiced bruting shards of gemstones at Abigail's mills in the attic. Daniel attempted to cheer him and listless David with jests and sleight of hand tricks he learned from Rocamora. Between teaching her younger brothers and expanding her own education, Sara took lessons in the harpsichord and served her father tea each evening.

One day in late spring, Geitl approached Rocamora when he came into the cooking kitchen to wash. "Doctor, I must speak with you. It is intolerable. Those women, your Touro in-laws … they must be watching the house. Whenever you leave to see patients, they arrive like a flock of crows. They come not to help with my cooking and cleaning, which they criticize, but to pry and question the children."

Joseph and Tiña also had complained about their aunts and cousins. Rocamora did not want those women snooping. "Geitl, there is no reason for anyone to visit when I am not at home. You may prevent them from entering, by force if necessary."

"Thank you, Doctor." She shook her kneading roller. "It will be my pleasure."

After the midday meal, Rocamora went to his study. It seemed moments later when Solomon awakened him from his unplanned siesta. "*Abba*, the bells …."

Plague struck Amsterdam in the summer of 1664 as it had in 1655. With Solomon at his side, Rocamora treated his patients. Again, he saw strong and healthy men and women succumbing to the plague and could not understand why Daniel and David, his sickly and frail youngest children, survived. Had it been the extreme measures he had taken to ensure their home was clean and they washed regularly? Did the de Rocamora and Touro bloodlines have some magical immunity? By the time the magistrates declared the plague officially ended, more than ten percent of the city's population had been buried, over a thousand in one week.

The passing of his great friend Jacobus Velde that summer saddened Rocamora. The gregarious surgeon had not died of plague but from food poisoning.

Three months before the year of ritual mourning for Abigail ended, her unctuous cousin Solomon Eliahu Touro visited, and Rocamora took him into the study.

"I shall speak frankly, Don Isaac, I have come here to again offer my sincerest condolences and to speak on behalf of my sister, Sara Eliahu."

Rocamora glared at the man for his effrontery. "Understand this. I do not love your sister. I never shall."

"Yes, yes, of course, but at our ages, it is more important that marriage offers comfort and companionship. If love comes later, as it usually does, so much the better. It is not good to be without a wife. You have six children. A man cannot care for so many alone, and my sister may yet conceive even if she will soon be forty. Our Touro women are fertile as you well know. Your year of mourning is almost over, and …."

"Over, you presume to say? Over? Know this, Solomon Eliahu, I shall mourn my beloved Abigail, may she rest in peace, until the day I die."

The power of Rocamora's voice and the green fire in his eyes caused Solomon Eliahu to shrink. "Still, you must think of your children, especially the youngest."

Rocamora gestured toward the door. "Have you not understood a single word I have said? It is best you leave."

Solomon Eliahu stood and groveled. "Forgive me, Don Isaac, I did not mean to offend."

"You have indeed offended me. Get out of my home, and do not speak another word."

63.
Yèyīng's Story

"Another draw."

Rocamora studied the remaining few elaborately carved jade chess pieces on the board. "So it is. Neither of us has yet to win."

"That is because we are well-matched and cannot cheat the way we do so well at cards and dice."

Rocamora sipped tea with Yèyīng atop cushions of silk and breathed sweet scents from incense and floral perfumes. After the year of ritual mourning ended, he had first gone to Peter Velde to have his hair, beard, and mustache cut and trimmed. Next, he visited *The Fragrant Peony* for Pablo's companionship and a bath.

That was when Yèyīng challenged him to their first game of chess. He welcomed her as a gift. She did everything possible to distract him from his grief. Her suite at *The Fragrant Peony* became an exotic world where he forgot everything and lived the moment. Yèyīng also told him her story without his asking in increments each time he visited. Soon it became a coherent narrative.

Yèyīng's parents came from families of prosperous Chinese merchants in Macao. They disowned her mother after she eloped with a Portuguese sea captain. Yèyīng's father decided that being a pirate was the most profitable business of all, but he was killed in battle when she was eight. The crew abandoned them, and they returned to Macao. Rejected by her parents, Yèyīng's mother turned to prostitution. The women who ran the brothel forced Yèyīng into the same servitude.

The day Yèyīng's mother died, members of her father's pirate crew visited the brothel, and the sixteen year old girl ran away with them. She learned to wield dagger and sword equal to any man and challenged the captain for control of her father's ship. After slaying him in a duel, Yèyīng led her men in raids and plunder throughout the Indies.

One night, she led a daring raid on Macao to loot and burn the home and business of her grandparents. Yèyīng would not tell Rocamora if she killed them. She also attacked the brothel where she had been enslaved, freed the women working there, and sold the owners to slavers. After more night raids, she became known as Night Hawk, feared throughout the Indies and along the South China coast.

A significant part of Yèyīng's story differed from Pablo's version. As she told it, he did not capture her. True, Pablo and his men boarded her ship and won the battle, but Yèyīng faced him with her sword and a primed pistol prepared to die fighting. During the standoff, Pablo offered her generous terms if she would join him. Wanted for piracy by several sultans, the Spanish, Portuguese, and English who offered high prices for her head, Yèyīng accepted Pablo's offer of a new life in Amsterdam but on her terms. She would not tell Rocamora her age or her birth name.

During each of Yèyīng's narratives, Rocamora instinctively assumed his familiar role of royal confessor. He listened and offered no advice. When Yèyīng expressed regret for certain acts, he almost suggested penance or offered absolution. Rocamora interlocked his fingers to avoid crossing himself. He did ask the occasional question.

"Do you miss the sea?"

"That was another life. I am content with this one."

"Will you return to the Indies or Macao one day?"

"Who can say? Pablo told me the story of your life and his, and you have heard mine. The paths we choose always lead to forks in the road, and each provides many surprises for good and for ill."

"Yes, Dame Fortune, Kismet, Fate, or whatever else we choose to call it, can be most capricious."

Yèyīng looked away from Rocamora. "Before I left the brothel, I became pregnant, and my masters forced me to abort, which left me incapable of bearing children." She paused and frowned. "This is most puzzling."

"What is?"

"I have never spoken about my life to anyone else. What is it that impels me to reveal myself to you? Pablo said you were a royal confessor. I suppose I should not be surprised."

"Your secrets are safe with me, Yèyīng."

"Yes, I know. I sense your restlessness. You wish to leave me now."

"I would prefer to linger here, for in this suite with you I forget all my cares. I have an important matter to settle and patients to see."

"You will return tomorrow?"

Rocamora donned his hat. "Perhaps sooner, perhaps this evening?"

"That will please me."

64.
"My Son, my son."

After Rocamora left Yèyīng, he walked to the Santcroos warehouse at the docks. David Samuel welcomed him in his office.

"Doctor, what a pleasant surprise. Please sit. Would you prefer coffee or tea?"

"Coffee. I have become addicted to the brew."

"I cannot fault you for that. One day it may surpass tea as a favorite drink if we can reduce the cost."

"I saw your eldest, Samuel David, recording inventory with my Moses. He is looking well."

"He has been in excellent health ever since you cured him of his respiratory problems."

Rocamora savored a sip of coffee. "I see so much of your father in you. He would be pleased to see how well you are running the company."

"Thank you, Doctor."

Santcroos asked no questions, which he appreciated. Rocamora had hoped Moses' infatuation with Delia would end during the year of mourning. It had not, and he intended to delay his son's sailing for as long as possible. "I have come here to ask on behalf of a friend about booking passage on one of your ships bound for New Amster ... I mean New York, now that the British took it from us last September. Perhaps late spring or early summer might be best."

"Yes."

"Is that rascal Gaspar Hendrijks still at sea?"

"Gaspar returned from Rotterdam this morning after what he said was his last voyage. I believe you could coax him out of retirement. He always speaks of the time you saved his life during the crossing of the North Sea."

"Gaspar in Amsterdam? I look forward to seeing him" Rocamora stood. "You have given me much to think about. I thank you for your time and your excellent coffee."

On an afternoon the following week, Rocamora stood with Solomon at his shelves of herbs in the basement. Now fifteen, the boy had developed into a fine young man, a brilliant scholar, serious of mind, with unshakable loyalty to his brothers and sister.

"Have you memorized their efficacies?"

"I believe so, *Abba*."

"We shall see." Rocamora touched a jar. "What is this?"

Solomon did not hesitate. "*Althea officinalis*, true marshmallow. Hippocrates wrote it is effective for treating wounds, and Dioscorides infused it with vinegar for toothache and its seeds as a poultice for stings from the bee and other insects. It also has been used to treat problems of the stomach, soreness of throat, and various infections."

"Excellent, my son. And this?"

"*Paeonia officinalis*, commonly called the peony, used since the time of Hippocrates to treat epilepsy."

"And?"

Solomon hesitated and blushed.

"My son, you will have to become more at ease with the female body and the ailments unique to women. Did I not tell you that its root is favored by Chinese physicians in the treatment of women who have problems with their monthly rhythms and the time when they begin to change as they age?"

"Yes, *Abba*."

After he further tested Solomon's herbal knowledge, which the boy passed with ease, Rocamora sat with him by the fire in his study. "You are going to be a fine physician, better than I. Are you looking forward to medical school next year?"

"Impatiently, but your teaching is helping to pass the time quickly."

"You alone of all my sons have a calling to medicine. Joseph will apprentice himself to a diamond polisher and learn the trade. Daniel and David lack the stamina for rigorous study."

"You omitted Moses."

Rocamora had not told his other children he had given permission for his eldest to leave for the New World. Even now, Moses was at the docks with Pablo and Captain Hendrijks discussing the best day for him and Delia to sail in the spring on the safest, cleanliest vessel in Santcroos' fleet.

"Moses will find himself."

"*Abba*, tell me, is it true you are to wed our cousin Sara Eliahu?"

Rocamora saw Solomon's look of distress aware the boy had more than a natural reluctance to accept a substitute for his beloved mother. Persistent Sara Eliahu had yet to endear herself to any of his children. The time had come to tell that woman and her brother ....

Before Rocamora could finish his thought, Joseph ran into the room crying and incoherent. He shook the boy until he made sense.

"Moses has been injured."

"Where is he?"

Pablo and a burly sailor carried Moses into the basement. Blood saturated a cloth wrapped around his head.

Rocamora cried out horrified, "My son, my son. What has happened to you?" He fought panic and fear. No time to summon Peter Velde, he had to be both physician and surgeon and treat Moses as a patient, not as his son.

"Pablo, place Moses on the table and stoke the fire. Solomon, tell Geitl to bring pots of boiling water. Joseph, find Sara and keep her, Daniel and David out of the way. Solomon, you will assist me. Light more candles, as many as we have."

"Pablo, who did this to my Moses?"

"Fortunately, I was on the docks, so I saw everything. Moses climbed a mast against my advice. You know how adventurous he can be, and he fell."

Rocamora stifled an urge to weep and focused on what had to be done. The winter sun was setting early. He lit several more candelabras and scrubbed his hands before he removed the blood soaked wraps. He recoiled at the severity of Moses' injury.

"Solomon, this is going to be the most delicate of operations. Note how bits of bone have penetrated the brain. They must be extracted with the greatest of care to avoid harming or removing too much brain tissue."

"Trepanning?"

"No, I will not need to bore into Moses' skull. As you can see, his wounds are open to the brain. Pablo, please bring that candelabrum closer. Solomon, I need another for more light."

"Yes, *Abba*."

Rocamora spoke aloud to teach Solomon and to calm himself. "Always concentrate on the specific and not the whole during an operation. First, we must see if the flesh around the bone is in danger of suppurating. The wound should be made to ripen and discharge pus as quickly as possible. Once cleaned the wound must be kept dry, for then it will heal quickly. What I have said holds true for the membrane surrounding the brain."

"*Abba*, why are you leaving those shards of bone in the wound?"

"They are too small and it would be injurious to the brain if I tried to remove them. They will ascend naturally and be flushed away with the discharge of pus." Rocamora washed, cauterized, and dressed Moses' wounds with clean linens. "One day, perhaps in your lifetime Solomon, we will be allowed to be both physician and surgeon."

"Will Moses awaken soon?"

"I cannot say. Let us pray he does. Now, I wish to speak with Pablo. If Moses awakens, give him the opiate I have prepared." Rocamora saw Joseph and Sara weeping at the bottom of the steps. "Control yourselves. None of this will help Moses. Tiña, I want you to watch over Daniel and David. Joseph, you must do whatever Solomon asks of you."

Rocamora took Pablo to his study. "Tell me the truth. What really happened to Moses?"

"I did not want to speak in front of your children. Moses brought Delia to the dock to show her the ship they would be taking to the New World, but her father and two older brothers followed them. Before we could come to Moses' aid, one hit him from behind with a mallet, and the father carried off the girl. After Moses fell, her second brother tried to bash his skull with a brick. He got in one blow before we chased them away. I would have run after them, but it was more important to bring Moses to you."

"You did well, my friend. You saved his life. Now, where are the dogs who hurt my son?"

"Captain Hendrijks had one of his crew follow them. He will tell us where they are."

Rocamora felt rage and desire for revenge no less than the day the Anglesolas assassinated his beloved father. He had given full retribution to those swine and would do the same with the vermin who had assaulted his firstborn. He led Pablo to the attic and unlocked a trunk. "I thought I was forever finished with vengeance and vendetta."

Rocamora attached belt and sword. He primed a brace of wheel locks and held the dagger he had used to dispatch Enríque Anglesola, murderer of his father, and for his self-circumcision.

"We will need help, Vicente. Even if you and I catch them unawares, we are but two, and they are three large and strong men."

"Put away that garrote, my friend. I have in mind a better fate for them. We must hasten. They shall pay dearly for what they did to my boy."

Solomon waited for them at the front door holding a surgical knife. Rocamora had never seen his son so angry.

"*Abba*, I will go with you. They tried to kill my brother."

He placed his hand on Solomon's shoulder. "Your manliness makes me proud of you, my son, but your place is with Moses. Watch over him."

Hendrijks insisted on being part of Rocamora's party and helped select four of the strongest dock rat veterans of many a battle and brawl: two Poles, a Swede, and an African. They snuffed their torches and took positions near a bridge by the tavern where Delia's father and brothers were drinking. Night fog reduced vision to no more than a few yards, and before long they saw three men emerging through the mist staggering and singing. Rocamora assigned two seamen to each brother. He, Pablo, and Hendrijks would deal with Delia's father.

A hard blow to the back of the head, a second to the knee, and a third or fourth to their thick skulls, and the assault ended in seconds. "You selected good men, Gaspar."

"They have proven themselves many times before."

They dragged Delia's father and brothers a short distance to the docks. Hendrijks led them to a ship scheduled to sail at first light. Rocamora heard voices on the deck, and Hendrijks called out, "Where is your captain?"

"I am Captain Abel Muelen. Who are you?"

"Captain Gaspar Hendrijks. I have brought the extra cargo I promised you, three sturdy men who wish to sail with you."

Rocamora stood at the gangplank and looked at the fierce black bearded man. Muelen's reputation for harshness and cruelty was so notorious few willingly sailed with him. Equally vicious, his chief mates sought prey in the taverns and plied them with drinks or waylaid them in alleys. Their victims awakened aboard too late when the ship was at sea.

Muelen stepped onto the dock followed by several crewmen who carried chains. "Aye, they are of good size. How much do you want for them?"

Rocamora took charge of the negotiating even though he would have given them to Muelen at no charge. "Ten guilders."

"I already have a full crew. Make it five."

"Eight."

Muelen's eyes narrowed. "More vengeance than business for you, is it?"

"Well?"

'Six."

"Seven."

"Agreed." Muelen paid Rocamora. "I can make a good profit when I sell them in the Indies. By tomorrow, they should be whipped into shape."

Rocamora watched satisfied when Muelen's crew put the Schiffers in chains and dragged them aboard. "Captain, be sure you let them know that the father of Moses Isaac de Rocamora arranged their voyage and destination."

He paid each dock rat two guilders, much more than he had promised them, and embraced Pablo and Hendrijks. "I thank you for your help, my friends, but now I must hasten to Moses."

65.
Family Conferences

Rocamora sat with Sara Eliahu and her brother Solomon in his study. Forty and never wed, the woman's large dark eyes feasted on him ravenous as a vulture, as they always had, but this day her facial expression also conveyed hope and at times a surprising softness. That was the mystery of Sara Eliahu. She could be a warm and kind person, or she might become angry and speak sharply for no discernible reason.

Rocamora had agreed to a meeting because raising six children on his own had become too much for him and aging Geitl. "Doña Sara, I have been told by your brother and others of your family that you wish to marry me. Am I correct?"

"Yes."

"Remember, I have six children. Each one is a different person. Moses and David need extra care."

"I know I can be a loving wife and mother."

"That may be true, but I want to make this clear to you and your brother, Doña Sara. I do not love you. I will not … I cannot share the conjugal bed with you."

"I can be patient. Love comes after marriage."

"In truth, love came to Abigail and me several years before we wed." Rocamora saw Sara Eliahu's expression darken. She would be forever jealous of Abigail. "Be that as it may, you must understand exactly how you will have to care for my children and run my house were we to wed."

"I will do whatever you say."

Rocamora removed a paper from his doublet. "I have written a list …."

"Excuse me for interrupting, Don Isaac, but my sister cannot read. Our father did not believe in educating girls."

Rocamora masked his disappointment Sara was illiterate. "Very well then, I shall explain what I have written. Moses, my eldest, injured his head in an accident last week. He is still bedridden and must be washed often because he soils his bedclothes. I do not know if he will regain his full mental capacity. Solomon is my responsibility, for he will be at my side to learn all he can about medicine until he leaves for a university next year. Joseph has his mother's talent and a great interest in diamonds. He is already a competent polisher. When Joseph is not at the *Yesibôt*, he must be free to spend all his time learning to work the diamond mills. Daniel is deformed and frail. David is sickly. I fear he may not live to his bar mitzvah. You must give my youngest sons much care."

"I can do all that."

"Now, about my daughter, Sara …."

"She will help your servant and me market, cook, and clean the house."

"No, my Tiña will not. You will help Geitl." The power of Rocamora's voice and his stern expression caused both sister and brother to recoil. "Understand this. I shall never allow my daughter to become an old woman before her time. She will continue her studies and lessons with the harpsichord. Your main obligations will be to give my children all the attention and love they require and provide a clean well run home for all. Do you understand?"

"Yes, of course I do."

I wonder.

"Then, Doctor, we can sign the banns?"

"Not so fast, Solomon Eliahu. I have not yet agreed to wed your sister. First, I must speak with my children."

Sara Eliahu brought her hand hard on the arm of her chair. "But why should they be consulted? They are children and must obey their father."

"And because I am their father, I need to know their thinking and consider their feelings. You shall have my decision in due time."

Rocamora thought about the ebb and flow of his life. A great tide now seemed about to engulf him. His beloved Abigail had left a void no one could fill. Their firstborn Moses may have sustained permanent injuries. Solomon, who had become an inseparable companion during the day and tended to Moses at night, would be leaving for medical school next year. Inconsolable, Joseph mourned his mother to obsession. Daniel and David needed much nurturing. Tiña, the sole light of his life, could not do it all, teach and watch over her younger brothers and help Geitl with her household tasks.

Sara Eliahu had promised to care for Moses and the boys, leave Tiña alone to continue her lessons, and help Geitl market, cook, clean, and do the wash. Would she? Could she? He had told her he must first speak to his children about their marrying. He summoned Solomon to his study.

"*Abba*, Sara Eliahu can never replace my mother, may she rest in peace. Her presence will not affect me, for I will be spending most of my time accompanying you on your rounds or studying for medical school. You have great wisdom, *Abba*. I know you will decide what is best. If you want to marry Sara Eliahu, I will not be pleased, but I shall not object."

"All right, Solomon, tell Joseph I wish to speak with him."

Rocamora asked his third son to sit opposite him by the fire, wishing he could give the boy more attention. Joseph spent nearly all his time at home in the attic where he practiced with Abigail's diamond mills at the expense of continuing his lessons in languages and geography. It seemed as if the boy believed his mother was present whenever he touched them.

"Joseph, my son, I want the very best for you, and because you are old enough to understand my dilemma, I need to know your opinion."

"Is it about cousin Sara Eliahu?"

"Yes, but how did you know?"

"When you are away seeing your patients, she visits and asks us if we would approve of your marrying her."

"She has? Thank you for telling me, and what did you say to her?"

"I told her I did not know."

"When I am not here, is she good to you and Sara and the smaller boys?"

"She is more fussy than *Eemah* was about little things. She becomes annoyed if anything appears to be out of place."

"Such as?"

Joseph thought for a moment. "If a vase is not placed exactly in the middle of a table, if a picture on the wall is not perfectly straight. She does not smell as nice as *Eemah* either. Geitl does not like it when Sara Eliahu visits and tells her how to cook or that she missed dusting a table."

"Then, do you or do you not want me to marry her?"

"*Abba*, I do not know. She leaves me alone when I practice with *Eemah's* diamond mills. You must decide because you are wiser than any of us."

Rocamora told Joseph to send for his sister. He would let Tiña's opinion be the deciding factor. When his daughter entered, he invited her to sit in the other chair. Almost ten years of age, she was too old to cuddle in his lap. They grew so fast.

"And how is my Tiña today?"

"I miss *Eemah* so."

"Dry your eyes, my precious jewel, for we can do nothing to bring her back."

"Yes, *Abba*, I know."

"Has Sara Eliahu been helpful when she visits?"

"Geitl does not like it when Sara Eliahu tries to take charge of the kitchen."

"Does Sara Eliahu give attention to Moses, Daniel, and David?"

"No."

"Tiña, I want you to think carefully about what I am going to say. I do not love Sara Eliahu, and no woman will ever replace your mother in my heart. But, I cannot allow you to become an overworked second mother to your brothers. You are a beautiful girl, and one day you will be an even more beautiful young woman. We shall find a handsome prince worthy of you, whom you will marry and live with happily."

"No, I never want to leave you, *Abba*."

"We have many years before that choice arises. I have not yet come to a decision, but would you say yes or no if I asked your permission to marry Sara Eliahu?"

"Whatever you decide, *Abba*, will be best for all of us."

Rocamora did not ask Daniel and David for their opinions. They were too young. He promised himself that Sara Eliahu would have to understand one thing above all else. His daughter must be free to decide what household chores she would do were he and that woman to wed.

Rocamora changed his mind and let Tiña sit on his lap while he stared into the fire seeking Abigail's face within the flames.

66.
Conjugal Beds

Rocamora tore quilt, sheets, and mattress from the bed in the great hall. With an axe, he brought down the four bedposts and canopy while his children and Geitl watched. He sawed the posts and frame into pieces small enough for Solomon and Joseph to carry to the yard.

After they piled the bedding and debris between house and outdoor privy, Rocamora faced his sons and daughter. "This was your mother's bed. No other woman shall ever sleep in it. A replacement will arrive tomorrow."

In the yard, he lit the pyre and with tears in his eyes watched the flames burn to the last ember.

Two weeks later, Rocamora wed Sara Eliahu Toura on the twenty-third of May 1665. Only her brother and immediate Touro relations attended. Rocamora decided his children should stay at home. No one objected. Throughout the ceremony, he remembered his marriage to Abigail. During the meal at Daniel Touro's home, Sara Eliahu clung to his arm and more than once proclaimed she was now the wife of the esteemed Doctor Isaac de Rocamora.

By the time they arrived home, the children had fallen asleep and Geitl had gone to her room. Rocamora left Sara Eliahu in the great hall. He went to the study, poured a glass of strong brandy, and lit his pipe. He reminisced about his life with Abigail and her wish for him to marry her cousin.

"Isaac, my husband, I have awaited you this past hour."

Sara Eliahu stood in the doorway holding a candelabrum. She wore a white silk robe over a shift. Her hair fell to the small of her back. Rocamora could summon no passion for Sara Eliahu, which had nothing to do with his sixty-four years of age. He did not desire her.

"Doña Sara, I told you and your brother more than once that I did not intend to fulfill any conjugal duties should we wed. I shall not this night or any other night."

"But …."

"You agreed to my terms in his presence."

"Where will you sleep?"

"Here on the divan or on the cot in my laboratory."

At night the week before Rosh Hashanah, Rocamora brooded in his study. He spoke to Abigail about his regrets marrying Sara Eliahu Toura who brought with her dowry a pall over his home. Within days after their wedding, she revealed herself a household tyrant. She fired Geitl. No servant stayed for more than a few days.

Sara Eliahu's temperament and rules differed in the extreme from Abigail's gentle yet firm treatment of their children. She complained that Rocamora and Abigail had raised them too leniently. She refused to understand why he continued to leave Abigail's chairs shrouded. She also nagged him to be more observant and encouraged her Touro cousins and aunts to visit daily.

No matter how many times Rocamora reminded Sara Eliahu, she forgot to have hot water ready so he could wash upon coming home. Had Moses not been so severely injured Rocamora would never have married a second time.

Healed externally, physically healthy and strong, his eldest had become simple and needed much care. Moses lived and slept in a small separate room on the fourth floor. Despite her promises, Sara Eliahu would not go near him. Solomon bathed the older brother he adored and took him for walks when he was not studying or assisting Rocamora.

Sara Eliahu also ignored the younger boys. It did not matter to Joseph who was away from home most of the time, either at the *Yesibót*, or learning to polish diamonds at the home of his cousin Reuben Judah Touro.

Despite his physical infirmities, Daniel helped Tiña care for Moses when Solomon could not. He also watched over David and each day told Rocamora if the health of his younger brother improved or declined.

Tiña, with Rocamora's full support, continued her studies. She had tried to help Sara Eliahu cook and clean, but the woman criticized everything she did. Tiña continued to teach her younger brothers what little she had learned about languages and geography, which Rocamora enjoyed watching.

Rocamora faced the unpleasant reality he had wed a virago. Were they Catholic, he would have sought an immediate annulment, for they had not consummated their marriage. As a Jew, he had to seek permission from the *Bet Din* to divorce Sara Eliahu. He would do so after Yom Kippur.

Tiña called him from the doorway. "*Abba*, hurry, come with me. A woman is at the door with a baby."

Rocamora followed his daughter to the open front door. A woman he did not recognize held a newborn wrapped in a blanket. "Please, come in. Is the baby ill?"

She continued to stand outside. "You are Doctor de Rocamora, father of a boy called Moses?"

"I am."

She thrust the baby into his arms. "Here. Take your son's bastard."

"What? Who are you?"

"I midwifed its birth."

Rocamora studied the baby's features searching for any resemblance to Moses. Too soon to tell. "And the mother ... Delia ... her condition?"

"In the grave where she can no longer shame her family. After I delivered it, they said I should drown it, but I could not take that sin upon myself."

"You are a good woman. I will pay ...."

"I want no payment except your promise. You must never tell anyone I brought him to you."

"Your secret is safe."

The woman left, and Rocamora carried the baby into the vestibule.

"*Abba*, can I hold him?"

"Here, but be careful. A baby is not one of your dolls."

Tiña cuddled the newborn. "I understand, *Abba*. Look how he smiles. He is so beautiful."

Rocamora summoned Solomon from the basement, Joseph, David, and Daniel from the attic, and Sara Eliahu from the parlor. His children congregated at the dining table.

Solomon examined the baby in his sister's arms. "It is a healthy boy, *Abba*."

Sara Eliahu entered frowning. "What is all this commotion? What is that baby doing here? Is it ill? Where is its mother? Whose baby is it?"

Rocamora took the newborn from his daughter. "He is my grandson, the son of Moses and Delia, the girl he loved."

"Then he is a bastard."

Rocamora felt his face aflame. The power of his deep, authoritative voice shook the walls and the fury in his eyes cowed all. "Sara Eliahu ... if you or anyone else in my house speaks that word or another similar to it, I promise I shall recite *Kaddish* for you. Do you understand?"

The force of Rocamora's words and threat of the awesome Prayer for the Dead silenced his children and Sara Eliahu, who glared at him and the baby.

His grandson's crying assuaged Rocamora's anger. "What healthy lungs you have. Hush, my little one. Yes, I know ... my raised voice did not cause you to cry. Solomon, he needs nourishment. Go quickly to our patient, Doña Rebecca da Silva. I believe she is available to wet nurse. My sons, *mi infantiña*, this is your nephew, son of your brother Moses, and of our flesh and blood. We shall raise him. We shall love him."

Rocamora turned to Sara Eliahu. Her expression could not have been more resentful. "I need not tell you what the consequences will be if you do not welcome my grandson into this house."

Her lips disappeared. "I understand."

"Good. Now, my grandson must meet his father."

Tiña and her brothers followed Rocamora to Moses' room. Sara Eliahu did not. No one missed her.

Moses sat on a chair playing with his *bilboquê*. He never missed catching the ball in the cup. He seemed not to notice he had company.

Rocamora stood over his eldest. "Moses, Moses, please put away your toy. Look at who I brought you. You are now a father." Rocamora offered him the newborn. "Here is your son."

Moses dropped his ball and cup on the floor. He gaped confused at the red-faced crying baby. When Rocamora placed the newborn in Moses' lap, Tiña began to sing one of Abigail's cradle songs. Her brothers joined in.

Rocamora could not have been more pleased when Moses held the baby in his arms, gently rocked him, and hummed the melody, which stopped the crying. While Joseph, Daniel, and David admired their nephew, they reminded Rocamora of the three Magi who appeared at the Nativity. His children giggled when Daniel extended a small finger to the baby who clutched it.

"May I care for him, *Abba*?"

"And I, *Abba*?"

"Yes, Daniel. You and Tiña may bring him to Moses every day."

Rocamora delighted in watching his children laugh and show pleasure they had a nephew. He experienced a surge of energy, a renewed zest for life for the first time since Abigail's passing and Moses' injury. He had a grandson to raise, the firstborn of his firstborn. He would take charge of his education in languages, literature, history, and geography; teach the boy to skate, play games, and master weapons; and prepare him for a life of his own choosing. On the day of his *berit milah*, he would receive the name Jacob Moses de Rocamora.

67.
Necessary Amputation

Rocamora held his grandson at the dining table. Tiña, Joseph, and Daniel tried to stop its crying with distractions. Sara Eliahu went to her bed in the great hall. Just as well, Rocamora thought.

Solomon arrived with the wet nurse, and Rocamora took Doña Rebecca to Geitl's former room on the fourth floor. She brought with her a small basket for the baby to sleep. Tomorrow morning, Rocamora intended to give Doña Rebecca the bed in the great hall until she weaned his grandson. This was to be Sara Eliahu's last night in the house.

He sent the younger children to bed and sat with Solomon in the study. "Say nothing about this to your brothers and sister. After your morning ablutions and prayers, go to your great uncle Daniel Touro and bring him here. I shall divorce Sara Eliahu."

"Yes, *Abba*."

Rocamora did not sleep that night. He sat in the third floor parlor alert to any noise. He had seen a malevolent look in Sara Eliahu's eyes when she looked at his grandson. He feared the woman might try to harm him.

Whenever the baby cried, Rocamora went to see if Doña Rebecca was feeding him. In between, he imagined Abigail receiving their grandson with love and nurturing, and Solomon, Joseph, Tiña, and perhaps Daniel too giving him many grandchildren. Rocamora visualized the fruit from his seed proliferating through the centuries and scattering to cities and continents until he laughed at himself for his grandiose *hidalguía*.

By morning, Rocamora no longer thought of his grandson as a newborn or the baby. He had named him. He was Jacob.

At daybreak, Rocamora looked in on Jacob. The wet nurse had awakened. "Doña Rebecca, please stay here for the next hour or so. My daughter will bring you bread, cheese, and tea."

Rocamora went to the serving kitchen surprised none of his children sat at the eating table. He saw the shroud missing from Abigail's chair and heard a commotion coming from the cooking kitchen below.

Tiña ran to him crying. "*Abba, Abba*, she slapped me. I tried to stop her. She is burning *Eemah*'s shrouds."

Rocamora lifted Tiña's chin and kissed the red mark on her cheek. "I promise … that *bruja*, that witch, she will never strike you again."

He strode into the cooking kitchen. Sara Eliahu stood by the fire cackling with each thrust of the heated stoker at Joseph and Daniel to prevent them from salvaging the shrouds. She saw Rocamora and Tiña and waved it at them. "Yes, yes, I slapped your precious little princess' face. I will do it again. She deserved it. She was disrespectful to me. Abigail is dead. I am your wife. I am the Señora Doctor de Rocamora."

Rocamora seized the stoker from Sara Eliahu's hand. He did not shout or speak a single word to her. He had already amputated the gangrenous shrew from his life.

Solomon arrived with Daniel Touro and two of his sons. Sara Eliahu's uncle and cousins stared shocked at her while she laughed hysterically and repeatedly shouted, "Abigail is dead. I am the Señora Doctor de Rocamora."

"Don Isaac, Solomon told me, that you will divorce Sara Eliahu."

"Yes."

"I understand. What is it you want me to do?"

"Please, take her with you now. Send her back to Rotterdam for all I care. If she will not begin divorce proceedings then I shall. Solomon, Joseph, gather that woman's clothes and carry them to your great-uncle's house."

Sara Eliahu screamed, scratched, and kicked when Daniel Touro took her arm. His sons helped him drag her from their home.

That noon, Rocamora brought Geitl home. His children welcomed her with hugs and kisses. He took her to the great hall where he had installed the wet nurse. Tiña and her brothers followed.

Rocamora introduced the women to each other, pleased the way Geitl fussed over Jacob in the *rolkoets*. "Doña Rebecca, has he been fed?"

"Yes, Doctor, half an hour ago. He has a healthy appetite."

"Excellent. Geitl, will you please go to the cooking kitchen and make us a midday meal."

"My pleasure, Doctor."

Tiña took her hand. "I will help you."

Again, hot water awaited Rocamora day and night. Favorite dishes returned to the table. He had the added pleasure of seeing Jacob at each meal with the wet nurse. Tiña provided tea and tranquility in his study every evening. Joy, laughter, and music returned.

The first Sabbath Eve without Sara Eliahu, Rocamora took his daughter's hand and led her to Abigail's chair at the dining table. "Sit here, Tiña."

She backed away horrified. "*Abba*, this is *Eemah's* chair."

"No more shrouds, Tiña, this will be your place now. My sons, your sister is now the lady of the house."

When Tiña lit and prayed over the Sabbath candles, Rocamora remembered Abigail performing the same rituals. Uncanny how much his daughter resembled her mother, his beloved, feature for feature.

In the basement on a morning shortly after the Day of Atonement, Rocamora closed his satchel filled with medicines and prepared to leave with Solomon when Joseph leaped over the steps into the basement out of breath.

"*Abba, Abba.*"

"Why are you home so early from the *Yesibót*? Your face is flushed. Are you ill?"

"No, *Abba*. I ran all the way. Rabbi Aboab dismissed us. He said the Messiah has come."

Rocamora arched an eyebrow. "The Messiah? Here? In Amsterdam?"

"My classmates believe the rabbis are going to close the school because everyone will be going to Jerusalem."

"*Abba*, listen."

"I hear it too, Solomon. Let us go see."

Tiña and Daniel had already opened the front door and stood on the steps with Geitl.

Rocamora stared aghast at a great procession of Sephardim singing and dancing to tumbrels and drums along Jodenbreestraat and crossing the bridge at St. Anthony's Lock. He recognized Chief Rabbi Aboab and members of the *Ma'amad* at the front carrying ornamented scrolls of the Law they had taken from Talmud Torah. Practical businessmen and leaders of the Iberian community sang and danced behind them as if in a trance no different from the cultist *alumbrados* he had seen in Spain. More Jews ran from their homes and joined the procession.

When they passed, several called to Rocamora:

"Doctor, come join us. Come proclaim the Messiah."

"He has come. It is true. He has come."

"The *Moshiach,* our Messiah, the Anointed One. He has come."

"We must sell everything and leave for the Holy Land."

Rocamora told his children to go inside. He took a last look at the procession and shut the door. "Those fools, those pathetic fools."

68.
A Different Plague

That evening in his study Rocamora reflected on the folly of men. After the procession earlier in the day, Chief Rabbi Aboab and other sages of the community proclaimed a man named Sabbatai to be the true Anointed One and Nathan of Gaza his prophet. They believed Sabbatai would bring spiritual redemption and judgment to the Jews, reestablish the Kingdom of David, rebuild the sanctuary of the Temple, and gather the dispersed of Israel under his dominion.

A congregant challenged the rabbis. He demanded Scriptural proof Sabbatai was the Messiah. Did the prophet Elijah appear and bring the tidings? Did the Celestial Temple descend upon Jerusalem? Was Sabbatai a descendant of King David? Outraged, the rabbis and nearly the entire congregation ridiculed and discredited him. Young men and boys influenced by Aboab harassed the unfortunate man all the way to his home where he died of a heart attack.

The *Bet Din*'s decree did not surprise Rocamora. The pot of messianic expectations had been brewing to boiling temperatures throughout Vlooienburg during the previous months. Many anticipated an imminent appearance of the Anointed One because the Jews were now scattered to the four corners of the world, a necessary prelude to a new Messianic Age. They conveniently ignored a salient fact.

Although more than twenty years had passed since Montezinos claimed to have found a lost Tribe of Israel, Jewish and Protestant messianists continued to believe all he said without demanding proof. After all that time, no other explorer came forward to corroborate his story. No Hebrew speaking Indian appeared anywhere in the New World. Montezinos never returned with new evidence. No one heard from or about him again. Yet they believed.

Rocamora could not dispute one fact. Jews could now live and worship in England for the first time in four hundred years. King Charles II approved their denization, a limited form of naturalization through private Parliamentary bills provided they "behaved themselves peaceably and quietly with due obedience to the King's Laws." Menasseh's efforts succeeded after all.

Over the next several weeks, belief Sabbatai was the Messiah spread from the Ottoman Empire throughout Europe and infected what seemed to be the entire Jewish community in Vlooienburg and many Protestants in the Dutch Republic and England. Even the most demanding hardheaded men of business gave credence to outrageous accounts. Typically, they believed a ship manned by sailors speaking Hebrew appeared off the north coast of Scotland carrying a flag inscribed with the twelve tribes of Israel.

Rocamora compared the epidemic of messianism to the plagues of bulboes and expected it to last no more than a year. Christian and Jewish authors had been writing for decades that in 1666 the Jews would be returned to Jerusalem, and the Messiah would appear, a second time for the former, a first for the latter. They even had a precise date for the great miracles, the eighteenth day of June. Rocamora looked forward to that day when Sabbatai would join a long line of false Messiahs.

The ecstatic singing and dancing throughout the community, their blind faith in a man they had not seen and miracles not confirmed reminded Rocamora of the rogue *alumbrado* Padre Begoña and his followers in Spain. While a Dominican royal confessor, he learned where Begoña and his followers met. In disguise, Rocamora infiltrated the congregation. Shocked to see a grandee amongst Begoña's acolytes and a lady in waiting to the queen participating in the heretical rituals, he reported all he saw and heard to the Count-Duke de Olivares and António de Sotomayor, the King's confessor and member of the *la Suprema*, the Supreme Council of the Holy Office.

After Familiars arrested Begoña and his followers, Rocamora received unwanted rewards. The Inquisition sent him to exhort the heretics to confess and reconcile with the Church in their Toledo dungeons during sessions of torture. At a grand *auto de fé* in Madrid's Plaza Mayor, Rocamora castigated Begoña and his acolytes with a long sermon in front of the royal family, Count-Duke, *la Suprema*, and thousands of spectators. At the *quemadero*, he harangued them to reconcile one last time before the fires were lit.

True, differences existed between the Jews of Vlooienburg and the *alumbrados* of Spain. The former believed in the Scriptural prophecies of their religion. The Spanish *alumbrados* had lost faith in Catholicism and followed a man who preached that individual spiritual union could be achieved only through sexual union. Their main similarities were trust in a charismatic man of flesh and blood and surrender to religious ecstasies.

From the start, Rocamora decided not to question the credulous rabbis and members of the *Ma'amad*. He had no theological standing. If he attempted to use his great rhetorical skills that compelled men and women to weep and repent in Spain during his sermons and harangues, the congregation would shout him down. Rocamora saw himself at the edge of an ocean raising his hands to stop a great tidal wave and failing.

The messianist folly continued through the end of 1665 and into the new year. Many neglected their businesses and spent all day and night at the synagogue, which overflowed with congregants and strangers. Some sold their homes and possessions and left Amsterdam for the Holy Land. The entire Jewish community of Avignon planned to emigrate after the spring thaws.

Parents named newborn males Sabbatai or Nathan. The rabbis added new prayers, and Jewish publishers produced Hebrew, Spanish, and Portuguese editions of a prayer book composed by Nathan the Prophet. The *Bet Din* had no time for divorces and other mundane matters.

When Rocamora and his children placed rocks of remembrance on Abigail's gravesite at the Ouderkerk cemetery, they saw congregants making plans to exhume their dead relations for reburial in Jerusalem.

Sabbatai and Nathan never came to Amsterdam. The Jews of Vlooienburg did not leave en masse for Jerusalem. Before the first day of spring, the Ottoman Sultan arrested Sabbatai for sedition and immorality. Most refused to believe those reports or waited until reliable sources confirmed the shocking events.

Although the eighteenth day of June 1666 passed without messianic signs occurring anywhere in the world, many clung to their belief in Sabbatai. Rocamora witnessed a chastened congregation during the High Holy Days of Rosh Hashanah and Yom Kippur. Word arrived a few days before that Sabbatai converted to Islam.

The merchants had other more practical concerns. Plague ravaged London. Seven thousand perished in one week. The city barely survived what the populace called The Great Fire. All that was bad for business. The Dutch East India's worries increased after the English attacked its fleet.

War, commerce, and other worldly concerns restored reality to Vlooienburg, and Solomon matriculated at Utrecht Medical School.

69.
Two Significant Events

Because Sara Eliahu had not begun divorce proceedings, Rocamora went to the *Bet Din* for his *Get*, decree. Not yet recovered from the Sabbatai affair and now having to deal with a backlog of decisions, the rabbis did not reply until early the following year.

Rocamora sat at a table across from Sara Eliahu and her brother Solomon in the conference room at Talmud Torah awaiting the three rabbi-sages' decision. A *sofer*, religious scribe, waited to write the *Get* as a new document to ensure it was not predated.

Earlier, Rocamora described to the rabbis Sara Eliahu's failure as a mother and her disobedience and that he never shared her bed. He promised to return the full portion of her dowry as specified in their marriage contract.

Sara Eliahu stared at the table and did not speak. Rocamora could not bring himself to look at her. He did not doubt the *Bet Din* would give him his *Get* even if Sara Eliahu did not want their marriage dissolved. The Talmud specified a man could divorce a woman for the most trivial of reasons to the most serious because it was preferable to a couple living together in discord and hatred.

The rabbis' ended their brief conference and returned to the table. Aboab's expression could not have been more austere. "Isaac Israel de Rocamora, are you asking for this *Get* of your own free will and not from fear, obligations, or other pressures?"

"I am."

"And you, Sara Eliahu de Rocamora y Toura, do you accept this *Get* of your own free will and not from fear, obligations, or other pressures?"

She hesitated, then mumbled a barely audible "I do."

Aboab cleared his throat and recited the date and location of the *Get*. "Don Isaac Israel de Rocamora and by all other names you are known, we give you your *Get*, your decree of divorce from Doña Sara Eliahu de Rocamora and all other names by which she is known. You are free to marry again this day if you so choose. Doña Sara, you must wait ninety-one days before you may wed again."

Rocamora took the *Get* from Aboab and handed the document to Sara Eliahu, which was the final validation of their divorce. He turned from her and left without saying a word.

This year Passover had more significance becausethe children saw the Hebrews' liberation from Pharaoh and the Egyptians in the context of their freedom from Sara Eliahu. All missed Solomon who continued his studies at Utrecht and celebrated Passover with a Jewish family in nearby Gouda.

That evening at the *Haggadah* Feast, which Geitl persisted in calling a Seder, Rocamora looked at each child while he read aloud the Ten Plagues, Exodus, and hair-splitting commentary by several rabbis. Moses sat at his right uncomprehending. By tradition, the youngest son read the Four Questions, but listless David was recovering from another bout of ague. Beside his younger brother across the table from Moses and Joseph, Daniel, the next youngest had developed into a handsome intelligent boy with a normal size head on his frail deformed body. He recited the Four Questions from memory.

At the other end of the table, Tiña and Geitl to her left took care of Jacob in his high chair between them. Doña Rebecca had weaned the boy two months earlier.

Tiña wiped her nephew's chin. "*Abba*, Jacob is going to be handsome like Moses."

The boy was large for his age, blond, with his mother's fair coloring. "Yes, Tiña, and the way you take care of him, I know you will be a wonderful mother one day." He saw her blushing. "And, we shall seek a proper husband worthy of you."

Daniel poked her. "Tiña likes Benjamin David de Santcroos."

"He likes me more."

Daniel encouraged David and Joseph to sing repetitively, "Tiña loves Benjamin."

Rocamora believed David de Santcroos would approve of their union. Aware of Tiña's discomfort, he returned to the subject of his grandson. "It is too soon to know if Jacob will have de Rocamora features or that of his mother. Regardless, we will continue to raise him with all our love."

After the *Haggadah* Feast, final prayers, and joyous singing, Tiña helped Geitl clear the table, Joseph went to his mother's diamond mills in the attic, and Daniel took David to their bedroom. Rocamora carried Jacob and led Moses to his room. He watched his eldest amuse the infant with his *bilboquê* until Daniel limped into the room.

"*Abba*, hurry, Tiña is screaming."

"Stay here with Moses and Jacob."

Rocamora hurried to his daughter who lay on the floor of the withdrawal room whimpering in a fetal position. Geitl stood over Tiña so distressed she spoke in Yiddish. Rocamora saw blood on Tiña's dress and around the chamber pot.

He kneeled beside her. "Tiña, please stop your weeping. You are not injured, and you are not going to die."

His presence and confessional tone calmed her. "*Abba*, why am I having these painful cramps and bleeding?"

Tiña's first menses surprised Rocamora, and he berated himself for failing to observe his daughter's maturing. Because Tiña twelfth birthday was two months away, he had continued to think of her as a child. No excuse, he should have spoken to his precious princess and prepared her for this significant event. As Rocamora had done many times as a friar confessor with similarly terrified young female penitents, he explained the monthly rhythms of her gender.

"Yes, my beautiful Tiña, you are no longer a girl. You are a woman. Feel no fear or shame. Your body will continue to change. You will grow breasts and hair where none existed before. You will have strange feelings and not know why. Geitl will tell you all you need to know about the *mikvah*."

Assured Tiña understood all he said, Rocamora kissed her cheeks and forehead and left the withdrawal room. "Geitl, bring hot water so she may clean herself. You have my permission to speak frankly with my daughter about her monthly cycle."

Rocamora told everyone to gather around him in the great hall. He stood and faced his sons with a grave expression. "Your sister is no longer a girl. She has become a woman. Treat her as such. Beginning tonight, this bed shall be hers."

When Rocamora spoke to Abigail that night, he told her of his desire to live long enough to shepherd their sons and Tiña into full adulthood and independence. He smiled at a devious thought. Another young woman in the house would be of great help to Tiña and Geitl.

Rocamora sat at his desk and by candlelight wrote to a different Eliahu and Sara Touro who lived in the Venice ghetto. They were stepfather and birth mother of a young woman close to Solomon's age described by many as an intelligent, literate, and dutiful daughter of sweet disposition. He listed his son's virtues, prospects, and lineage and inquired if they were open to the possibility of marriage between Solomon and their daughter, whose name was Abigail.

One may not carry a pistol, wear spurs, or raise
one's voice during services.
—Rule of the Amsterdam Synagogue, Talmud Torah

Part V
Ornament of
The Community
1668-1688

70.
Doctor Solomon Isaac de Rocamora

Rocamora waited on an embankment for Solomon's canal boat to arrive from Haarlem. His second son had received his diploma two days earlier at the University of Utrecht on the eighteenth of August 1668.

Rocamora held a large bag filled with marzipan infused cookies and cakes, a farewell gift from Vrouw Cornelia, whom he had visited earlier to say goodbye. His former landlady sold her home because she wanted to live her last years with a daughter and grandchildren in Delft. She no longer bred Chartreaux, and Rocamora remembered Hombrecillo's companionship during his travels, adventures, and quiet evenings. He never forgot how tenaciously the cat defended his trunk during that violent voyage across the Channel to England.

The canal boat arrived at six in the evening, and Solomon disembarked carrying a coarse canvas trunk. He dropped it on the embankment when he saw his father.

Rocamora embraced his second son "Welcome home, Doctor Solomon Isaac de Rocamora. Doctor, how does that sound to you?"

He kissed Rocamora. "I have not yet become used to it."

"You shall. Do you need help with your trunk?"

"I can manage, *Abba*."

Rocamora stepped back to look at Solomon. Swart, slight of build with long flowing dark brown hair and a stylish vandyke, the eighteen year old resembled the Touros and carried himself with typical Spanish reserve. "It is too late today, but tomorrow I will accompany you to the *Collegium Medicum*. I want to have the pleasure of seeing my son register there." He led Solomon to a nearby two-horse coach. "I arranged for transportation to our house."

They stepped inside and sat facing each other. "You are looking well, *Abba*. You seem never to change. I see you have a new satchel."

Rocamora handed Solomon the black leather bag. "It is yours. My gift to you for receiving your diploma. Look. Tiña stitched your name, Dr. Solomon de Rocamora, in gold thread below the handle."

"Thank you, *Abba*. It is heavy."

"I filled it with medicines and a new set of instruments. Solomon, you have realized one of my most cherished dreams, to have a son working at my side who will carry on my practice. True you had done the same before you left for medical school, but now it will be official after you register tomorrow."

"I shall not disappoint you."

"You never have."

Rocamora brought Solomon to the great hall after they washed and told him to drop his trunk by the bed. Tiña, Joseph, Daniel, and Geitl welcomed him with hugs and kisses. His sister frowned at him. "You are so thin. You have lost too much weight."

"Geitl and I will soon fill you out. We have prepared a welcoming feast for you this evening."

"I am sorry to have missed David's funeral."

Rocamora's sickly youngest child had died in April, never reaching his tenth birthday. "There was no way for you to come home in time for his burial."

Solomon went to Moses who sat in a corner of the room playing with Jacob on his knee. He kissed his brother, who did not recognize him, and ignored Jacob.

Rocamora intended to learn Solomon's thoughts about Jacob later.

Geitl called that she was ready to serve their supper. Tiña and Daniel took Jacob's hands. Joseph and Solomon guided Moses from the great hall.

During a meal of steaming bowls of soup, lamb, vegetables, and rice, Daniel entertained everyone with coin tricks Rocamora taught him and mimicry of Rabbi Aboab and other dignitaries of the congregation. After supper, Tiña played the harpsichord. Rocamora praised her skill and sweet voice and invited Solomon to the study for a glass of Port and a smoke. His son accepted the first and refused the latter.

"Solomon, I have made changes in our home this past year. We converted the parlor to a room for Tiña after her menses arrived. I sleep on the divan in my study."

"Why do you not prefer the bed in the great hall?"

"This is where you shall sleep … and not alone for long if all goes well."

Solomon raised his eyebrows. "Am I to understand you have chosen a wife for me?"

"That depends upon you and the young woman. I have been corresponding with your mother's kin in Venice, and they have assured me their daughter is comely, dutiful, observant, and pleasant of temperament."

"And if I find her displeasing and disagreeable?"

"I shall not force you to wed."

"What is her name?"

"Abigail Abraham Toura."

The mention of his mother's name startled Solomon. "When shall we meet?"

"The young woman and her parents should arrive in Amsterdam sometime in the spring of next year."

"Her age?"

"She is two years older than you."

"If Abigail of Venice has so many virtues, why is she not married?"

Rocamora appreciated Solomon's thinking. "From what her parents have told me, I believe she may be more particular about marrying than you are. Now tell me, what do you think of your sister and brothers?"

"Tiña is beautiful like *Eemah*. Joseph has grown, but Daniel is so frail."

"Yes, Daniel has the mind and desire but lacks the stamina to become a physician. While you were away at medical school, he acquired much knowledge of herbs and spices. I have trained him to prepare and measure medications. I believe Daniel's cheerful temperament contributes to his survival."

"My heart breaks for Moses."

"I remember how close you were. He was your protector. After I depart from this world, you will be his guardian."

"Always, but *Abba*, what you said … is something wrong with you?"

"Nothing serious, except all clocks eventually slow and stop."

"Not for many years, I pray. Does Moses understand Jacob is his son?"

"I prefer to think so, but I cannot say for certain. Moses has somehow bonded with the boy, or he sees him as a playmate. What do you think of Jacob? He is almost three, intelligent, and large for his age."

Solomon hesitated for a moment. "I am surprised how much Jacob resembles Moses, but his blue eyes, fair skin, and blond hair … he looks gentile. Will the community accept him?"

Rocamora did not miss Solomon's disapproving tone of voice. "Do you?"

"Yes, yes, of course, *Abba*."

"Always remember, Jacob is your brother's son, your nephew. We cannot control what others may think or say, but we can do our best to shield the boy from the worst of it." Rocamora placed his hand on Solomon's shoulder. "You must be tired from your journey."

"I do not know if I will be able to sleep tonight. That I have my diploma and will be practicing medicine with you are dreams that have come true."

"Make dreams your reality, and you will lead the happiest of lives."

71.
Conversation with Abigail

Rocamora lay awake on his divan in the study and talked to Abigail. "I conjure you, and you are at my side again, the golden dream that is my true reality.

"Eleven years have passed since you left me, and they seem to have passed as rapidly as the blink of an eye. Will we meet again in some afterlife? There are times when I believe myself to be a spirit manifesting itself amongst the living but not existing at all, as if I am in a state of disengagement from life.

"The years bring so many changes. This past thirty-first of October, Solomon celebrated his fifth year of marriage to Abigail Abraham, whom you would have loved as your own daughter. I call her Biga, for you are the only Abigail in my life.

"Our granddaughters are healthy. Sara Solomon is now two years of age and Lea Solomon is one.

"My good friend Gaspar Hendrijks is no longer with us, nor are your *Tíos* Judah, Daniel, and *Tía* Ribcá. I seldom see Pablo. He has an incurable restlessness and can stay in Amsterdam for no longer than a month after an absence of a year or two.

"Dirck visits whenever he is in Amsterdam. He spends much of his time representing the House of Orange in England. Peace and prosperity have returned in the two years since Willem III became our *Stadhouder* after the murder of Grand Pensionary de Witt and saved our republic from the coalition of France, England, Münster and Cologne.

"Sara Eliahu has been deceased since the twelfth of October this year, the second day of our *Hesvan*, 5434. She lived less than a contented life, but it was one of her own making.

"More than three years have passed since our youngest child David died of ague despite the best I could do for him. We can take comfort that although he was frail and sickly from birth he lived a longer life than other children so afflicted.

"Moses is healthy of body but forever damaged of mind. I attend to our eldest and take him on walks. He enjoys watching the ships arrive and depart at the docks as if he somehow dreams he will sail to the New World with his beloved Delia.

"Except for Moses, our children thrive. Solomon has become so fine a physician, I have given him all but a few of my patients, and he is expanding our practice. I still consult and treat Pablo when he is in Amsterdam and other old friends.

"Joseph continues to be a sought after polisher of diamonds, but he has yet to express any interest in marriage. I must have a talk with him. Daniel has a natural bent as an apothecary and mixes medicines for Solomon. His sweet nature and wit charm all, but not enough for him to attract a woman, I fear. He is so terribly frail.

"Our own Tiña at nineteen years of age is a perfect incarnation of you, querida, feature for feature, sweet of temperament, and with your natural grace and serenity. She gives much tender care to Moses. Were I a selfish man, I would keep her at my side forever as a reminder of you, but I believe there is a young man she fancies and who adores her.

"I worry I have neglected Joseph and Daniel in favor of Moses, Tiña, and Jacob. Our grandson is tall for his age and sturdy with a quick mind, but there are times when I question my decision to have him circumcised and raised as a Jew. He has nine years now and attends the *Yesibót*. He has problems there with other boys and the rabbis. I fear the community will never accept Jacob. You know how malicious gossip can be.

"Miriam sent me a long letter. She writes they have changed their surname to Furman, appropriately, and now have two sons, and three daughters. Lyzor-Eliezer shortened his name to Eli and is a successful merchant in the beaver trade. I know you are as pleased for them as I. We did well, querida, giving Miriam and Eli an opportunity for a new life.

"And what of me? Age brings creaking limbs, cracking joints, and the removal of a tooth here and there. I need stronger spectacles every few years. Otherwise I am sound of body, heart, and mind.

"As you know, I am one of thirty founder benefactors for our community's *Maskil el Dal, atender el pobre* our society to help the poor and unfortunate. So many impecunious refugees arrive from Spain and Portugal each day. We offer financial support and services to those ineligible for the community's Poor Relief Fund, and I treat many of them gratis if they cannot afford our fees.

"I have made a new acquaintance, Manoel de Belmonte, also known as Isaac Nuñes de Belmonte. He is a member of the influential Sanpayão family of diplomats and successful merchants and a neighbor of Santcroos. The Portuguese king gave a *converso* antecedent of his the town of Belmonte early in the sixteenth century. He is the Spanish consul in Amsterdam and one of the official representatives of our congregation. Recently, María's son, Emperor Leopold III, made him Count Palatine. But that gossip probably does not interest you. These Jewish *titulos* follow all Sephardic customs and rituals in the community, claim superiority of blood as *hombres de nação*, and yet have insatiable appetites for titles granted by the gentiles. Preen as they may, not one has the quality of my lineage."

Rocamora laughed at himself for his own pride of blood and expression of *hidalguía*. He sobered and again reflected on how quickly time passed as if he slid toward a bottomless abyss. How many more years did he have left? How many more he loved would he see buried?

"And so, *mi querida, mi amor,* I bid you goodnight and await you in my dreams."

72.
Father and Daughter

In the great hall, Rocamora watched Tiña playing notes at random on her harpsichord and gazing out the window. "Tiña." She did not hear him. "Tiña?"

She blinked as if emerging from a trance. "*Abba?*"

He offered his hand. "Come, walk with me. It is a lovely spring day."

During their stroll along teeming streets to the center of town, many *yonkers* approaching them slowed to flirt with Tiña. She did not notice the young men. Rocamora guessed why his daughter was so distracted.

They reached the great floating flower market in the center of town on the Singel, the great canal crowded with barges containing flowers and plants from outlying areas and overseas. Boxes of vivid tulips, geraniums, roses, and other spring flowers represented every shade of the rainbow. A breeze wafted their heady sweet scents toward them and took Rocamora back to another time in the gardens of the Casa de Campo at the Alcazar when he confessed Infanta María under shady elms.

He purchased a bouquet of roses and handed it to Tiña. "This will have to do, *mi infantiña*, until a suitor will have the courage to court you." He smiled at her maidenly blush.

"*Abba*, they are so lovely. Thank you."

Rocamora led his daughter to a nearby park, and they sat on a stone bench beneath great oak trees. Never before had he spoken of marriage to Tiña. Were he a younger father, he might have postponed this conversation for many more years to keep his *infantiña* at home by his side.

Rocamora heard himself sounding like the confessor he had been for more than twenty years. "Tell me, my daughter, is there a young man you fancy?"

Tiña's face reddened a deeper hue. "Has someone told you so?"

"No, but you did not answer my question."

"Yes, there is one young man."

"Would he be Benjamin David de Santcroos, grandson of my dear departed friend Samuel?"

"Yes, but how did you know?"

"I have eyes behind my thick spectacles, and I have heard Daniel tease you about him. Does Benjamin return your love?"

"I want to believe he prefers me above all others, but I dare not hope until he tells me so."

"Dare not hope? Why do you say that?"

"*Abba*, as you know, Benjamin comes from one of the wealthiest families in Amsterdam. Do they not always arrange marriages for financial alliances?"

Rocamora recalled that Samuel de Santcroos had offered him his daughter Lea in marriage when he had no income and was not yet a physician. "We are de Rocamoras. I am a citizen of Amsterdam. Our name and bloodline count for more than wealth in the eyes of many."

"Yes, you are right, and so does your reputation. Many in Vlooienburg refer to you as an Ornament of the Community."

"Benjamin is how old now?"

"Twenty-two."

"And you will be twenty-one in a few months. Do you think he has spoken of you to his family?"

"I cannot say. Benjamin has not said as much to me. We are never alone. We seldom exchange words. It is the way Benjamin looks at me when I go to the warehouse to purchase tea and coffee that makes me believe he shares my feelings."

"Shall I speak to his father?"

"I am fearful. What if he says Benjamin does not love me? What if he disapproves?"

"Then it is best you know that sooner than later."

Rocamora walked with David Samuel de Santcroos through the merchant's warehouse at the docks. Samuel David, the eldest son named for Rocamora's great friend, recorded figures in a ledger, and second son Benjamin David supervised the crating of goods to be shipped.

Rocamora evaluated the young man as a potential mate for his *infantiña*. Benjamin was solid of body with manly features sun bronzed from journeys on behalf of his father. Rocamora recognized features similar to Benjamin's grandfather.

"How quickly time passes. I clearly remember supervising Benjamin's birth as if it were yesterday. He has grown into a fine young man."

"Yes, Benjamin is a good son. As you know better than anyone, my eldest lacks robust health, and that he has lived so long I attribute both to the Lord, Blessed be He, and to your skills as physician. Benjamin is better suited to run my company than Samuel, who prefers to keep the books, which is why I have been sending him to seek goods and deal with my factors in the New World, the Baltic, and two days from now to the East Indies. He will be gone for about two years."

Rocamora did not like what he heard. "Those absences would be most difficult for a wife to bear."

Santcroos beckoned a servant to bring them some recently arrived tea to sample, which he always had ready for customers and friends to taste. "Isaac, my friend, it is not like you to row to your objective with muffled oars."

"I shall be direct. My daughter would wed Benjamin if he loves her and you were to give consent. Has he mentioned any interest in Sara?"

"No, he is not the most talkative of men, but let us ask him directly and now. In truth, I would be honored to have a grandchild with the blood of the de Rocamoras and that of my father's dearest friend and mine too if I may so presume. I owe my life to you, and my father wanted you to marry my sister Lea." Santcroos raised his voice. "Benjamin, will you come here for a moment?"

The young man made a deferential bow to Rocamora. "How are you enjoying that tea, Doctor? It is the finest we have ever imported."

"Delicious."

"Benjamin, we have something of great importance to ask you, and above all else, we want truthful answers."

"I have always been truthful with you, Father."

"Yes, of course. I have given Doctor de Rocamora's permission to question you."

"Do you think I am ill?"

Rocamora smiled to put him at ease. "Benjamin, you and my daughter Sara have been acquainted since childhood. She told me if your parents approved and you were similarly agreeable she would wed you."

Benjamin's reaction amused and pleased Rocamora, surprise at first followed by a broad grin. "Father, Doctor, are you both giving us permission to wed?"

"I believe we are. Am I not correct, Isaac?"

"Absolutely correct, David."

"I believe I have loved Sara since we were children. I did not know she felt the same about me. We can marry, Father?"

"Yes."

"When? How soon?"

"You understand you cannot wed Sara de Rocamora until you return from the East Indies. At that time, we shall announce the banns. Do you agree, Isaac?"

"I do." Rocamora placed his hand on the young man's shoulder. "Benjamin, you must see my daughter before you leave and do her the honor of a proper proposal of marriage."

"Doctor de Rocamora, I have rehearsed that speech many times, and now that I have your permission and my father's, I shall call upon Sara and offer marriage this evening. That is, if it is convenient for you."

"Come at eight, speak to my daughter, and stay for supper."

Santcroos placed his cup atop a crate and took their arms. "Enough of this tea. Come to my office so we can seal the union of our two families with a toast. Isaac, I shall open the finest brandy you have ever tasted."

73.
A Plan for Jacob

In his basement laboratory, Rocamora peered into the microscope he purchased for Solomon fascinated by the organisms swimming in a few drops of swamp water. That invention had brought with it more than an expansion of knowledge. Discoveries of the female egg and male sperm now divided scientists into two camps.

Animaculists believed a preformed human existed in the head of each sperm. Ovists asserted to the contrary that it waited to be fertilized in a female's egg. Yet no one had seen a preformed human in any egg or sperm. This was not the first time Rocamora observed that faith based theories divided dogmatic scientists the same as theologians.

"*Abba*, look who is here."

Tiña escorted van Noordwijk into the basement. His hat brushed against the low ceiling.

"Dirck, what an unexpected and pleasant surprise to see you."

Tiña curtsied. "Please excuse me, *Oom* Dirck. I am helping Geitl and Biga prepare our midday meal. You will stay of course."

"Yes, Tiña, he shall." Rocamora and Dirck hugged each other. "Has it really been four years?"

"My only regret during that time, Isaacus. My visit is for more than friendship. I have need of your services. Is there some medicine that can stop the burning when I urinate?"

"Each time?"

"Often enough."

Rocamora gave van Noordwijk a glass beaker and a chamber pot. "I will need a sample."

"Here?"

"And now. Drop your breeches. Please." After van Noordwijk finished urinating, Rocamora examined his friend's privates. "No external evidence of Cupid's malice."

"I should hope not. I have been loyal to my wife."

Rocamora recalled that several years after Arabella and his son died of smallpox, van Noordwijk married the wealthy widow of a Zeeland magnate. "Your family is well?"

"Charlotte and her three daughters are plump, robust, and cheerful."

"A happy home can be the healthiest of homes."

"And so yours must be from the laughter I hear above. Your daughter Sara is charming and beautiful, the image of her mother."

"Yes, she is, and you will have to meet my two granddaughters. They enliven our home. Biga, Solomon's wife, is expecting her third child next month. We hope it will be a boy." Rocamora shook the beaker and studied its contents by the window. "You have a mild infection of the bladder. Nothing serious." He handed van Noordwijk a basket of small red berries. "Eat some with each meal, and the burning should end in a few days."

"What berry is this? I have not seen it before."

"The English call it a cranberry. It comes from their northern colonies across the Atlantic and has been proven effective in cases such as yours."

"You work miracles in your own way, my friend."

"I credit nature and our ingenuity to exploit it. Now, for how long shall I have the pleasure of your company?"

"For the entire day and evening. Tomorrow I must return to The Hague, and after that, I shall rest at my estate in Gouda through spring and summer before I return to England. We were fortunate not to be there during another outbreak of plague three years ago."

"Fortunately those sporadic recurrences can be contained before they become an epidemic."

Jacob rushed into the laboratory. "*Abuelo*, grandfather, I …."

"Where are you manners, Jacob?"

"Excuse me, *Abuelo*. I did not know you had company." He stared at the huge man surprised. "*Oom* Dirck?"

"Yes, Jacob. I am flattered you remember me. How old are you now?"

"Almost eleven. Are you a marshal in the *Stadhouder's* army now?"

"No, but I have been raised in rank to Ambassador."

"Is that more important than a marshal?"

Rocamora guided his grandson to the steps. "Very much so, Jacob. Now, go wash your face and hands. We will be called to the table in a few minutes."

"Not yet eleven, Isaacus? The boy is tall for his age."

"I shrink. He grows."

"Jacob is so ash blond and fair he looks very much like a Hollander."

"His mother's coloring." A plan for Jacob formed in Rocamora's mind. "Dirck, your visit is most opportune. There is something I want to discuss with you after we dine."

In Rocamora's study, Van Noordwijk savored the coffee Tiña served. "I must remember to take a bag of beans with me when I leave Amsterdam. Coffee adds a perfect finish to a wonderful meal. I am delighted to see how much your family has grown. Your granddaughters are delightful. I am amazed both are learning to read."

"Tiña is teaching them. Jacob helps when he can."

"Jacob too? He is a handsome, sturdy lad. Are you encouraging him to be a physician?"

"My grandson has no interest in medicine or trade. He is more likely to choose a life of adventure."

"Boys have their dreams."

"As I once had. Jacob does have a keen mind. He is fluent in Spanish and Portuguese. He reads Hebrew, Latin, and Greek. You have heard him speak Dutch, and I have begun to give him lessons in English."

"English? You have something specific in mind for him?"

Rocamora did not believe it necessary to tell van Noordwijk about Jacob's current and likely future difficulties in the community and at home. No classmate dared to be friends with "the gentile bastard" their parents called him behind his back. For that reason and because Solomon never warmed to Jacob, Rocamora had become his grandson's shield. But for how much longer?

"I believe Jacob may want to seek adventure in North America where knowledge of English is essential, or he may choose to be a soldier."

"You know that no Jew may serve in the Army."

"He looks like a Dutch Christian."

"Yes, he does." Rocamora poured more coffee. "Jacob has become a superb skater and excels at sport. He is stronger than boys several years older."

"I am not surprised."

"Unfortunately, Jacob spends mornings and afternoons at school. He has little opportunity and space to ride in Amsterdam. I cannot teach him swordsmanship because I lack the reflexes and stamina of earlier days."

"That is unfortunate." Van Noordwijk seemed to be deep in thought until he flashed a broad smile, his voice conveying enthusiasm. "Isaacus, I told you I am going to rest at my estate in Gouda during the summer. Why not send Jacob to me? Better yet, I insist you come with him."

"Yes, I can arrange to be away for a few weeks."

"Excellent. With your approval, Jacob can stay with me the entire summer until I leave for England or he must return to school. I will let him ride my finest Frisian mounts. A master swordsman who lives nearby can give him lessons. We will speak English day and night. In a few years, I may begin taking him to The Hague, with your permission of course."

"You have that in advance, my friend."

"I promise you I shall do all I can for Jacob, the same as I would have done for my son had he not died from smallpox. And now I have a favor to ask of you."

Rocamora satisfied van Noordwijk's curiosity and brought him to the grand new synagogue for the congregation Talmud Torah dedicated the previous year on the second day of August 1675. Envy of the great Ashkenazim's synagogue completed several years earlier spurred the Sephardic community to surpass it.

"Dirck, that gilded inscription in Hebrew over the entrance includes the year 1672 when our *esnoga* was supposed to have been completed and Rabbi Aboab's name because he insisted it be built. The verse is from Psalm 5:8 and translates as 'In the abundance of Thy loving kindness, will I come into Thy House.'"

Van Noordwijk admired the *esnoga's* façade of rust-colored bricks and abundance of square windows. "I have been told it is now the largest Jewish house of worship in all Europe."

"Of more importance, Dirck, it is a monument to your tolerance of our faith.

"So many people coming and going. They cannot all be Jews."

"No, most are curious. Many have come to Amsterdam to see for themselves this Wonder, as you call it. Unfortunately, in their own kingdoms and principalities, they refuse to follow the example of Amsterdam when it comes to religious tolerance. Also, many a spy from Portugal and Spain will report what they have seen. After we go inside, wash your hands in the vestibule and do not remove your hat."

They entered the *esnoga* crowded with Sephardim and many foreigners. Fine sand covered the floor to absorb dust, moisture, dirt from shoes, and to mute the noise.

"Dirck, that raised section in the center is where the rabbis and *hazzans* read from the Torah and at the far end below those windows is the *tiváh*, the Ark that holds dozens more Torahs. Those chandeliers can hold a thousand candles, which are lighted for services."

Van Noordwijk studied each detail of the interior: benches facing each other separated by a central aisle, walls of dark wood from Italy, cylindrical columns lining the aisle, lamps hanging from plaster sunflowers, fine tapestries covering the pews, and countless candles glowing from chandeliers. "Most impressive, Isaacus. We Dutch call our Town Hall the Eighth Wonder of the World, and surely this must be the Ninth."

"The twelve stone columns along the side aisles supporting the women's galleries represent the tribes of Israel. The *tiváh* holds more than fifty scrolls of the Torah."

"Now I understand why the Senate has decreed your synagogue to be a Glory of the Amstel."

"There is another glory you must see."

74.
A Sense of Mortality

Van Noordwijk touched *flapkans* with Rocamora and Pablo in a heated pool at *The Fragrant Peony*. "Isaacus, you were right. A comfortable tavern, tables for wagering, exotic women and décor, and now these baths. This is truly another glory of Amsterdam."

"You must also experience the cold and sea water pools. Going back and forth from hot to cold helps soothe aching muscles."

"With the assistance of lovely attendants who give our customers the most delightful massages. Something we did not have at *el Paraíso*, Vicente. Am I not right?"

Pablo was in a garrulous mood. He regaled van Noordwijk with stories about their life in Valencia. He told anecdotes of banditry, debasing coinage, and blood feuds. Rocamora heard a yearning in Pablo's voice. It seemed his friend was reliving their youth while he spoke.

"You should have seen Vicente run from my sister when she tried to kiss him. Later he chased Moraíma and caught her, but never permanently." Pablo enthralled van Noordwijk with vivid descriptions of *ellParaíso* in Madrid, his sister's brief time as King Philip's mistress, and Vicente's exploits in disguise.

"All that at the same time you confessed the Infanta?"

"I had more energy in those days, Dirck." Rocamora did not like to be the subject of another's conversation. "Come, let us enjoy the buoyancy of sea water without fear of drowning and predators of the deep."

Pablo took Rocamora aside when van Noordwijk stepped into the adjacent pool. "I am surprised that mountain of a man did not create an overflow." He lowered his voice. "Before we join him, I have something of importance to tell you. My old friend, I am going to make another journey."

"But you returned from the West Indies only two weeks ago."

"Ay, Vicente, I have seen the world, East and West Indies, New Grenada, Africa, and North America. Now, I shall return to Valencia. When, I cannot say. Please, do not look at me like that, *amigo*. Our enemies are dead and the Holy Office will have forgotten me. I want to spend my remaining days in fields of melons and groves of palm where the sun shines."

Pablo's decision to leave Amsterdam intensified Rocamora's growing sense of mortality. So did the passing of many from his generation. The following day, the first of April, shortly before his seventy-fifth birthday, he met with the notary Adriaen Locke to write his will.

"I, Don Isaac Israel de Rocamora, being of sound mind, bequeath one thousand florins to my simple and incompetent son Moses Isaac.

"I bequeath one thousand florins to my son, Daniel Isaac, who is unhealthy and deformed.

"I bequeath five hundred florins and two diamond mills of five hundred florins value to my son, Joseph Isaac.

"I bequeath the rest of my wealth and estate to my obedient son, Solomon Isaac, who has contributed much to my wealth and prosperity.

"Solomon Isaac is obliged to pay costs of my burial and any debts.

"Solomon Isaac is to be the guardian of his brothers Moses Isaac and Daniel Isaac, and executor and administrator of my will."

"Is there more, Doctor de Rocamora?"

"I have two more bequests that I do not wish to add to the will." Rocamora handed Locke two sheets of paper. "This is for Sara Isaac. It is an inventory of my daughter's portion of her mother's estate, which we registered with the Chamber of Orphans at the time of my beloved Abigail's death, may she rest in peace. Here is a separate list of all items I have included in her dowry to be given to my daughter Sara Isaac at the reading of my will should I die before she weds."

Rocamora waited until the notary signed the documents as a witness, placed them in an envelope, and sealed it in wax. "Mynheer Adriaen, the contents of this envelope are for my grandson, Jacob Moses de Rocamora, which no one else may view after my passing."

"It shall be secure in my possession."

Upon his return home, Rocamora went to the attic, unlocked one of the trunks, and carried a smaller chest filled with papers to the study. He took out the chart of the de Rocamora genealogy that his kinsman Abbé Pierre de Taurelle gave him at Abbaye de St. Roch in Roquemaure. It traced the de Rocamora roots to the Houses of David and Arnulf.

His children and succeeding generations should know their origins. Regardless of wealth and station, his descendants would be able to hold their heads high with justifiable pride.

Rocamora first added to the chart that Gaspar de Rocamora, second son of Don Jerónimo, passed away, and his younger brother Juan, who had loved Brianda, was now the Third Marqués de Rafal.

Next, he began with the story of his distant ancestor, Natronai Bustanai of the House of David in Baghdad, whom Pepin the Short invited to be the first *Nasi*, Jewish Prince of the Exile, of Narbonne-Septimania. Natronai married Alda, daughter of Charles Martel and sister of Pepin. Rocamora took the name of their warrior-scholar son Isaac, also known as Guillherme of the *Chansons de Geste*, the day he declared himself a Jew.

Rocamora wrote until he fell asleep at his desk.

75.
Pater Familias

Each Sabbath Eve and holiday feast, Rocamora sat at the head of the table with a sense of accomplishment mixed with regret his beloved Abigail had not lived to enjoy with him their growing family. Five of their children had survived into adulthood although thirty year old Moses would forever be slow of wit and unable to function without help. Twenty four year old Joseph had established himself as a sought-after diamond polisher, and Daniel approached the age of twenty-one despite his frailties.

His *infantiña* glowed with happiness. Earlier in the week, she received a letter from Benjamin David de Santcroos dated six months earlier that arrived by boat. He promised the day after his arrival they would sign the banns. Rocamora calculated it should be in another month or two at the most.

At age twenty-eight, brilliant Solomon had a loving wife, three healthy and lively children with another due. If all went according to hopes and plans, two year old Isaac and pregnant Biga's next child, if a boy, would become physicians and ensure a de Rocamora dynasty in medicine.

He approved of how Jacob cared for Moses at the far end of the table. Not yet bar mitzvahed, the boy had become a man physically, taller than anyone at the table.

Rocamora's eldest granddaughter six year old Sara Solomon sought his lap and pulled at his white beard. He favored her of all Solomon's children because she had been born with the unusual green eyes he had inherited. Would she be as beautiful as his mother and Brianda, may they rest in peace. It was difficult to tell because the features of children changed over the years. He acquiesced to little Sara's pleas and produced coins from her nose and ears and made them disappear as quickly.

Rocamora watched Geitl help serve the meal concerned about her worsened arthritis. She had trouble holding the smallest plate. He decided to give her an adequate stipend to pay for food and lodging in a clean comfortable house. Geitl had been part of the family for two decades and deserved no less.

After the meal, Jacob asked for everyone's attention. "I have a surprise for all of you. May I use your guitar, *Abuelo*?"

"Yes, of course, for did I not teach you to play?"

Jacob summoned Solomon's daughters, Sara and five-year-old Lea, to stand beside him. "Tiña and I have taught the girls to count the way she taught me. I will call out the numbers, and each will respond. Sara, Lea, are you ready?" The girls said they were, and Jacob sang the melody:

"Who knows and understands what is one?"

Sara responded, "One is God in Heaven."

"Who knows and understands what is two?"

Lea took her turn. "Two are … are …." She smiled when Daniel whispered in her ear. "… are Moses and Aaron."

"Who knows and understands what is three?"

Both girls replied, "Three are our forefathers, Abraham, Isaac, and Jacob."

They continued through twelve, that number being the tribes of Israel. Rocamora led the applause and praise for his granddaughters and rewarded them with the coins he pretended to take from their faces and clothing. After they left the table, he invited Jacob to come with him to the basement.

"You have done well teaching the girls, but that is not why I wanted to speak with you. I have reached my seventy-fifth year now, and I do not know how many more I have been allotted." He placed a hand on the boy's shoulder. "You will be bar mitzvahed soon and become a man in our community. Do you think you can be happy in Vlooienburg?"

"I cannot say. Not everyone accepts me as a Jew."

"I know, and I worry I may be doing you a great disservice by having you bar mitzvahed. I have told you often the story of your father's love for your mother, her great beauty, and the plans they made to live in the New World. I still weep over Delia's death and what happened to Moses. I also grieve for the other children they might have had and often ask myself if I have done right by you. You might be better off in the faith of your mother, may she rest in peace."

"But I am also your grandson. You gave me the de Rocamora name. I will be bar mitzvahed to honor you. Though in truth, I cannot imagine making my life here in Vlooienburg. I want to experience adventure the same as you and *Oom* Dirck."

"I suspected as much. I will now tell you something important that you must never repeat. Do you so swear?"

"Yes, *Abuelo*. I so swear."

"Now, listen carefully and do not interrupt. After I die, you must go in secret to the notary, Adriaen Locke. Remember his name. I have given him a sealed package meant for you alone. Although I did not mention you in my will, I have provided well for you. Jacob, I want you to be free to make a place in this world one of your choosing, not that of others."

"Then I can be a soldier like *Oom* Dirck."

"Yes, or you may change your mind and seek adventure in the Indies or the Americas. That is why I have assured your financial independence."

"But if I leave, who will take care of my father?"

"Your *Tío* Solomon adores Moses and will always assure his comfort and wellbeing." Rocamora wanted to say more, but Daniel limped into the room. "What is it?"

"David de Santcroos' servant is at the door. He says his master asks you to come to him this night."

"Did he say why?"

"No, but I think someone may be seriously ill."

Rocamora's instincts alerted him to an unwanted possibility. "Say nothing about this to your sister."

The instant he arrived at Santcroos' mansion, Rocamora understood why he had been summoned. The family was in mourning, tearing clothes, and reciting the prayer for the dead. David de Santcroos clung to Rocamora weeping.

"My beautiful boy, my son, my son. Death by infection from an insect bite. That a father should live to see his son die."

"How well I know."

Rocamora offered condolences to the family and comforted each as he had done so often as physician and earlier in life as a Dominican friar. He joined them in prayer while searching for the best words to ease the blow he was about to deliver to his daughter. He would first speak with Solomon, Joseph, Daniel, and Jacob and prepare them to do everything possible to comfort her.

His plan went awry when Tiña greeted him at the door. "They said you were summoned by Don David. Is there word of Benjamin? No, I see it in your face. Something has happened to him. *Abba*, tell me. Tell me the truth."

Rocamora held her shoulders. "Benjamin will not be coming home. He died of an infection after being bitten by an insect."

Tiña shrieked a shrill *crie de coeur* and beat her fists against his chest. Her screams brought everyone into the room, and she fainted in Rocamora's arms.

"All of you, listen to me. Be attentive to Tiña. Benjamin David de Santcroos died in the Indies. She will be going through a terrible time."

"Drink this soup, *mi infantiña,* it will give you the necessary strength."

Rocamora forced a spoon between Tiña's lips. They went slack, and the liquid dribbled from her mouth as drool.

Solomon stood worried on the other side of his sister's bed. "If we cannot make her eat and drink, she will surely die."

Rocamora repeated what he had said to her many times since Tiña had taken to bed. "*Mi infantiña,* you are young. You have much to live for. You will meet many other young men. They will love you. I, your father, your brother Solomon, our entire family, we all love you."

Solomon bent and kissed her forehead. "Listen to our *Abba,* my dearest sister. We all love you."

Solomon's wife approached them. "She is not eating the soup we prepared?"

Rocamora rose and handed Biga the bowl and spoon. "Perhaps you will have better success with her. Solomon, let us consult."

They sat facing the fire, father and son, both physicians, both experiencing frustration over Tiña's refusal to eat.

"My sister will die if we cannot feed her."

"She wants to die. I believe that if Tiña could obtain poison, she would take it. That we cannot allow. Tiña is so much like your mother it would be as if I lost my beloved twice, and no father should ever witness the death of his child as I have seen happen to Brianda, my own David, and the three who failed to live more than a few days. May you be spared that."

"Surely, we can find a way to feed her."

"It is always the body we can heal more easily than the mind and spirit."

"*Abba.*"

Rocamora turned and saw Daniel in the doorway. "You heard our conversation?"

"Yes, and I want to tell you that I will stay at Tiña's bedside and encourage her eat, amuse her if I can, and try to make her laugh."

Rocamora beckoned Daniel to come closer. "She may not respond to your attentions."

Solomon agreed. "She seems to be unaware of her surroundings and simply stares into space."

"But I must try, *Abba,* Solomon. I love my sister. I want her to be well."

"As we all do. Yes, of course, sit at Tiña's bedside and do whatever you can."

Although midday, Rocamora sat in darkness still brooding over his *infantiña's* passing two weeks earlier. From the moment his daughter learned of Benjamin's death, she did not eat or leave her bed and declined both physically and mentally. Tiña became so weakened, she fell ill and succumbed to pneumonia. It was as if he had buried his beloved Abigail a second time. Tiña had been so like her mother feature for feature and identical of temperament.

Although tempted to do as others during mourning, Rocamora did not rend his garments or tear at his beard. Instead, he wept when alone and cursed God and all the fates for ending the lives of children before their parents' time to die.

"*Abuelo?*"

Rocamora realized he was sitting at Tiña's harpsichord as if he were with his daughter. He placed his eldest granddaughter, five-year-old Sara Solomon, on his lap and guided her fingers along the keys. "Would you like to take lessons, my precious jewel?"

"And play like *Tía* Sara? Yes, *Abuelo*."

"I shall arrange it. And now, let me teach you a song my Tiña learned when she was your age."

76.
A Career for Jacob

Rocamora greeted van Noordwijk in his study and poured him a glass of Port. "Back so soon from England?"

"And with a report of great success. Our *Stadhouder* Willem will wed his cousin, York's eldest Protestant daughter, and we shall have another Mary Stuart as Princess of Orange. King Charles has no legitimate children, which makes it more likely that Willem will be King of England one day and rule jointly with Mary."

"How can you be so sure of that? York may yet sire a son with his Catholic wife."

"There is none so far, and if that should happen, it could lead to another civil war James would surely lose."

"If what you hope for comes about, that means an end to wars with England."

"And great prosperity for both our nations. Have you seen the latest bulletins announcing that we now have a coalition including Spain, Austria, Denmark, and German principalities against France?"

"No, I have been in mourning for my beloved daughter."

"I am sorry. I did not know. My condolences. May I ask what happened?"

"Tiña passed away from melencholia after learning her intended, Benjamin de Santcroos, died from an untreated infection in the East Indies."

"She was a lovely young woman."

"And so much like my beloved Abigail, may she rest in peace." Rocamora breathed deeply. "As is written, the Lord giveth and taketh away. Solomon has become a father again. I have a new granddaughter they named Ester. May she have all the qualities of my *infantiña*."

"Perhaps I should leave you to mourn your daughter."

"Please, stay. Your visit is most welcome. I mourn when I am alone."

"You are still seeing patients?"

"A rare few friends and others from my charities, I have been appointed to the board of *Abi Yetomim* Father of Orphans, our community orphanage. You are well?"

"Aside from aging, yes. Your cranberries cured the problem."

"I thought they might. Dirck, I am delighted to have this opportunity to speak with you about my grandson Jacob. Too many in our community will never accept him because he was not born of a Jewish woman, and they consider him to be a bastard even though I adopted him."

"I am sorry to hear that."

"His uncles treat him well, but I sense a distance between him and Solomon, who will head the family after I am gone. Solomon cannot help himself and blames Jacob for the assault that affected Moses' brain."

"He is a reminder of that day."

"Unfortunately."

"As I told you before, he cannot be a practicing Jew if he wants to soldier for the House of Orange."

"If he is a man of honor, I care not what religion he follows. As you have seen, Jacob is skilled at weapons. He is fluent in Spanish, Portuguese, Dutch, and most important for his future, English. I have personally schooled him in the classics and secular writings, the same as my mentor taught me. I thought Jacob might go to one of the English colonies to make his fortune the same as Moses wanted with Delia. After what you have told me, his future might well be in England."

"When Jacob is sixteen and if he can live as a Christian, I shall accept him as my protégé and treat him the same as I would have done with the son I lost."

"Thank you, Dirck. You have put my mind at ease."

Jacob's sixteenth birthday arrived as if Rocamora had gone to bed the night of his conversation with van Noordwijk and the next morning more than three years had passed. He sat by the fire in the study and reviewed what had transpired over that time.

In 1678, Jacob was bar mitzvahed, and a treaty of peace with France signed at Nijmegen ended the long war and once again confirmed the independence of the United Provinces. The peace was short lived, and war resumed the following year when the French moved into adjacent lands.

East India Company shares fell several hundred percent and rose at the same pace with each defeat and victory. Tolerance of the United Provinces expanded to allow marriages between Christians and Jews, too late for Moses. The legislative body of the Estates General instructed its Counsels to protect the safety and security of Dutch Jews no less than if they were Christians.

Rocamora continued to ruminate about his life and how many years he might have left. Physically, he had minor aches, pains, and stiffening of joints. His clock still ticked but at a slower pace. Some men and women younger than his eighty years of age went to their beds and gave up. His will to live was rooted in simple curiosity. He wanted to know what would be happening next and to see more advances in science and medicine.

The discoveries of Anton van Leeuwenhoek had been as significant as that of the Americas. His microscope revealed a New World of previously unknown tiny organisms inhabiting bodies, plants, soil, and liquids. Perhaps they caused disease and other ailments. Perhaps they held the secrets to their cures.

Lost in thoughts, memories, and speculations, Rocamora fell asleep in his chair until someone entered the room. "Jacob?"

Well over six feet of height with a trimmed blond mustachio and goatee, Jacob kissed Rocamora and stood before him. "I came to say goodbye and ask for your blessing."

"Have you said your farewells to everyone?"

"It was difficult. My father tried to understand, but I believe he did not. *Tíos* Daniel and Joseph were sorry to see me leave, but *Tío* Solomon and *Tía* Abigail … I have never told you this, but I feel as if they never approved of me."

"Solomon adored, still adores your father, who was his protector. He does not understand your ambition to be a soldier and seek adventure. It reminds him of Moses' plans to sail to New York."

"I understand and wish it were otherwise. *Abuelo*, I will miss you, and I worry about my father."

"Moses will be fine. He lives here with two physicians, and your cousins Sara and Lea help care for his daily needs."

"Yes, I know. He plays with them and little Isaac and Ester as if he is a child."

"A blissful existence given the alternatives. Now, if I should pass away while you are gone, you must see the notary Adriaen Locke."

"You will live many more years, *Abuelo*."

"I have accumulated more than most. But please, sit, for I wish to counsel you. Do not worry about being an observant Jew. Dirck will not mention how you have been raised, so let everyone assume you are a Protestant. Should you see battle, know that there shall be much confusion. The noise, the screams, the dust and smoke. Never waste your shot. Most important of all, to survive, you must have a sense of your surroundings at all times. If you feel fear, so do your enemies. That is why men shout in battle."

"I shall remember all you have said and taught me."

Rocamora next allowed himself a moment to remember the day in the gardens of the *Casa de Campo* when he gave Brianda the same advice. "As you know, I lived at the Spanish court for many years."

"I always enjoyed listening to your stories about your life there."

"I want to give you some useful, extremely important advice, for I believe that you will be welcomed at The Hague and perhaps later at the English court should the Prince of Orange become King of England."

"That seems likely according to *Oom* Dirck."

"Courts are filled with intrigues within intrigues. The ambitious would sacrifice their mothers, daughters, even firstborn sons to advance. Keep your counsel and trust no one."

"Not even Oom Dirck?"

"He is an exception, a proven friend, but if he had a son who was your rival for a post, he would do all he could to ensure your destruction. As I would with his were our positions reversed."

"You are telling me that I can earn enemies simply by being?"

"Yes, that is the way of the world. You are handsome of face and sturdy of body. Many ladies will adore you. Do not offend the powerful by having casual liaisons with their women. Instead charm their wives as a son or brother would."

"And you taught me well how to avoid *mal frances*."

"Good. Also, never trouble the powerful with trivial matters, nor ask for inconsequential favors, for that will annoy them. Compliment often those who can advance your career without unctuous obsequiousness. Surprise them with delightful yet inexpensive gifts. On important occasions when you give any significant present, let it be something they will see every day, so they will be favorably reminded of you."

"I fear I may be a poor courtier."

"I think much will come naturally to you. To survive and advance in any court, you must be both humble and generous to your superiors. Be familiar yet respectful with your equals to enhance your reputation as a well-bred young man. And to inferiors, show them kindness without familiarity. Then all will think well of you. One more thing. A quick tongue can be as sharp as a Valencian dagger. Use it to defend yourself, but never sacrifice the powerful or a friend to a pointed jest. Charm and gentle wit will take you farther."

Rocamora rose, and so did Jacob. They embraced, kissed, and walked to the door where Solomon's daughters waited. They gave Jacob parcels of bread and cheeses, which reminded Rocamora of the day when eleven year old Abigail did the same for him in Antwerp.

Jacob thanked and kissed each girl, and Sara Solomon clung to him as if never wanting to let go. After Jacob left, she followed Rocamora to the study and sat in his lap.

"*Abuelo?*"

"Yes, Sara."

"Jacob looked so handsome today."

"Yes, he did."

"Do you think we will marry some day?"

Rocamora was amazed how Sara Solomon in spirit was so much like his beloved Abigail and physically identical to Brianda. "Life is filled with unanticipated outcomes. Did I ever tell you about the first time I met your grandmother?

Sara listened to Rocamora's story and said nothing until he finished. "Like *Abuela* Abigail and you, I shall wed Jacob."

May I live long enough to ensure your marriage. Should I die before that day, Solomon will never consent to any wedding between you and Jacob.

77.
Harmonious Applause

Three weeks after his eighty-first birthday, Rocamora grieved with Solomon and Daniel over Joseph's fresh grave at Ouderkerk. On the twenty-sixth day of April 1682, sixteen *Nissan* 5442, his third son died of consumption, the result of working in dank conditions for a diamond merchant despite his admonitions. Within days of Joseph's burial, Biga gave birth to a second son, whom they named at his *berit milah* Abraham bar Solomon after her deceased father.

Now retired from active practice, Rocamora gave his time, medical care, and contributions to the Sephardic orphanage and poor relief. He also served as an official of *Maskil el Dal,* the congregation's philanthropic burial society.

Each day he went to the *Collegium Medicum* to discuss with his colleagues new scientific discoveries or to attend one of its many banquets. He never failed to stop at the Town Hall to read bulletins and chat with friends in the government. Magistrate van der Waag had informed him that Jews were now ten percent of Amsterdam's population. Rocamora remembered when a few hundred Iberian families resided in the city.

He also visited with Pablo and Yèyīng several days each week at *The Fragrant Peony,* but this day his childhood friend had left a laconic note for him.

To Valencia.

Pablo had sailed to the *Costa d'Azahar,* their Fragrant Coast of Orange Blossoms. Rocamora sat at a table reminiscing about the past, which often seemed to be clearer in memory than what happened the day before. He envied Pablo. His friend would die a Spaniard on Spanish soil, whereas he, despite his success as both physician and founder of a dynasty, was an adrift widower in exile.

"You are still the most difficult man I have played against."

"And you have been my most tenacious opponent."

For more than two decades, Rocamora and Yèyīng failed to defeat the other at chess. They used every proven tactic and strategy against each other, invented others, and applied their innate wile and guile, all for naught. He had come to believe a draw was the best outcome.

"Now that Pablo has sailed, what are your plans, Yèyīng?"

She sat behind Rocamora on the cushions and massaged his forehead and temples. "I will continue here as before while you live."

"And after?"

"I do not think beyond that."

"It may not be for very long. Not many men live beyond my eighty-one years of age."

"You are ageless."

Rocamora closed his eyes and surrendered to her skilled fingers. Yèyīng had called him ageless, but in truth, she was the one who looked no different from the day of her arrival in Amsterdam. "Yèyīng, I am pleased you have decided to remain here."

"I stay because of you."

"You have said that many times but never told me why."

"First, I want you to know my real name, the name I was given at birth by my mother. It is Cháng-lì, beautiful elegant Moon goddess."

"So you are, and so you shall be throughout eternity. But why have you told me your birth name now?"

"Do you believe we humans have a soul?"

"For most of my life, I asserted no such thing existed. Now, I am not sure."

"It is so. Cháng-lì's soul died when they forced her into servitude. Night Hawk, who replaced her, had no soul, but now Cháng-lì's soul has returned."

"How can you know that?"

"After your wife died, her soul came to me and filled the void so I could comfort you."

"And you have done so these past years."

"I believe your wife's soul has left me so it can become one with yours when the time comes, and as a gift she found Cháng-lì's soul and returned it to me. Yèyīng no longer exists. I am Cháng-lì again with all the felicity of my lost childhood."

Are you telling me my death is imminent? Or yours?

Solomon and Daniel awakened Rocamora from his siesta. He had fallen asleep in the study. They had broad smiles. So did Biga and his grandchildren.

"What is it? Why is my entire family here?"

Solomon showed him a book. "*Abba*, you have been honored."

"Honored? Why? And by whom?"

"My good friend, Daniel Levi de Barrios."

"De Barrios? Yes, I remember him now. It has been several years since we met at our *tertulias literarias*, literary gatherings, when I was a judge of poetry for our group *la Academia de los Sitibundos*, the Academy of the Thirsty."

"*Abba*, de Barrios published this book of poetry titled *Aplauso Harmonico*, honoring the greatest men of our community. And you are foremost."

"Am I? Let me see it." Rocamora found his spectacles, turned to the pages where de Barrios mentioned him, and read:

Al muy Ilustre Señor Doctor Ishac De Rocamora
Por Daniel Levi de Barrios. Ano de 5443

Noble Doctor, magno Ishac,
benerable Rocamora
ilustre por tu ascendencia
mas por la Ley heroyca.

Digalo tu insigne patria
Valencia: digalo aora
con tu ley al Judaismo,
el pobre con tus limosnas;

Noble Doctor, Great Isaac,
venerable Rocamora
illustrious because of your ancestry
and more because of your heroic loyalty

Said of your famous fatherland
Valencia: said now
With your loyalty to Judaism.
And to the poor with your alms,

In the following stanzas, De Barrios praised Rocamora's brilliant example of religious faith and philanthropy, his great reputation as a healer, and that Empress María esteemed him. De Barrios even mentioned his self-circumcision. Rocamora could not have been more pleased that the poet described Abigail as a beautiful woman of impressive virtue and glorious honesty. De Barrios also mentioned their children and praised Solomon as a brilliant physician like his father.

Rocamora smiled at de Barrios' effusive hyperbolic praise proclaiming his medical skills as so great he belonged amongst the effigies of Apollo. He frowned when de Barrios mentioned Sara Eliahu as a dawn of his new love, but the final two stanzas pleased him:

> *Tienes ochenta y dos años,*
> *la Eterna Misericordia*
> *te de tantos, que el tiemp*
> *los vorazes dientes rompan.*
>
> *Paraque Eterno en el Mundo*
> *dilates su generosa*
> *descendencia, con la vida*
> *que mi humilde Mus honoras.*

> You have eighty-two years.
> much Everlasting Compassion
> to you, which time's
> voracious teeth shreds.
>
> So that Everlasting in the World
> your excellent descendants
> continue with the life
> that my humble Muse honors.

De Barrios' mention of Valencia, María, and his beloved Abigail aroused memories of other times, other lives. He must have closed his eyes, for he heard Solomon's voice:

"*Abba*, is something wrong?"

"I am weary. We are both physicians. I know my own body, and I can feel my strength decline daily and my aches increase. No, do not weep, Daniel. I am not yet ready to leave you. There is so much more I want to see and know. What will happen next? Who will be my next grandchild? Will Isaac and Abraham become physicians? Who will Sara, Lea, and Ester wed? And Jacob, where will life lead him? My sons, have I been a good father to you? I fear there were times I neglected you."

Daniel protested, and Solomon kissed Rocamora's forehead. "No better *Abba* exists in the world. Now, please, you must rest."

I resist sleep. I cannot let devious Morpheus carry me away to permanent rest. Not yet.

78.
Old Dreams, New Reality

The boy frolicked in the waves off the Valencian beach, wallowing in the foam, sand, and salt air under a blazing sun. He yearned to taste melons from a nearby field. He had not experienced so intense a feeling of well-being in years.

"*Abba*, can you hear me?"

Another voice, more insistent. "*Abba*, please."

The boy saw someone approaching through the palm grove. Brianda?

"*Abuelo*, I am here."

Rocamora opened his eyes. He was lying in his basement bed and saw Moses, Solomon and Daniel at his bedside. Grandson Jacob too. Abigail Abraham and her children stood behind them.

Which is the reality? Which is the dream?

Solomon checked his pulse. "Can you hear me, *Abba*?"

"He has closed his eyes again. Has he passed on?"

"No, Daniel, not yet. Father still breathes."

The boy slit the throat of Enrique de Anglesola, the swine who murdered his father, and he wept over the loss of his parents, noble Don Luís and beautiful Doña Gabriela de Rocamora. He inhaled the essence of orange blossoms in a clearing between the pines beyond Elx as he lay entwined with Moraima, his morilla encantadora.

The boy has become a man, and la Hermosura, the beauty, sings and dances at El Paraíso. He cavorts with his kinsman Ramón and beloved pícaro rogues, *Pablo, Yusef, and Koitalel.*

As if ensconced in a baldacchino, the beauty of golden Infanta Doña María captivates him.

"Here *Abuelo*, we have prepared this broth for you."

Rocamora opened his eyes. "Brianda, how beautiful you are."

"No, *Abba*, she is my eldest daughter, Sara."

"Yes, yes, Solomon, of course, my beloved mother's eyes, the green eyes of Bodo, and I see all my sons, Lea and Esther and Isaac too. But where are David and Joseph?"

"They are with our mother and sister, may they rest in peace. But my wife Abigail is here too, with our youngest Abraham."

"Of course, the reality, not the dream. Or is it the opposite?"

"I do not understand, *Abba*."

"What day is it, Solomon?"

"The twenty-fourth day of Nissan, 5444."

"The eighth day of April 1684? I do not remember celebrating my birthday three days ago."

"You are fevered *Abba*. You had, still have pneumonia."

"Yes, I feel the effects. So tired, so very weak. Need to sleep ... but, I must speak. Solomon, remember ... go to the notary, Adriaen Locke. Take care of your brothers."

"Yes, I promise."

"Solomon, you have made me proud. You are one of the finest physicians in all Amsterdam, a loving husband and father. Daniel, you have been a great joy in my life. May you find happiness. Moses, my blessed firstborn, forgive me. I set in motion events that caused your permanent childhood."

Moses did not understand. "*Abba*?"

"Worry not, Moses, your life will continue as it always has. Jacob, you are here at last. Come closer."

Jacob knelt at the bedside, and Rocamora rasped in English so no one else could understand them. "Remember, you too must see the notary. Marry your cousin Sara if she will follow the life you choose to lead. She loves you, the same as my beloved Abigail loved me. Daniel will be of help."

"*Abuelo*, without you, what is my place to be in this world?"

"I asked the same question often and did not learn the answer until now."

"What is the answer?"

"Jacob, you will know the place you have made when you come to the end of your life, as I have, my boy."

"*Abuelo* ...."

Rocamora closed his eyes. "So tired, so very tired."

He saw Abigail at the diamond mill. A soothing warmth blanketed him. They embraced in bed, their world complete.

Floating together.

A scent of orange blossoms.

A taste of melon.

A blinding light.

79.
The Package

On the fifteenth day of April 1684, 1 *Ijar* 5444, Jacob stood with his uncles at Rocamora's fresh grave surrounded by rabbis and congregants of Talmud Torah, city magistrates, friends, and patients who had come to pay their respects, Jew and Christian alike. He experienced more than a sense of great loss. His closest link to the Sephardic community had been irrevocably broken. *Abuelo* Isaac had been his protector, mentor, and despite the great gulf of many decades, his best friend.

"I wish I could have known *Abuelo* when he was a young man. And you, *Abba*." Jacob hugged Moses, who seemed not to comprehend what had happened.

Solomon comforted Daniel who was weeping. "Our father is now with our mother and brothers and sisters, may they all rest in peace. Jacob, will you be joining us at *Shiva*?"

"Today and part of tomorrow morning, for I must leave with Ambassador Dirck and rejoin my regiment."

"You are still an observant Jew and not living as a gentile?"

"As best I can. Although the current fashion is to have a clean shaven face, you can see I still have my mustache and beard."

"But so closely trimmed, and with your blond hair barely noticeable."

"No soldier wants to have a beard so long that it can be seized by an enemy in combat."

Solomon frowned at Jacob. "But you are still trimming your facial hair in violation of our ritual year of mourning."

Van Noordwijk approached them. "Doctor, Mynheer Daniel, my sincerest condolences and grief. Your father was my great friend and the most interesting of men. I shall miss him as if he were my brother. Jacob, we depart on the morrow at two in the afternoon."

After van Noordwijk left, Solomon walked with Jacob at a slow pace so Daniel would not be left behind. "How long will you be away this time?"

"I cannot say, *Tío*. It may be another several years."

"You will continue to do your best to be an observant Jew?"

"No less than I have to this day."

"If ever you need anything, remember you have family here in Amsterdam."

"Yes, I know."

"Daniel and I are surprised even disappointed that our father did not provide for you in his will."

Jacob suspected Solomon was fishing for information. "*Abuelo* had confidence in my ability to make my own fortune."

"So have I. No one could have had a better mentor."

The following morning, Jacob went to the fourth floor to say farewell to his father. Moses offered him his *bilboquê*. Downstairs Solomon, Daniel and members of the community sat Shiva, praying for the dead patriarch, which was heard throughout the house. The women grieved separately.

Jacob took the toy and played with Moses. "*Abba*, I do not know when I shall see you next. I love you. Please, understand and know that I love you."

"You play good. You do not miss."

Jacob returned the cup and ball to Moses who said nothing more. He sat fixed on his ability to flip the ball into its holder.

Jacob kissed his cheeks and forehead and stifled an urge to weep over Moses' lost years. He cursed his maternal grandfather and the uncles he had never seen until his cousin Sara appeared at the top of the stairs with a sack filled to bursting.

"I baked some delicacies for you, your favorites, and I added some cheeses and dried kosher meats for your journey."

"Thank you, Sara."

"I so love your smile, Jacob."

He took the bag. "You have reminded me of a story *Abuelo* told …."

"About the first time he met our grandmother."

"You heard it too? *Abuelo* told me that *Abuela* Abigail knew in her heart of hearts, even when she was a child, that one day they would wed."

She is looking at me as if … but, no Sara is still a child. Impossible. She cannot know what love is. Still, Abuelo, *may he rest in peace, said she adores me and he wanted us to marry.*

"Do you know why *Abuelo* called me Brianda the last time I saw him."

"You reminded him of his first daughter."

"I wonder if I really look so much like her."

"*Abuelo* told me once that Brianda had his unusual green eyes, the same as you."

"And he said often that she was beautiful. Am I beautiful, Jacob?"

"Everyone agrees that you will be the great beauty of the community."

"But do you see me as beautiful?"

"Have I not praised you since you were a small child?"

"Yes, you have, but not since you returned for *Abuelo's* funeral." Sara moved closer until her body touched his. The top of her cap reached no higher than his chest "When will we see each other again, Jacob?"

"I cannot say."

"Do not stay away for long."

"I shall try not to."

"Jacob, can I sit in your lap and cuddle, the way I used to?"

"That was years ago. You were a little girl. It is not appropriate now, Sara."

"Why?"

"You are too young."

"Not too young to know I love you, Jacob. I have all my life. I have told no one this except *Abuelo* that I want to marry you when I am older."

"Sara, by the time of my next visit, you will have many suitors and be ready to wed one of them."

"No, never. I will wait for you, Jacob." She clung to him and sobbed.

Jacob held Sara and calmed her. The repetitive thumping from Moses' wooden ball landing in the cup and relentless chanting of prayers below filled the silence in the room. No mistaking it, the girl loved him, and in truth, she had grace, charm and appeal. Sara would be a loving wife for any man. Their grandfather wanted them to marry, but not Solomon and Abigail Abraham. Jacob did not doubt that if he and Sara were to wed, her father would recite the same prayers for the dead he was now chanting for *Abuelo*.

Notary Adriaen Locke handed Jacob a package. "This is what your grandfather, the esteemed Doctor de Rocamora, instructed me to give to you upon his passing. As you can see, the seal has not been broken."

Jacob thanked him and left for a private place where he could inspect its contents. He found an empty bench in a nearby park, sat, and broke the seal. The contents included a manuscript, a letter, a dagger, and a magnificent ruby ring.

Jacob, my beloved grandson,

Know that I love you as much as I do your father, Moses, my firstborn.

Know that I desire your happiness above all else.

That is why I am freeing you to be your own man in this world, to live a life of your choosing instead of one others may try to force upon you as happened to me in my youth.

Live in Vlooienburg, or become a soldier, or go to the English colonies in North America. As I told your father, Moses, live the free life of choice I was denied in my youth.

That is why I have provided an account of five thousand guilders for you to draw upon at the Wisselbank, of which no one in the family is aware. Use the money wisely.

The ruby ring was bestowed upon me by Infanta María. I had hoped to give it to my daughter Sara on her wedding day. I bequeath it to you so you may give it to Sara on your wedding day.

The manuscript I have included in this package is a history of the de Rocamoras. I give it to you so you may remember that no noble, king, or emperor has superior bloodlines.

You know of the vengeance I took upon the murderer of my father. I bequeath you the instrument of that revenge.

Make your place in the world. Marry well and have many children.

I regret I shall not live to know all the adventures you will have and the children you shall sire.

May God, if He exists, bless you.

Your loving Grandfather

Despite his grief, Jacob laughed aloud when read his grandfather's signature not as Isaac Israel but as Vicente de Rocamora y Cornel, Sixth Señor de Benetorrente.

80.
Queen of Hearts, Ace of Sorrows

As he had done each visit to Amsterdam during the four years after Rocamora's passing, Jacob placed a stone of remembrance at his grandfather's grave in the Ouderkerk cemetery. "I pray you are resting well and are with your beloved Abigail and all the wonderful friends you spoke of so often. I wish I could have met them all. And I thank you for the education you gave me in arms, sport, and ways of the world. I shall do all possible to honor you and our name in the great adventure awaiting me."

Jacob left his grandfather's grave and placed another stone on that of *Tío* Daniel who died of pneumonia in October the previous year. "You were the kindest of all my uncles. May you also rest in peace."

After Jacob placed stones of remembrance at the graves of Abigail, Joseph, and Tiña, he mounted his horse and rode to the home where he had been raised to see his *Abba* and settle the matter of marrying Sara. Each time he saw his cousin she had become more desirable, and their love for each other intensified. He still did not know if Sara would follow him as a soldier's wife. If not, could he turn his back to the army and a new life in England and settle here in Amsterdam as a member of the community? Solomon might forbid a marriage between them in any case.

Does Sara love me enough to go against her Abba's wishes? I must know this day.

Jacob stared surprised at what Solomon had done to the de Rocamora crest above the front door. His uncle had replaced the mulberry branch with a gilded six-pointed Star of David.

A servant let him in, and he went to the basement where Solomon was preparing medicines. "*Tío.*"

Solomon squinted through his spectacles. "Jacob, this is a surprise. I thought you would have sailed by now. I have never seen you with so negligible a mustache and beard. Are you now living as a gentile, clean-shaven, with a recently grown a bit of hair knowing you would visit us? Tell me the truth."

"The fashion is to be free of facial hair, but as I am blond, I can avoid questions with a tightly trimmed mustache and beard."

"Have you been observant?"

"It has been difficult. *Tío*. I would like to see my father. Is he well?"

"In perfect health. Moses has the strongest constitution of all. He is in his room."

Jacob went first to the kitchen where Abigail Abraham, pregnant again, and her daughters were preparing the midday meal. Sara Solomon, now sixteen, hugged and kissed him on the mouth. Both fifteen-year-old Lea Solomon and shy eleven-year-old Ester Solomon gave him perfunctory kisses on the cheek.

Abigail Abraham stopped slicing carrots and looked askance at Jacob. "We thought we would never see you again."

A wish as well as a thought?

"For how long do you intend to visit us?"

Not the warmest of welcomes. "Tomorrow when I must return to my regiment. If the winds shift direction, we can set sail for England."

"No."

Abigail Abraham glared at Sara, and Jacob saw his aunt's eyes narrowing, first at him then at her daughter. He excused himself and went to Moses. Jacob found his father to be well cared for with clean clothes and bedding. At age forty Moses had streaks of grey in his hair and beard, skin smooth as a baby, and he in fine physical condition. He did not recognize his son until Jacob sang him a favorite child's song. Or was it the melody he remembered?

When the boys returned home from the *Yesibót,* Jacob complimented twelve year old Isaac Solomon's height and wished him well for his bar mitzvah next year. Six year old Abraham Solomon stared at him without speaking. Both resembled their lean and swarthy father.

During the evening meal, Jacob did not worry that Solomon and Abigail Abraham watched every glance and gesture between himself and Sara. Better they should know how much he and their daughter were in love. The silence and tension were palpable until Solomon spoke.

"Tell me, nephew, is it really necessary to invade England?"

"So the English Protestants and Prince William believe, *Tío*. Their Parliament has decided James II had to be removed from the throne once and for all after his Catholic wife gave birth to a son this past June. That was why both Whigs and Tories united to prepare a letter to Prince Willem urging him to invade England and save the country from the papists. We have assurances that nineteen of twenty English will welcome us."

"Then why has it not happened yet?"

"The gales are still too strong, The Pope's Wind, the Catholics call it. We do not want to suffer the same fate the Spanish armada experienced a hundred years ago."

"Does your army have adequate physicians and surgeons? My father, may he rest in peace, described the latter as little more than filthy horse gelders."

"I prefer to believe they are better than that."

The meal ended, and Sara went unbidden to the harpsichord. She fixed her eyes on Jacob and sang a plaintive English air she translated to Spanish:

> To the Queen of Hearts,
> He is the Ace of Sorrows.
> Here today and gone tomorrow.
> Young men are many
> And sweethearts few.
> If my love leaves me,
> What shall I do?

Solomon stood, his complexion coloring from red to purple. "Enough, Sara. You, all you children, leave us. Wife, tend to them. Jacob, come with me."

They went to the study. Solomon lit his pipe, and now calmer, he offered tobacco to Jacob who refused.

"As you know, Jacob, I wish you success in whatever endeavor you choose, and be assured of this. I promise to continue giving Moses the very best care."

"I never doubted that, *Tío*. His health and comfort attest to that."

"Have you decided to make your life in England, or will you return to us after James and the Catholics are defeated?"

"That depends upon your answers to my questions."

Solomon peered at him above the spectacles that had dropped lower on his nose. "What have I to do with your decision?"

From the moment Jacob realized the intensity of his feeling for Sara, he had planned how best to ask Solomon for her hand in marriage. No easy approach existed. He decided to be direct.

"*Tío*, I ask for your consent. Sara and I wish to wed."

Solomon's face reddened again. He breathed deeply until he could modulate his voice. "Understand this. I shall never give my consent for you and Sara to wed."

Jacob felt hot blood rushing to his face. "Why? Is it because you have always resented my existence, that I remind you of what happened to my father?"

"Yes, I confess it is so. I cannot help how I feel, Jacob, and I wish it were otherwise. I have great affection for you and know how much my father loved you. I have always been honest in my speech, and I shall be so with you. Were you to marry, I would sit *Shiva* for Sara. She will be dead to me, no longer my daughter."

"That is unfair."

"Yes, Jacob, I concede that I am being unfair to you, but I am thinking first and foremost of Sara's well-being and our standing in our community. Circumcised and bar mitzvahed you may be, I still cannot accept you. You were not born of a Jewish woman. You are perceived as illegitimate even though my father gave you his name. That is why you have never been a Jew in my eyes and in the eyes of many of our congregation. That is why I shall never give my consent for you and Sara to wed."

Solomon's response did not surprise Jacob, but the rejection of his person infuriated him. He would have drawn his sword against any other man who would have spoken so. "*Tío* Solomon, the last words of my grandfather to me were his wish and blessing for Sara and me to wed. He also said you would oppose our marrying, and to speak truthfully, I have always felt a chill in your presence. Now, you have essentially told me I can never be part of this community or even a member of your family even though your brother is my father and I was raised in this home."

"I am head of the family de Rocamora now, and I make all decisions in the best interests of my children."

Jacob stood. "I cannot stay here any longer, for now I know how unwelcome I am. I shall see my father now and speak with Sara."

"Say your farewell to Moses, but I forbid you from this moment to speak with Sara. The sooner you leave my house the better for both you and my daughter."

Moments after Jacob reached the room where Moses slept soundly, Sara followed him upstairs crying. "I heard everything. We all heard."

"I did not realize how much I love you until this day."

"Jacob, Jacob, what shall we do?"

"Could you live the life of a soldier's wife? Can you accept the long absences, the possibility of my death in battle?"

"I would bear all if you were that soldier."

Jacob attached his cloak. "Then leave with me this night. Leave with me now."

"But you heard my father. I would be dead to him and my family."

Jacob took her hand. "Yes, my love, I know, but we can find someone to marry us without his consent and start our own family. Your parents will reconcile with us in time, most likely after we have a grandchild for them."

"My father will see to it that no rabbi in Vlooienburg will marry us."

"There are other communities."

"None will accept us as Jews once my father sits *Shiva* for me."

"Sara, I love you enough to turn my back on a promising career in the army and life in England to marry you, the woman I love. We can sail to New York and begin a new life there. That is what *Abuelo* wished for my father and mother to do."

"But who would marry us?"

"A ship's captain, anyone in the Protestant faith."

Sara recoiled horrified. "Never."

"If you love me …."

"I do, Jacob. I do, but I need more time to think."

"If you will not leave with me this night, I shall await you until I sail from Hellevoetsluis, our embarkation port."

He kissed Sara with all the love he felt for her. She responded until she needed to breathe.

"Jacob, why am I so dizzy?"

"Sara, I beg you. Leave with me now."

"I cannot. I am not prepared."

"Then make an excuse to visit your cousins in Rotterdam. It is but a few miles from Hellevoetsluis."

"Sara, come down this instant."

"My father. I must go. I love you, Jacob, love you with all my heart."

"Then prove it." He gripped the hilt of his sword. "Your father cannot prevent your leaving with me."

"No, I dare not. I cannot."

"Then come to me before I sail."

"If I can."

81.
Captain Jack

"Must you leave so soon, my handsome lover?"

Jacob washed his face in the stale water of a porcelain bowl on a dresser in the elaborate suite at Prince William's palace in The Hague. He looked into the gilt framed wall mirror at voluptuous Joan Woodhill, famous outside the bedroom as Lady-in-Waiting to Princess Mary and Duchess of Fairfield, a title bestowed by Charles II for her services as his mistress.

Daughter of an ambitious squire, Joan Woodhill had been renowned as one of England's great beauties since age fifteen when she caught the connoisseur's eye of Charles II. The last year of his life, he made her a duchess, the same as he had done for other mistresses.

Jacob had spent yet another night with Lady Joan, who had been the aggressor in their relationship. Van Noordwijk introduced them upon his return from Amsterdam. That first night, Jacob was overcome with guilt because of his disloyalty to Sara, but not for long. Joan had skills in lovemaking he never dreamed possible. Even so, each day he waited for Sara to appear or send a message in which she declared her love and intention to come to him. Each night throughout October and into November he slept with Lady Joan.

She lay naked atop the bedding and beckoned him. "Come here."

"Your Grace, Ambassador van Noordwijk awaits me."

"Can you not call me Joan?"

He sat beside the thirty-three year old blonde and held her hand. "I fear I might commit a gaffe in public were I to become too comfortable using your given name."

"If we were to wed, you would have a title of your own after my good friend Mary Stuart is Queen of England."

Jacob kissed her and they entwined. "I cannot think of marriage until after our work is done."

"When will that be? I shall be a gap-tooth old hag by the time Prince William overthrows the tyrant."

"You will always glow with the fresh loveliness of an adolescent, and your beauty is far greater than its fame."

"Flatterer."

"No flattery, ma'am, but an objective appreciation of your charms."

"Jack, for shame. You have deserted me for your thoughts."

He smiled at Lady Joan's preference for Jack instead of Jacob, the same as the soldiers of his English regiment who addressed him as Captain Jack. "I am sorry about that, my lady."

"Then make love to me one more time before you leave me this morning."

Jacob did not hesitate. He had never lusted so after any woman, and Van Noordwijk urged him to pursue the affair as a practical matter. Playing stud for an amorous titled mare could make a man's career in England.

Not until the second week in November, did the Papist wind become the Protestant Wind. The fleet reassembled on the eleventh day of November, and Jacob supervised the boarding of his regiment against a din of men shouting, horses neighing, and the creaking of artillery caissons and supply wagons moving across docks and up ramps to the ships.

The time for military action had come now that Prince William's brilliant diplomacy had succeeded. He convinced Leopold I that he would not persecute the Catholics in England. In return, the Emperor sought peace with the Ottoman Empire and alliance with the Dutch against France. William also encouraged Hanover and Saxony to declare their neutrality. The Amsterdam magistrates, wealthy Francisco López Suasso, and Pope Innocent XI, who hated King Louis XIV of France, loaned William millions of guilders for the great enterprise.

In advance of the invasion, supporters of William in England distributed more than sixty thousand pamphlets titled the Declaration of The Hague. It assured the populace that the Prince of Orange was a true Stuart and a devout Protestant free from the family's usual vices of crypto-Catholicism, absolutism, and debauchery. The pamphlet also emphasized that William sought to protect the Protestant religion, install a free parliament, and investigate the legitimacy of the Prince of Wales while continuing to respect James as King of England. Jacob had learned differently from van Noordwijk. William intended to be King of England.

He moved closer to one of his regimental musicians seated on a barrel and plucking the strings of his lute. The soldier sang of disappointed love, which suited Jacob's mood because he had heard nothing from Sara.

> *"How now shepherd what means that?*
> *Why that willow in thy cap?"*
> *Why thy scarfs of red and yellow,*
> *Turned to branches of green willow?"*

Despite his dallying with Lady Joan, Jacob had not lost hope Sara might appear or at least send some word. He could well imagine Solomon and Abigail Abraham watching her every move. Perhaps they had locked her in a room until he sailed.

> *"They are changed, and so am I;*
> *Sorrows live, but pleasures die:*
> *Phyllis hath forsaken me,*
> *Which makes me wear the willow-tree."*

His Phyllis, my Sara.

Van Noordwijk approached Jacob. "A magnificent sight, it is not? Our fleet is four times larger than the Spanish Armada with more than five thousand mounts and sixty thousand soldiers and sailors. Our navy is more experienced and better manned than the Spanish were. Jacob, you know we placed you with the English regiment because of your fluency in their language. Can we still rely on them?"

"Completely. King James made a great mistake this past January when he demanded we allow our mercenary Scot and English soldiers to return to England. Prince William agreed so his army would be free of potential Catholic traitors. They are fit and ready to go. This time I hope the winds remain Protestant."

> *"She that long true love profest,*
> *She hath robbed my heart of rest."*

"Good fortune will favor us, Jacob, as it has you this day."

"Good fortune for me? How so?"

"You have been assigned to Prince William's staff, which means you will sail to England on his flagship."

"How is that possible?"

"Do not be so naive. Your duchess must have spoken to Princess Mary who used her influence on your behalf. But your expression and reaction ... you seem to be disappointed rather than pleased. Are you still hoping your Sara will come?"

> *"Yet, Phyllis, shall I pine for thee,*
> *And still must wear the willow-tree?"*

"No longer, but I hoped for the courtesy of a letter to let me know her mind. It would be different if my grandfather still lived."

"Then always remember the examples and standards he set for you to follow."

"There are so many. I would like nothing more than to be like him."

"Your grandfather lived a most unique life. He was of the Spanish *caballero* caste and a Dominican royal confessor. Of necessity he had to leave his beloved Spain and make a new life, which he did with great success. He found true love with your grandmother and became the esteemed physician Don Isaac de Rocamora. Jacob, as he did with Spain, so must you turn your back on Amsterdam and face the future for which you have been so well prepared. Our prince will soon be King of England, and as he shall, so must you also become more English than the English."

"It seems I have already made a start. My English comrades prefer to call me Jack Rockmore."

"Then that is the name you must have. Remember this. Since it cannot be with Sara, court your duchess. Lady Jane has the ear of the future queen. She can help make a great career for you in England. A title awaits you if you woo her with passion and wed her.

"I would have to be baptized a Protestant."

"That is inevitable anyway. You could do worse than marrying a titled beauty who adores you."

"But I do not love her. I should ride to Amsterdam and carry Sara away, but I cannot read her mind. I do not know if she will choose me over her family."

"I cannot encourage you in that venture. Sara is an obedient daughter. She will not ... she cannot bring herself to disobey her father. Several days ago, while in Amsterdam on a mission for Prince William, I went to see Solomon on your behalf."

Jacob stared at him surprised unable to speak.

"Sara has promised her father she will wed the man of his choosing, David Gaon, an observant Jew from an esteemed family."

Jacob recoiled as if he had been struck a blow. "How can she? Has she no words for me? No feeling?"

"Sara asks you to forgive her weakness and to forget her. She wishes you well and much happiness. She wept throughout our brief conversation."

"That is all?"

"Yes."

"So it ends with a pathetic impersonal goodbye."

"Believe me. She suffers no less than you."

"Perhaps, but Sara loves her family more than she loves me."

"That is true, I regret to say." Van Noordwijk placed his hand on Jacob's shoulder. "Prince William awaits us. Within the half hour we shall be setting sail for *Het Glorieuze Overtocht*, the Glorious Crossing."

Jacob walked with van Noordwijk toward Prince William's flagship. He turned his head one last time to the streets leading to the docks and despaired Sara had not and would not appear. The ruby ring his grandfather bequeathed weighed heavily in Jacob's hand.

To whom shall I give it now?

Jacob strode toward the flagship and his future with new resolve.

> *"Henceforth I will do as they,*
> *And love a new love every day."*

Historical Notes

Although Vicente-Isaac de Rocamora is more documented in Amsterdam than he was in Spain, none of his writings have survived. His true thoughts, feelings, and beliefs remain buried with him at Ouderkerk.

That leaves many questions unanswered.

What did Rocamora do from the day of his arrival in Amsterdam in 1643 to his matriculating at Leyden Medical School in August 1645?

Why did the respected scholar Vossius write this letter dated the twenty-ninth of March 1647 on Rocamora's behalf to Anthony van der Linden, a former Professor of Medicine at Leyden translated in Cecil Roth's *A Life of Menasseh ben Israel, Rabbi, Printer, Diplomat?*

> Yesterday, Rabbi Menasseh ben Israel came to me, accompanied by Isaac Rocamora, a Portuguese Jew. The latter has been studying medicine for the past two years and has made such progress that he is confident that his standard is such as to qualify him for the highest degree in the subject. Owing to his slender means, he prefers that Academy where the fees of graduation are least. This Rocamora has been warmly recommended to me by your friend, Menasseh, whom I know has no deficiency in your eyes excepting for his religion. I, for my part (and I would say this of few, not only of that sect, but also of any other), consider him a man of true worth albeit he lives in darkness. He has requested me to write you a letter informing you of his protégé's intention. Unless I am mistaken, religion is no impediment for the conferring of a degree, for while you were still in your native city, this honor was bestowed by the University of Leyden upon David Haro. I remember, moreover, having heard from my old colleague Adolf van Voost (God rest his soul!), in talking about this matter, that medical knowledge only comes into the question, and not religious belief; especially in these parts, where Jews are licensed to practice the art."

Yet a few days later on the First of April, Rocamora obtained his license to practice medicine from the University of Franeker without having attended classes there.

Documents regarding Rocamora's intentions to convert to the Dutch Reform Church can be found in the Archives of the 8th protocol of the Church Council, fol.274/275, 12 NS 199, dated May 12 and 19, 1650.

Rocamora's will is recorded in the Amsterdam Municipal Archives. In it he describes Moses as slow of wit, simple, and incompetent, Daniel as deformed and sickly. I could find no source that explained if Moses' limited mental ability originated at birth or if it resulted from injury or illness. The origin of the two diamond mills bequeathed to Joseph is not documented. I assumed it must have been part of Abigail's dowry.

The Chamber of Orphans protected the inheritance of minor children who lost a father or mother and because of minority could not receive it. If no will existed, the Orphan Chamber supervised the inheritance until the child reached age twenty-five or wed.

I found no declarative sentence that explained why Amsterdam granted Rocamora citizenship. The Amsterdam Municipal Records do not show if he owned property or had significant income or wealth from trade.

Rocamora's second son Solomon died in 1719 at age sixty-nine and Moses his eldest in 1721 at age seventy-three having outlived all his siblings.

Solomon's sons Isaac and Abraham became physicians. They married daughters from the prominent families Méndez da Costa and da Costa Athias. Their sons also became physicians.

Solomon's daughters married into the prominent families Gaon, da Costa Athias, Abarbanel, and Abarbanel Brandón.

Solomon's grandchildren married spouses from the prominent families dela Penha, Abendena Belmonte, Valhe del Saldanha, Santcroos, and Abendena Méndez.

And so, Vicente-Isaac de Rocamora's descendants through Solomon were fruitful and multiplied.

Jacob's story is yet to be told.

Acknowledgements

To Pam Marin-Kingsley, Acquisitions Editor and Creative Director at Briona Glen for discovering me, *A Gathering of Vultures,* and *Rocamora* and for her continuing belief in my writing.

To Dana Blythe, Director of Operations at Briona Glen, and Jason Reilly, Director of Marketing at Briona Glen, for their instant responses, excellent communication skills, and wonderful sense of humor.

To Tammy Andrew, President and editor at Briona Glen for her "eagle eye" editing and ease with whom to work.

To William Birch, Director of Technology, for being the "backbone" of Briona Glen.

To Helga Becker-Leeser of Arnhem, my long distance genealogist friend of more than twenty years, whose invaluable research contributed as much to *House of Rocamora* as it did for *Rocamora.*

To Dr. Wilhelmina.Chr. Pieterse, past Director of the *Amsterdam Municipal Archives,* and to current Director Harmon Snel for sending information about Rocamora's life and family in Amsterdam and generously answering my questions.

To the following for doing more than encouraging my writing with words and by their actions:

Amanda and William Chohfi

Dr. Christiane and Steve Engel

Dr. Claudia and Sandy Samuels

Aplauso Harmonico

Al muy Ilustre Señor Doctor Ishac De Rocamora
Por Daniel Levi de Barrios. Ano de 5443

Noble Doctor, magno Ishac,
benerable Rocamora
ilustre por tu ascendencia
mas por la Ley heroyca.

Digalo tu insigne patria
Valencia: digalo aora
con tu ley al Judaismo,
el pobre con tus limosnas;

Con tu exemplo el virtuoso;
con tu fe la Sinagoga;
las Yesibót con tus dones,
y el Pueblo con tus victorias.

En, to sana edicacion
adquiriste de edad poca
por la enseñança la cienccia,
y el aplauso por la honra.

Estimaronte los Grandes,
y hasta la Infanta Española
Doña maría de Austria
del Gran Ferindando esposa.

No estimaste las grandezas
como la Ley que gloriosa
te asseguró en los peligros,
y te iluminó en las sombras.

Cinco mil y quatrocientos
y tres años la vistosa

casa universal ténia,
con orden maravillosa;

Quando te circuncidaste
por verte con luz debota
clara estrella de Jacob,
en Firmamento de Gloria.

Aprendiste medicina,
con sapiencia tan notaria
que el Docto la solemnize,
y el Enfermo la pregona.

Con Abigail casaste
de Mosseh Toro hija ayroía,
per la vertud tan solemne,
como honesta por si íola.

Siete hios de ella tuviste
y dos hijas, que oy gloriosas
te serven de resplandores
en la Celestial alcoba.

Tus nietos sus dos hijos
y sus quarto hijas, pregorian
en tu Selomoh tu ciencia,
en su educacion tu Gloria

Entre tus hijos campéa
Selomoh, di tan copia
que acierta en la medicina,
y en Colegios assombra.

Diez y nueve años depues
caso con la virtuosa
Abigail de Abraham Toro
hija y de su Amor corona.

Los Israelitas y quantos
Amestelodamos, os nombran
por sus Medicos, os hallan

de Apolo effigies famosas.

Con salutiseras luzes
deshazeys nubes diversas,
de enfermedades diversas,
y de nocivas çoçobras.

Casaste segunda vez
con Sara, hija primarosa
del estimado Eliahu Toro,
y de tu Amor nueva Aurora.

Oy biudo, mas no de Fama,
la estiendesen las memorias
que tus primores aplauden,
y tus atenciones loan.

Tienes ochenta y dos años,
la Eterna Misericordia
te de tantos, que el tiemp
los vorazes dientes rompan.

Paraque Eterno en el Mundo
dilates su generosa
descendencia, con la vida
que mi humilde Mus honoras.

HARMONIOUS PRAISE
(Translated by the Author)

To the most illustrious Señor Doctor Isaac de Rocamora
by Daniel Levi de Barrios. Year 5443 (1683)

Noble Doctor, Great Isaac,
venerable Rocamora
illustrious because of your ancestry
and more because of your heroic loyalty

Said of your famous fatherland

Donald Michael Platt

Valencia: said now
with your loyalty to Judaism.
And to the poor with your alms,

With your brilliant example,
with your faith at the Synagogue,
the Yeshiva with your donations
and the People with your triumphs

Esteemed by the Great,
and also the Infanta of Spain
Doña María of Austria
married to Grand Emperor Ferdinand

In your education as a healer
acquired in a short time
because of training in science
and praise for your reputation.

You did not value their esteem
as much as the glorious principles
that enabled you to survive dangers,
and enlighten you in the darkness.

Five thousand and four hundred
and three years and colorful
house universal had
with wonderful order;

When you circumcised yourself
because you saw religious light
the clear star of Jacob,
In the Glorious Firmament

You studied medicine
with wisdom so remarkable
that the learned
and the praise you.

You married Abigail,
beautiful daughter of Moses Toro

because of her virtue so impressive
as her obvious honesty.

Seven sons she brought you
and two daughters, who today
serve you as glorious splendors
in the Heavenly bedroom.

Your praiseworthy grandchildren,
Two sons and four daughters
of your Solomon, your science
and his education are your Glory

Standing out amongst your sons
Solomon so much like you
who successfully in medicine
amazed the Colleges.

Born after fifty-four
centuries the torch of
the sun has ten Januaries
and ten and nine dawns

Nineteen years after
marriage with the virtuous
Abigail, daughter of Abraham Toro
and the crown of your love.

The Jews and many
Amsterdammers, nominated you
because of your Medicine to be
amongst the famous effigies of Apollo.

With welcome light
clearing away many clouds
from assorted sicknesses
and from malignant ailments

The Forlorn and the Suffering
from your generous hands

besides being restored to health
received the favor of your charity.

You married a second time
Sara, excellent daughter
of the esteemed Eliahu Toro
Dawn of a new Love.

Oh, widower, but Fame does not
does not diminish the records
that extol your excellences,
and the courtesies of your charity.

You have eighty-two years.
much Everlasting Compassion
to you, which time's
voracious teeth shreds.

So that Everlasting in the World
your excellent descendants
continue with the life
that my humble Muse honors.

Abbreviated Genealogy of The House of Orange-Nassau and The Stuarts

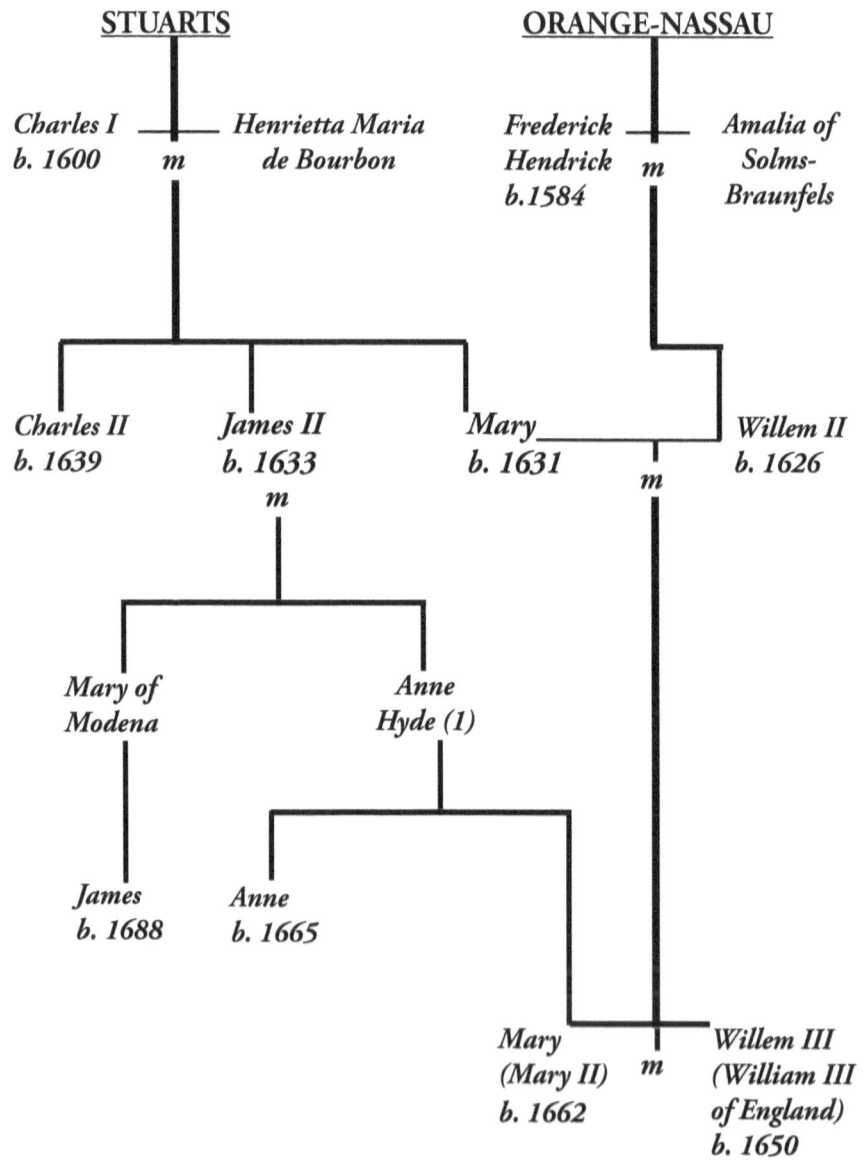

VALUE OF MONEY

1 Spanish *escudo*	1 gold sovereign or 1 guilder
1 guilder	15 silver florins.
1 florin	20 *stuivers*
1 *stuiver*	16 *penningen*.
1 duit	1/8 *stuiver*

FOOD AND DRINK

Average tankard of ale	8 *penningen* (1/2 st.)
13 lb. loaf of rye	4.5--7.5 (6-9) *stuivers*
pair of cured red herring	1 *duit*
fresh new Holland herring	1/2 st.
Gouda Cheese	2½ st. per Amsterdam pound.
Butter	5 st. pound
Chicken	11 st. at market.
Veal	4 st./pound
Beer	¼ st./tankard

CLOTHING

Man's shirt averages	1 fl.
A man's house gown	10 fl.
A man's plain coat, vest, and breeches	30 fl.
Man's elaborate coat and vest	50gl
Woman's chemise	1 gl.
Ordinary skirt	2 gl.

WAGES

Artisan	30 st./day
A skilled worker	3 to 5 fl./week.

Journeyman	27 st./day
Schoolmaster's annual wage	200 fl.
Physician charges	4 st. to 1 fl. for consultation
University professor's wage/yr.	1100 fl.
Municipal physician wage/yr.	2000 fl.
Municipal official wage/yr.	5000 fl.

HOUSING AND FURNITURE

A small house	300 hundred fl./yr. lease
Apartment in subdivided home	2000 fl. per year's lease
One room	5 fl./week
Straight back chair	20 st.+
Simple table	1 gl.+
Simple wall-bed	15 to 25 gl.
Ornate, free-standing canopied bed	100 gl. +
Single cup-board or wall-bed and rust bank couch	3 to 5 gl.
Oak chests	10 gl.+
Linen cabinet	20 to 60 gl.
Small mirror	3gl
Fancy mirror	10-15 gl.
Stew Pan	1½ to 2 gl.
Kettle or tart pan	3 gl.
Biggest pans	5 gl.
Copper bed warmer	5 gl.
Pewter bowl	2 to 3 st.
Floor tiles	1½ to 4 st. ea., 25 gl./1000
Engravings	2-7 st.
Major Painting in gilt frame	up to 25gl.
Small landscape	3 to 4gl.
Major landscape	30 gl.

About the Author

In Hollywood, Donald sold his writing to the TV series, *Mr. Novak*, and worked for and with diverse producers. After moving to Jupiter, Florida, Donald co-wrote *Vitamin Enriched*, 1999, for Carl DeSantis, founder of Rexall Sundown Vitamins; and *The Couple's Disease*, 2002, for Lawrence S. Hakim, MD, FACS, Head of Sexual Dysfunction Unit at the Cleveland Clinic.

Born and raised in San Francisco and a graduate of Lowell High school and U.C. Berkeley, Donald also has taught History, English, and Creative Writing and has been an Adjunct Professor of Writing at Polk Community College. He currently resides in Winter Haven, Florida with his wife, Ellen.

Donald is currently being house trained by his new cat, Bodo, a loquacious tyrant.

Photograph of Donald Michael Platt, courtesy of:
Richard V. Pezzimenti, Pezzimenti Photography
356 3rd St. NW
Winter Haven, FL 33881
Web site: http://pezzimenti.com/

www.ingramcontent.com/pod-product-compliance
Lightning Source LLC
Chambersburg PA
CBHW021138080526
44588CB00008B/118